h. 02104104

MATURITY AND MODERNITY

I know of no study which examines the intellectual trajectory of Nietzsche, Weber and Foucault in such an imaginative and instructive way. The work is thorough and thoughtful, yielding many important insights.

Keith Ansell-Pearson
University of Warwick

This text examines the work of Nietzsche, Weber and Foucault as a distinct trajectory of modern thought tracing the emergence and development of genealogy as a form of immanent critique. The book aims to clarify the relations between these thinkers and to respond to Habermas's charge that they are nihilists and that their approach is philosophically incoherent and practically irresponsible by showing how genealogy as a practical activity is directed towards the achievement of human autonomy.

The scope of the book covers the critical methodologies developed by these thinkers with respect to the analysis of how we have become what we are, their substantive reconstructions of how we have become what we are and the implications which they draw for the possibility of human autonomy in the present. It proceeds by detailed analysis of each thinker showing the structure of their approach, their historical accounts of the emergence of modernity, and the politics of their attempts to facilitate the achievement of human autonomy.

This is the first book to analyse these three thinkers as a tradition of theorising and to chart the development of genealogy as a mode of critique. It provides clear accounts of the main ideas of Nietzsche, Weber and Foucault (as well as a useful glossary) and illustrates the relations between these thinkers at methodological, substantive and political levels.

David Owen lectures in politics at the University of Southampton and is assistant director of the Centre for Post-Analytic Philosophy.

MATURITY AND MODERNITY

Nietzsche, Weber, Foucault and
the ambivalence of reason

David Owen

London and New York

First published 1994
by Routledge
11 New Fetter Lane, London EC4P 4EE

Simultaneously published in the USA and Canada
by Routledge
29 West 35th Street, New York, NY 10001

First published in paperback 1997

Reprinted 1998

© 1994 David Owen

Typeset in Baskerville by
NWL Editorial Services, Langport, Somerset

Printed and bound in Great Britain by
Mackays of Chatham PLC, Chatham, Kent

British Library Cataloguing in Publication Data
A catalogue reference for this book is available
from the British Library

Library of Congress Cataloguing in Publication Data
Owen, David, 1964–
Maturity and Modernity: Nietzsche, Weber, Foucault,
and the ambivalence of reason / David Owen.
p. cm.
Includes bibliographical references and index.
1. Genealogy (Philosophy)   2. Nietzsche, Friedrich
Wilhelm, 1844–1900.   3. Weber, Max, 1864–1920.
4. Foucault, Michel.   I. Title
B819.5.094   1994   93–38534
190–dc 20

ISBN 0–415–05398–6 (hbk)
ISBN 0–415–15352–2 (pbk)

For my parents
Ann and Jerry Owen
without whom nothing

CONTENTS

CONTENTS

ACKNOWLEDGEMENTS

I cannot note all the people who have supported my work and well-being over the period in which this book was written but I extend my gratitude to them and hope those I do mention will act as stand-ins for all.

The initial grant to undertake a doctoral thesis on Nietzsche, Weber and Foucault was provided by the University of Durham, and it is on that research that this text is loosely based. My supervisor during this time, Irving Velody, was a model of academic generosity; to him I owe my greatest intellectual debts and his friendship has remained an unlimited source of support without which this work would hardly have been possible. I would also like to acknowledge the other members of the Sociology Department for their encouragement, particularly Robin Williams for his commitment to intellectual clarity which pushed me to try to convert my thoughts into some order of intelligibility. The external examiner of my thesis, Zygmunt Bauman, gave me the confidence to try to publish and has continued to offer support; while my editor, Chris Rojek, has offered endless patience. I would also like to thank the two anonymous readers for Routledge.

In the last four years, I have been fortunate to receive encouragement from the Departments of Politics at City of London Polytechnic and Queen Mary and Westfield College, University of London; I would like specifically to thank Anne Phillips for our lunchtime discussions which always stimulated. More recently, colleagues in the Department of Sociology at the University of Essex have been generous in their encouragement; I would like to thank Ken Plummer and Nigel South for their practical support, and Ted Benton for our productive disagreements. I would also like to mention here the Nietzsche Society of Great Britain, the BSA Max Weber Studies Group and the History of the Present Research Network, each of which has been a source of collective engagement and support. Passages from *On the Genealogy of Morals* by Friedrich Nietzsche are reprinted by permission of Random House (copyright © 1967 by Random House, Inc.). Passages from *From Max Weber* are reprinted by permission of Oxford University Press, New York.

ACKNOWLEDGEMENTS

During these four years, several people have read individual chapters; for their critical aid and for sending me copies of their own work, I would like to thank Samantha Ashenden, Sebastian Barker, Daniel Conway, Joanna Hodge, Kimberley Hutchings, Kelly Oliver, Tom Osbourne, Noel O'Sullivan, Nik Rose, Tracy Strong, Arpad Szakoiczai, Sam Whimster, Tony Woodiwiss, and any others whom I have inadvertently failed to acknowledge. For reading the majority of the manuscript at various stages of development, I would especially like to thank Keith Ansell-Pearson, Howard Caygill and Ralph Schroeder who all sacrificed their own time to discuss, argue and critically comment on my work; without their scholarly readings, I would have made several more errors and missed numerous possibilities. I am grateful to them for combining intellectual rigour with generosity of spirit, even as they continue to query my more idiosyncratic moments. Needless to say those errors which remain are my own.

Throughout the period of composing this work, my family have offered essential support (particular thanks to my sister Cath for the computers) and I would like to thank my friends Simon Court, Kirsty Seymour-Ure, Tom Smyth and Jim Stretton for occasionally bringing me back to the planet. Finally, I thank Samantha Ashenden for becoming who she is; may we continue to share truth, time and trees.

ABBREVIATIONS USED IN THE TEXT

NIETZSCHE

AC	*The AntiChrist*
BGE	*Beyond Good and Evil*
BT	*The Birth of Tragedy*
D	*Daybreak*
EH	*Ecce Homo*
GM	*On the Genealogy of Morals*
GS	*The Gay Science*
HAH	*Human, All Too Human*
PT	*Philosophy and Truth*
TI	*Twilight of the Idols*
UM	*Untimely Meditations*
WP	*The Will to Power*
Z	*Thus Spoke Zarathustra*

WEBER

AJ	*Ancient Judaism*
ES	*Economy and Society*
FMW	*From Max Weber: Essays in Sociology*
GAW	*Gesemmelte Aufsätze zur Wissenschaftslehre* [Collected Essays on Methodology].
MSS	*The Methodology of the Social Sciences*
NSEP	'The Nation State and Economic Policy [Freiburg Address]'
PE	*The Protestant Ethic and the Spirit of Capitalism*
PV	'Politics as a Vocation'
RK	*Roscher and Knies*
SPWR	'The Social Psychology of World Religions'
SR	*The Sociology of Religion*
SV	'Science as a Vocation'

ABBREVIATIONS

FOUCAULT

AK	*The Archaeology of Knowledge*
DP	*Discipline and Punish*
FR	*The Foucault Reader*
G	'Governmentality'
HS	*The History of Sexuality*, vol. 1
LMC	*Language, Counter-Memory, and Practice*
OT	*The Order of Things*
P/K	*Power/Knowledge*
PPC	*Politics, Philosophy, Culture*
PTI	'The Political Technology of Individuals'
QM	'Questions of Method'
SP	'The Subject and Power'
TS	'Technologies of the Self'
UP	*The Use of Pleasure*
UR	'Is It Useless to Revolt?'

INTRODUCTION

It has become commonplace to comment on the affinities between the thinking of Nietzsche, Weber and Foucault; yet, despite the repetition of such remarks, the specific character and significance of these affinities have not been subjected to systematic scrutiny. It is this lack which this text attempts to fill by arguing that Nietzsche, Weber and Foucault can be read as constituting a distinct trajectory of critical thinking within modern thought and by specifying the character of this trajectory by reference to the topics of *maturity* and *modernity*. More particularly, the central thematic interests of this text are to trace the emergence and development of *genealogy* as a form of immanent critique and to elucidate the ethical and political character of this form of critique. In this introduction, I want to suggest a few reasons why I think that Nietzsche, Weber and Foucault are centrally relevant to our contemporary ethical and political concerns and, specifically, to our thinking of the question of critique.

THE QUESTION OF CRITIQUE

What do we mean by critique? This is a complex and contested topic yet, for post-Kantian social and political thought, it is possible to situate the sense of critique as the pursuit of *maturity* through reflection on *modernity*, where this reflection is articulated via a historical reconstruction of our being in the present. While Kant's critical enterprise is concerned with our maturity (or lack of it), it is only after Kant that the activity of critique becomes historical and the question of maturity (what is the possibility of achieving autonomy given the conditions of the present?) is tied to the question of modernity (what is the character of our historical being in the present?). In this context, we can suggest that to engage in critical reflection is to pose three questions: What is maturity? What is modernity? What is the relationship between maturity and modernity?

This clarification of what is involved in the question of critique is pertinent because it provides a route into reflecting on contemporary debates about the form of critical reflection. Initiated by Jean-François

1

Lyotard's reflections on the conditions of knowledge in contemporary society, these debates have been thematised in terms of the opposition of the terms *modern* and *postmodern* (and their various affiliates). The most prominent intervention within this arena of argument to date is Jurgen Habermas's *The Philosophical Discourse of Modernity*. In this text, Habermas claims that:

> Hegel inaugurated the discourse of modernity. He introduced the theme – the self-critical reassurance of modernity. He established the rules within which the theme can be varied – the dialectic of enlightenment.

> (Habermas 1987: 52)

From this claim for Hegel's foundational role with respect to the form of post-Kantian critique, Habermas goes on to expose the illegitimacy of Nietzschean claims to articulate a form of critique in either German anti-modernist or French postmodernist guises. For Habermas, the Nietzschean rejection of modernity betrays a nihilistic deficiency in the attempts of this tradition to articulate a critical knowledge of the present. Far from enacting a critical engagement with the present, the total rejection of modernity which Habermas claims characterises the philosophies of Nietzsche, Adorno, Heidegger, Derrida and Foucault produces performative contradictions which illustrate the incoherence of these so-called critiques and which reveal their unwitting complicity with the capitulation of rationality to irrationality, of thought to power, of right to might, which characterises neo-conservative politics.

But how convincing are Habermas's knockdown arguments? These arguments depend to a large extent on the narrative which Habermas constructs whereby Hegel is situated as the foundational legislator of the philosophical discourse of modernity. In other words, Habermas's highly critical readings of the Nietzschean tradition only stand up *if* he is justified in the claim that Hegel determines the form of post-Kantian critique, where this claim is grounded in the narrative he constructs. Against this narrative and its claim for Hegel's determination of the form of critique, this text will present the case for another discourse of modernity which cannot be judged by Hegelian rules in so far as it represents an alternative route out of the antinomies and aporias of Kant's philosophy. In other words, I am claiming in this text that the Nietzschean tradition should be read as emerging from reflection on the problems of Kantian thought and that this other form of post-Kantian critique which emerges in Nietzsche and develops through Weber to Foucault (as if to double or shadow the tradition of critique which emerges in Hegel and develops through Marx to Habermas) provides us with an alternative to the Hegelian tradition within which Habermas situates himself. Indeed, one way of reading this text would be as an extended reply to Habermas, as a counter-hegemonic intervention in the struggle over the meaning of critique which attempts to re-open the question of the form of critique against Habermas's efforts to impose closure on this question.

To give a brief sense of these two traditions, we can sketch very schematically their significant differences with respect to the question of critique by returning to the three questions which we have suggested characterise critical reflection after Kant: What is maturity? What is modernity? What is the relationship between maturity and modernity? Against Hegel's understanding of maturity as self-actualisation, as the realisation of one's authentic being as an ethical agent, we can place Nietzsche's understanding of maturity as self-overcoming, as the ongoing process of becoming what one is – an extra-moral agency. Against Hegel's understanding of modernity as the diremption of reason and reason's reconciliation with itself, we can place Nietzsche's understanding of modernity as the will to truth becoming conscious of itself as a problem. Moreover, in terms of how they think the relationship of maturity and modernity, we can point out that while Hegel situates maturity as the *telos* of modernity, as its redemption of its promise to itself and the realisation of its authentic nature, Nietzsche understands the relationship of maturity and modernity as ambivalent, modernity both creates and undercuts the possibility of maturity. Consequently, whereas Hegel locates the activity of critique as the reassurance of modernity through the heightening of its consciousness of its own authentic being, Nietzsche specifies the activity of critique as directed towards the confronting of the ambivalence of modernity and thereby facilitating the achievement of maturity. In other words, Nietzsche and Hegel present different understandings of maturity, modernity and their relationship.

It is not my concern in this text to argue for the superiority of one or other of these accounts of the form of critique (indeed, I am only concerned with examining one of them); rather, the interest of this highly simplified and schematic contrast is simply to signal the arena into which this text commits itself as structured by debates over the questions of maturity and modernity, and their relationship. Within this arena, the tasks of this text are twofold: (i) to ground the claim that Nietzsche, Weber and Foucault may be read as a distinct trajectory within modern thought with respect to the question of critique by placing this tradition in its Kantian context of emergence and (ii) to trace the development of *genealogy* as a specific form of critique, critically examining the ethical and political character of this form of critique.

THE STRUCTURE OF THE TEXT

In the context of the concerns outlined, we can specify the reasons governing the structure of this text by reference to both its general interest in showing that Nietzsche, Weber and Foucault constitute a particular trajectory of modern thought which constructs a form of critique distinct from both Kantian and Hegelian models, and its specific interests in showing the form of their approach to the question of maturity (and the development of this approach), the reconstructions of modernity through which they address the question of maturity (and the differences which mark their interpretations of modernity), and the responses to the question of maturity they offer (and the development of these responses).

With respect to the general interest of the text, the argument is organised in terms of the tracing of a historical trajectory from Kant to Foucault. I begin examining the way in which Kant sets up the question of maturity and the failure of his critical thinking to approach and answer this question adequately. Following this, I examine the transformation of critique wrought by Nietzsche in confronting the question of maturity as a historical question, before showing how both Weber and Foucault refine and reproduce the form of immanent critique which Nietzsche develops. This is facilitated by structuring the sections on each of Nietzsche, Weber and Foucault in terms of the specific interests of the argument. Thus I begin by showing that each thinker adopts a *genealogical* approach to the question of maturity; I then go on to examine the genealogies of *modernity* they construct before, finally, analysing the *politics* of their responses to the question of maturity. This strategy enables the argument to attend to both the developments which occur within this trajectory of thought and to maintain a structural form which exhibits the family resemblances between these thinkers. At this stage, having elaborated the reasons governing the structural organisation of the argument, we may turn to the detailed contents of each chapter.

In Chapter 1, I offer a detailed reading of Kant's essay on enlightenment as the text which first poses the question of maturity before placing this text in the context of Kant's critical philosophy in order to reveal the historical antinomy and political paradox which Kant unwittingly bequeaths to modern thought. The concern of this chapter is to specify the tasks that the question of maturity sets for modern thought as the elaboration of a historical form of immanent critique which is capable of accounting for its own conditions of possibility through a reconstruction of our modernity which simultaneously serves as the site of its critical and political concern with the achievement of autonomy.

The next three chapters explore the work of Nietzsche. In Chapter 2, I present Nietzsche's transformation of the form of immanent critique by focusing on the topic of *genealogy* and the project of the evaluation of values which it announces. The form of genealogical critique is presented by analysing Nietzsche's doctrine of *will to power* as providing principles of explanation *and* evaluation. We turn from Nietzsche's formal delineation of genealogical critique to its deployment in his historical reconstruction

4

of our modernity as *nihilism* in Chapter 3. The argument of this chapter is that through his concern with *ressentiment, bad conscience* and the role of the ascetic priest, Nietzsche is able to present an account of the ambiguity of modern culture in which the capacity of modern *Mensch* for autonomy is tied to the lack of the grounds of value which would enable the exercise of this capacity. Nietzsche's response to the ambiguity he diagnoses is taken up in Chapter 4 where his doctrine of *eternal recurrence* is identified as an attempt to provide a new ground of value for modern culture. The politics of this response are explored by reference to the ambivalence which characterises Nietzsche's notion of the *Übermensch*. I identify two types of *Übermensch* modelled on the figures of Napoleon and Goethe, and argue that while the legislative form of Nietzsche's Napoleonic politics reproduces Kant's political paradox, the Goethean model discloses a form of politics characterised by an ethic of exemplarity which overcomes Kant's paradox at the price of abandoning the utopian aspirations of modern thought.

Chapters 5, 6 and 7 take up Weber's thought and attempt to situate his work by reference to Nietzsche. This task is taken up polemically in Chapter 5 wherein the orthodox location of Weber's methodology in terms of Rickert's neo-Kantianism is subject to extended critique and the form of Weber's cultural science is shown to repeat the structure of genealogical critique. This polemic is grounded in a reading of Weber's famous 'switch-man' metaphor as reproducing the features of Nietzsche's doctrine of will to power, while refining and developing this doctrine through the specification of the distinctions between the dynamic of charisma and routinisation, the differentiation of the spheres of life and the inner logic of worldviews. Chapter 6 further illuminates the Nietzschean character of Weber's cultural science by showing how Weber's historical reconstruction of our modernity as *disenchantment* involves the repetition of Nietzsche's concern with the nihilistic effects of the Christian will to truth and its modern embodiment as secular scientific reason. However, Weber's refinement of the doctrine of will to power as a mode of accounting for cultural change, it is suggested, exhibits itself in terms of Weber's elaboration of the institutional features of disenchantment and, specifically, in his concern with bureaucracy. The concern both with disenchantment and bureaucracy is drawn out by relating Weber's analysis of the *Protestant ethic* to the spheres of science and politics in order to show how Weber argues that modern *Mensch* has the capacity to be autonomous but lacks *both* cultural grounds of value which would motivate the exercise of this capacity *and*, increasingly, the institutional conditions which facilitate or, at least, do not restrict the exercise of this capacity. Weber's response to the question of maturity is presented in Chapter 7 where it is suggested that he attempts to provide a cultural ground of value through the elaboration of a notion of *personality*, while he attempts to ground resistance to the dominance of *rational discipline* by constructing a vocational ethic around a secularisation of the idea of *calling*. The politics of this response is examined by reference to Weber's appeal to the figures of the *charismatic politician* and the *scientific genius*. It is argued that Weber's position reproduces both the legislative and exemplary forms of politics which characterise the dualistic ambivalence of Nietzsche's notion of the *Übermensch*, yet in Weber's thought these are tied together in an uneasy and unstable tension which is ultimately aporetic.

The following three chapters address the work of Foucault and attempt to exhibit how his concern with the question of maturity is related to the work of Nietzsche and Weber. This task is initially taken up in Chapter 8 through a focus on the development of Foucault's methodological reflections on the form of critique from archaeology to genealogy to the *double gaze* of archaeology and genealogy. Alongside this development, the chapter also examines Foucault's genealogical method as a further refinement of the doctrine of will to power in which the constitution of subjectivity is addressed in terms of the agonistic struggles of relations of *power* and *ethics* within regimes of *knowledge* which they transform and reproduce. In other words, the practice of critique is oriented towards forms of social practice and knowledge in terms of their implications for autonomy. This orientation is developed via the 'double gaze' in Chapter 9 in which Foucault's archaeological reflections on the form of the modern will to truth directs the historical reconstructions of our modernity presented by reference to the topics of punishment and sexuality, and drawn together in terms of *biopolitics*. Here it is argued that Foucault shows how humanist forms of knowledge and biopolitical technologies tie our capacity to transform ourselves to the intensification of power relations. Chapter 10 takes up Foucault's response to this dilemma as the elaboration of an *anti-humanist ethics of creativity* which displaces a politics of truth by a politics of struggle. Finally, it is argued that Foucault's refinement of genealogical critique produces an abandonment of the appeal to a world-historical genius/legislator which at least in part characterises the politics of Nietzsche's and Weber's responses to the question of maturity; this, it is suggested, results in the politics of Foucault's response appearing as an ethic of exemplarity in which critical activity exemplifies precisely that ethical stance which it attempts to entrench in modern culture.

In my conclusion, I attempt to draw together the significant features of my argument and to indicate the implications of the genealogical form of immanent critique developed by this trajectory of thought for contemporary thinking. Here my concern is both to delineate the family resemblances which constitute this trajectory as a distinct trajectory of thought and to suggest the tasks with which this way of thinking through the question of maturity confronts us.

1

KANT AND THE QUESTION OF MATURITY

KANT AND MATURITY AS ENLIGHTENMENT

Kant begins the essay 'What is Enlightenment?'[1] by posing the question of enlightenment as *'man's emergence from his self-imposed immaturity [Unmündigkeit]'* (Kant 1983: 41), this immaturity being defined as 'the inability to use one's understanding without guidance from another' (Kant 1983: 41). For Kant, this immaturity is *'self-imposed'*; as a species with the capacity for rational self-reflection, humanity has the ability to emerge from its immaturity but the majority of individuals – largely through laziness and cowardice – lack the drive to rely on their own understanding and, thereby, take responsibility for themselves. Kant, consequently, concludes his initial outline of the question of enlightenment with a positive definition of the spirit of enlightenment which functions rhetorically as an exhortation to the reader: *'Sapere Aude!* "Have the courage to use your own understanding!" – that is the motto of enlightenment' (Kant 1983: 41). The question having been defined, Kant's argument moves to its main concerns, namely, the determination of the conditions of possibility of enlightenment and the relation of these conditions to the actual conditions of the present (i.e. Prussia under Frederick the Great).

Kant initiates discussion of the conditions of possibility governing the emergence of enlightenment by distinguishing between the case of the individual and the case of the public. Kant suggests two grounds which render the individual's achievement of maturity problematic. Firstly, he states that laziness and cowardice result in the majority of individuals taking the path of immaturity – 'It is so easy to be immature. If I have a book to serve as my understanding, a pastor to serve as my conscience, a physician to determine my diet for me, and so on, I need not exert myself at all' (Kant 1983: 41) – and, moreover, it is this laziness and cowardice on the part of the mass of individuals that enables the few to constitute themselves as the guardians of humanity. The role of these self-appointed guardians is the focus of the second ground Kant presents; he argues that these guardians intentionally perpetuate the lack of resolve and courage that characterises the public:

The guardians who have so benevolently taken over the supervision
of men have carefully seen to it that far the greatest part of them
(including the entire fair sex) regard taking the step to maturity as
very dangerous, not to mention difficult. Having first made their
domestic livestock dumb, and carefully made sure that these docile
creatures will not take a single step without the go-cart to which they
are harnessed, these guardians then show them the danger that
threatens them, should they attempt to walk alone. Now this danger
is not actually so great, for after falling a few times they would in the
end certainly learn to walk; but an example of this kind makes men
timid and usually frightens them out of all further attempts.

(Kant 1983: 41)[2]

This combination of a certain natural timidity in the majority of humanity
and its social reinforcement by humanity's 'benevolent' guardians leads Kant
to suggest that, in practice, only a very few, no doubt exceptional, individuals 'have succeeded, by cultivating their own minds, in freeing themselves
from immaturity and pursuing a secure course' (Kant 1983: 41). If pros-
pects in the case of the individual are bleak, the reverse is the case in considering the public: 'that the public should enlighten itself is more likely;
indeed, if it is only allowed freedom, enlightenment is almost inevitable'
(Kant 1983: 41–2). The ground for Kant's claim lies in a conception of the
force of reason manifest in the catalytic role played by the few individuals
who have reached maturity (including even certain guardians) given the
condition of freedom of discussion within the public arena. In specifying
the nature of this freedom, Kant introduces a significant and curious distinction between the public use of reason and the private use of reason:[3]

By the public use of one's own reason I understand the use that
anyone as a *scholar* makes of reason before the entire *literate world*. I
call the private use of reason that which a person may make in a *civic
post* or office that has been entrusted to him.

(Kant 1983: 42)

Enlightenment, for Kant, requires only that the public use of reason be
free; indeed, not only does the restriction of the private use of reason not
hinder enlightenment, such restriction may be in the public interest. As
Kant notes:

in many affairs conducted in the interests of a community, a certain
mechanism is required by means of which some of its members must
conduct themselves in an entirely passive manner so that through
an artificial unanimity the government may guide them to public
ends, or at least prevent them from destroying such ends. Here one
certainly must not argue, instead one must obey.

(Kant 1983: 42)

Within a civic post, it appears, the individual must be conceived simply as an *instrument* for the achievement of public goals.[4] Stressing this feature of civic life, Kant gives an example which has sombre resonances for our age:

> it would be disastrous if an officer on duty who was given a command by his superior were to question the appropriateness or utility of the order He must obey. But as a scholar he cannot be justly constrained from making comments about errors in military service, or from placing them before the public for its judgement.
>
> (Kant 1983: 42–3)

Having specified the conditions under which enlightenment is possible, Kant turns to the relationship between the conditions requisite for enlightenment (i.e. a few enlightened individuals and freedom of public debate) and the actual conditions of his time.

Kant begins with a question: ' "Do we presently live in an *enlightened* age?" ' and an answer: ' "No, but we do live in an age of *enlightenment*" ' (Kant 1983: 44). The distinction between these two states lies, for Kant, in the form of legislation each embodies. That Prussia under Frederick II is an age of enlightenment is established by the freedom to reason publically set out in the formula ' "*Argue as much as you want and about what you want, but obey!*" ' (Kant 1983: 45); this, Kant asserts, is the primary principle of Frederick the Great's rule. Being both himself enlightened and possessing 'a well-disciplined, numerous army to guarantee public peace' (Kant 1983: 45), Frederick II is able to both encourage public enlightenment through freedom of discussion and to ensure obedience to the legislation he enacts. This form of rule, Kant suggests, is a prerequisite for the historical emergence of an *enlightened* age, for it is within the restrictions of their civil freedom occurring under an enlightened monarchy that individuals acquire 'the inclination to and vocation for free *thinking*' (Kant 1983: 46). Once acquired, this vocation

> gradually reacts upon a people's mentality (whereby they become increasingly able to *act freely*), and it finally even influences the principles of *government*, which finds that it can profit by treating men, *who are now more than machines*, in accord with their dignity.
>
> (Kant 1983: 46)

Although Kant does not, in this essay, go further than this general statement in characterising an enlightened polity, it is possible from his other political writings to determine the features of such a polity. Principal among these is the rational concordance of the public will and the legislative will. Following Rousseau, Kant constructs a contractarian model in which the legitimacy of a law resides in its expression of the public will (although, for Kant, this does not require the active participatory consent of the citizens; rather, it merely requires that the law in question

9

be rationally worthy of consent).[5] Consequently, Kant provides the following formula: '*Whatever a people cannot decree for itself cannot be decreed for it by the legislator*' (Kant 1983: 83). A polity in which the legislative will and the public will are identical expresses the existence of an enlightened age, for Kant, simply in that such an identity presupposes the existence of an enlightened public which embodies the recognition of individuals as ends in themselves. An enlightened age, in other words, is an age in which the realm of the political is consonant with the moral law. The age of Frederick marks, Kant argues, a necessary step towards such a 'kingdom of ends'.

At this stage, we may pause and reflect on this essay. Three questions immediately arise. What claims are involved in this identification of maturity with enlightenment? Why does Kant regard it as necessary that the public use of reason be free but not the private use of reason? On what grounds does Kant situate the potential concord of the political and moral realms? The issues raised here may be addressed by focusing on the theme of autonomy.

AUTONOMY, REASON AND HISTORY

Kant's essay begins, as we have noted, by identifying enlightenment with maturity, with reliance on one's own understanding, and ends by identifying enlightenment with the capacity to '*act freely*'. The initial definition presented by Kant links enlightenment with autonomy in a broad sense, that is, it represents enlightenment as self-determination, as a taking of responsibility for oneself. The latter identification, however, locates enlightenment in relation to autonomy in a more specific sense; enlightenment here is represented as *moral autonomy*, which in the context of Kant's system refers to the dutiful self-legislation of the moral law of freedom, that is, the categorical imperative. How though does Kant ground this identification of maturity (the determination of one's own will) with moral autonomy (the self-legislation of the moral law)? This crucial question for the coherence of Kant's notion of a kingdom of ends entails a brief examination of his critical philosophy.

Kant's system finds its starting point in a confrontation with what Kant termed the antinomies of pure reason and it is the third of these antinomies which provides a site of entry for this discussion.[6] In explicating this antinomy, Kant sets out two arguments concerning causality which appear to be equally grounded in reason:

Thesis Causality in accordance with the laws of nature is not the only causality from which the appearances of the world can one and all be derived. To explain these appearances it is necessary to assume that there is also another causality, that of freedom.

(Kant 1963: A444/B472)

10

Antithesis There is no freedom; everything in the world takes place solely in accordance with the laws of nature.

(Kant 1963: A445/B473)

The thesis involves the contention that, in accordance with the principle of sufficient determination, the idea of causality itself requires the existence of a free causality (a first or final cause). The antithesis, however, embodies the claim that, in accordance with the principle of non-contradiction, the idea of a free causality undermines the idea of causality itself in which all causes are themselves already effects.[7] Kant's resolution of this antinomy revolves about a positing of two distinct realms of reason, the realm of theoretical reason defined as a phenomenal realm of appearances determined by the laws of nature and the realm of practical reason identified as the noumenal realm of things-in-themselves governed by the law of freedom. The mutually exclusive positions expressed in the antinomy arise, for Kant, out of the tendency of theoretical reason to transgress its limits, to overstep the boundaries of experience within which it holds sway. In determining the parameters within which theoretical reason may legitimately make knowledge claims, however, Kant revolutionises the position of humanity. For, in contrast with the rest of nature, we know ourselves not only through the senses but also through 'pure apperception' (the faculties of understanding and reason); thus, one knows oneself both as a determined sensible (phenomenal) object and as a free intelligible (noumenal) subject.

It is on this location of the individual as constituted by both an empirical self and a transcendental self that Kant grounds his account of the individual as both natural and supra-natural, as both a being constituted by natural desires existing within the chains of cause and effect which define nature and as a being constituted by a rational will capable of initiating causal sequences within nature and, thereby, transforming nature. Our constitution as both natural and supra-natural beings emerges in the sphere of morality. This is evident, Kant argues, from

the *imperatives* which in all matters of conduct we impose as rules on our active powers. '*Ought*' expresses a kind of necessity and of connection with grounds which is found nowhere else in the whole of nature.

(Kant 1963: A547/B575)

Thus, to act freely is, for Kant, to act morally. In a way directly analogous with the scientific laws of nature which define the phenomenal realm of theoretical reason, the noumenal realm of practical reason is governed by the moral law of freedom which Kant renders comprehensible as the maxim: 'Act always according to that maxim whose universality as a law you can at the same time will' (Kant 1981: 42). The imperative form of

11

this maxim grounds morality in the motive of duty, in the recognition that the essence of one's humanity lies in willing the moral law for its own sake as the condition of one's freedom.

How does this relate to Kant's identification of maturity, the ability to act according to one's own understanding, with moral autonomy, the rational self-legislation of the moral law? Kant's identification of these two concepts of enlightenment is predicated on his identification of willing one's own will with willing the moral law (which is precisely the expression of one's rational will). On the one hand, immaturity as the reliance for understanding on the guidance of another indicates not a lack of knowledge concerning the character of the moral law but rather an inability to recognise this law for oneself as the ground of one's essential being and, consequently, the lack of a motive to realise one's will, to constitute oneself in accordance with the moral law. The role played by the guardians of humanity, for Kant, is that they actively operate to prevent the formation of such a recognition through such diverse tactics as a stress on the frailty of the individual, the elevation of heteronomous interests into ends, and the dismissal of the moral law as impractical or incidental.[8] On the other hand, enlightenment as reliance on one's own understanding indicates the moment at which one does recognise the essential ground of one's freedom in willing one's own will, in legislating the moral law for oneself, and, thereby, engages in the activity of transforming oneself as an empirical individual in accord with the dictates of the categorical imperative. Enlightenment, thus, appears as the project of bridging the gap between the noumenal and phenomenal realms, of transforming both oneself and the world into a form consonant with the moral law.

In delineating this project, however, Kant unwittingly constructs two problems internal to his philosophical system; a consideration of these difficulties is useful both in determining the relationship between the theme of autonomy and that of public and private uses of reason, and in specifying the problematic which Kant bequeaths to modern thought. The first issue to be addressed concerns the possibility of transforming the world of experience into a world characterised by moral freedom, that is, the problem of the possibility of maturity. The second issue relates to the coherence of Kant's resolution of the antinomies of pure reason through the introduction of a resolutely dualist philosophy.

How, given the distinction Kant draws between noumenal and phenomenal realms, is it possible to conceive of transforming of the world of nature in a moral direction? There are two related moments to the difficulty Kant's thought faces here: firstly, the teleological character of moral action logically requires for its possibility the existence of an end, and secondly, the very intention to act morally itself requires the possibility that moral action is effective in transforming the world.[9] The latter point has a significant psychological correlate in that the motive for taking the step to maturity is dependent on the possibility that enlightened action is causally effective in the world of experience. If Kant cannot ground this claim, the potential agent is liable to feel 'that his moral efforts would accentuate, not diminish, his alien and impotent position' (Yovel 1980: 102), thereby undermining the motive for maturity. How does Kant attempt to resolve these problems?

In relation to the determination of an end, Kant's problem is that of the radical autonomy he ascribes to the individual; in locating moral freedom as divorced from all man's natural (heteronomous) interests and desires, Kant rules out of court all those ends which are conventionally located as the ground of moral action (e.g. happiness and pleasure). Kant's attempt to overcome this dilemma relies on the introduction of a 'historical imperative' in the form of the idea of 'the highest good':

> The moral law is reason's formal condition for the use of our freedom and hence obligates us all by itself, independently of any purpose whatever as material condition. But it also determines for us, and *a priori*, a final purpose, and makes it obligatory for us to strive toward [achieving] it; and that purpose is the *highest good in the world* that we can achieve through freedom.
>
> (Kant 1987: §87, p. 339)

This 'historical imperative' is, for Kant, an elaboration of the categorical imperative in so far as the categorical imperative involves the presupposition that we, as rational self-determining beings, have purposes. As beings with purposes, it is entailed in Kant's system that we wish our purposes to count and, since to treat individuals as simply a means to a goal is to treat them as things (entities without purposes), it thereby follows from the condition of universality expressed in the categorical imperative that we must in locating ourselves as ends also recognise and treat all others as ends. The *'highest good in the world'* is simply this 'kingdom of ends' in which the greatest welfare of individuals is guaranteed by their treatment as beings with purposes which must be respected.

In setting out the idea of the *summum bonum*, Kant has established an end which appears consonant with the demands of his vision of radical autonomy; however, the possibility of realising this end (which is demanded for the intention of it) remains ungrounded. Moreover, Kant recognises that this possibility of realisation is necessarily cognitively ungrounded when he describes the idea of the highest good as a *matter of faith*. This is the meaning of the famous comment that he has denied knowledge in order to make room for faith. Kant's remarks in assigning this status to the *summum bonum* are revealing:

We cannot prove the concept of this good, as to whether it has any objective reality, in any experience that is possible for us, and hence adequately for the theoretical use of reason. But since pure practical reason commands us to use this concept in order to achieve that purpose [the highest good in the world] as best we can, we must assume it as possible [to realise]. This commanded effect, *together with the sole conditions conceivable by us under which [achieving] that effect is possible*, namely, the existence of God and the immortality of the soul, are *matters of faith*, and they are moreover the only objects which can be called matters of faith.

(Kant 1987: §91, p. 362)

The significance of this passage is twofold. Firstly, it illustrates that Kant can only provide for the possibility of moral action as causally effective by reference to a transcendental postulate, namely, God. Secondly, Kant thereby reverses the traditional relationship between God and humanity in so far as he does not deduce the moral law from the existence of God but, rather, deduces it from man as a being with the capacity for rational thought and only introduces the figure of God to facilitate the possibility of translating the moral law into causally effective action.[10]

The second problem posed for Kant is more serious. As has been noted, Kant grounds his identification of willing one's own will with willing the moral law on the distinction between noumenal and phenomenal realms; the question raised here is whether this dualism is coherent. The problem concerns the very idea of a history of reason in Kant's system and results in what has been termed Kant's *historical antinomy*.[11] To begin with, it is necessary to take up Kant's idea of a history of reason.

As Yovel has pointed out, Kant conceives of reason as a *system of interests* whose 'basic feature is *teleological* activity, pursuing its own "essential ends" or immanent tasks' (Yovel 1980: 14). Primary among these interests is the *architectonic* interest of reason, its interest in realising the unity of all its other interests (e.g. critical, metaphysical and totalising). The realisation of this architectonic interest has a history precisely because of the finitude of human reason:

Since it is finite, reason must inevitably suffer from a gap between its limited potential and its actual articulations; and it thus faces the problem of gradually closing this gap. Reason does not immediately possess the full, though limited scope that it can achieve in principle, but must be actualised in a progressive move of self-explication; and thus . . . human reason is subject to a history or becoming of its own.

(Yovel 1980: 14)

The difficulty with this, however, is that while Kant's system requires the idea of a history of reason (and indeed gains its authority from its claim to complete this history), it also rules out the idea of a history of reason.

This emerges when we consider that the concept of 'history' implies an embodiment in time, yet Kant locates time as a form of intuition which applies purely to the world of experience and thereby sites reason (which is a capacity of the noumenal self) outside of time.[12] Ironically, it appears that Kant's attempt to resolve the antinomy of causality, in which the principle of sufficient determination demands a free causality and the principle of non-contradiction rules out such a form of causality, ends by reproducing a formally isomorphic antinomy in which the principle of sufficient determination requires that reason have a history, while the principle of non-contradiction rules out the very idea of such a history. The significance of this antinomy is not simply that it cannot be overcome by reference to a transcendental postulate but moreover that it provides the impetus for the transformation of Kant's antinomy of causality into a *dialectic* of freedom and determination by Hegel and an *agonism* of freedom and necessity by Nietzsche.[13]

The discussion in this section began by suggesting that three questions arise from Kant's essay on enlightenment: What claims are involved in this identification of maturity with enlightenment? Why does Kant regard it as necessary that the public use of reason be free but not the private use of reason? On what grounds does Kant project the potential concord of the political and moral realms? We are now in a position to indicate answers to these questions. Firstly, the claims involved in the identification of maturity with enlightenment are that maturity consists of willing one's own will and that this is identical to willing the moral law. Secondly, Kant requires the free use of public reason on the grounds that it is critical and moral in that this use is addressed to individuals as rational beings, as entities with ends; by contrast, the private use of reason is both instrumental and immoral. Thirdly, Kant grounds the possibility of transforming the political sphere into accord with the moral law in the *faith* that practical reason requires of us, namely, faith in the effectiveness of moral action, which is grounded by reference to the idea of God. The final inescapable dilemma for Kant, however, is that the noumenal/phenomenal dualism which he requires to make these claims is itself entrapped within an antinomy isomorphic with what it was created to overcome.[14]

CONCLUSION

What, in the end, emerges from this brief discussion of Kant? We may note, firstly, the identification of maturity with willing one's own will, and secondly, the distinction between a public use of reason which is critical and addressed to individuals as ends, as beings with purposes, and a private use of reason which is instrumental and requires the treatment of individuals as things, as entities without purposes. Kant's ultimate failure to ground both his identification of willing one's own will with willing the moral law and his faith in the gradual withering away of the private use of reason as the political sphere progressed towards consonance with the moral law thus bequeaths a dual problematic to modern thought: firstly, the question of the relationship between thought and time, between the philosophy and history, *qua* the thinking of autonomy as maturity and, secondly, the question of the relationship between critical and instrumental forms of reason *qua* the achievement of maturity. This problematic, which erupts in the form of a historical antinomy and inerrs in the ambivalence of reason which characterises his thinking of the relationship of ethics and politics, entails that post-Kantian thought must confront the problem of its own historical specificity and that our interrogation of the adequacy of Nietzsche, Weber and Foucault with respect to this question requires that we are attentive to the relationship between ethics and politics in their texts, that is, the relationship between their ethical thinking of autonomy and their political thinking of the conditions of realising autonomy in modernity.

2

THE TRANSFORMATION OF CRITIQUE
Nietzsche and genealogy

To begin – a remark: 'in the presence of morality, as in the face of any authority, one is not *allowed* to think, far less to express an opinion: here one has to – *obey!*' (D Preface 3 p. 2). This comment of Nietzsche's occurs at the beginning of a critical discussion of Kant: what does it signify? In terms of Kant's discussion of enlightenment, it bespeaks an irony. Kant defines an age of enlightenment by reference to the principle ' "*Argue as much as you want and about what you want, but obey!*" ' (Kant 1983: 45), yet in articulating the categorical imperative, Kant seeks to foreclose arguments concerning the character of the moral law and to legislate obedience to this law for its own sake. For Nietzsche, one may suggest, this irony pervades Kant's philosophical project in which critique takes the form of legislation: a critique of pure reason to legislate the theoretical limits governing knowledge, a critique of practical reason to legislate the moral law governing freedom, and a critique of teleological judgement to legislate the purpose governing existence. In the grounding of its authority in a claim to complete the history of reason, Kant's system attempts to give definitive answers to the questions of reason – what can I know? what should I do? what can I hope for? – and thereby to rule out of court any further critical discussion of reason. It is precisely such discussion, however, that Nietzsche seeks to initiate. The concern of this chapter is to indicate the routes Nietzsche takes in re-opening the question of critique.[1]

The force of Kant's conception of critique, for Nietzsche, lies in its claim to construct a mode of critique which is *immanent* and, thereby, articulate a *total* critique. However, Nietzsche argues that Kant's critical philosophy fails to substantiate this twofold claim in both respects. With regard to the epistemological form of immanent critique deployed by Kant, Nietzsche poses an ironically rhetorical question: 'was it not somewhat peculiar to demand of an instrument [i.e. reason] that it should criticise its own usefulness and suitability?' (D Preface 3 p. 3).[2] The inability of reason to judge itself emerges in the metonymic form of Kant's critique: Kant's account is constructed about the claim that synthetic *a priori* judgements are possible by means of the faculty of reason – 'But is that – an answer?

17

An explanation? Or is it not rather merely a repetition of the question? How does opium induce sleep? "By means of a faculty", namely the *virtus dormitiva* – replies the doctor in Molière, ' (BGE 16 p. 24). Nietzsche's contention is that Kant's critique posits the possibility of synthetic *a priori* truths on the basis of the consequences of such truths, that is, the antinomies of pure reason; the antinomies which spur Kant's critical investigation already presuppose the faculty deployed to 'explain' them. It is the form of Kant's critique which leads on Nietzsche's account to its failure to articulate a total critique. As we noted above, Kant's critique expresses a project of legislation; however, this project (to which the form of his critique commits him) undermines its own claim to be a total critique in so far as the enterprise of legislation elides that of evaluation. In other words, in setting itself the task of delineating the laws governing the rights of claims to knowledge and claims to morality, Kant's critique fails to raise the question of the *value* of these ideals. Consequently, one might say that Nietzsche re-opens the question of critique by transforming this question from one of *legislation* into one of *evaluation*.[3]

How does Nietzsche effect this transformation? Two analytically distinct moments may be identified. Firstly, Nietzsche argues that we need to replace Kant's epistemological question – how are synthetic *a priori* judgements possible? – with a genealogical question: why are synthetic *a priori* judgements necessary? Secondly, Nietzsche suggests that we need to question the value of those judgements of this type which are constitutive of the history of the present. In advocating this transposition of the question of critique, Nietzsche sets himself tasks which require the articulation of a genealogical principle of immanent critique that operates at both the level of explanation and that of evaluation. Before attempting to delineate the characteristics of this principle, however, it is necessary to outline the grounds upon which Nietzsche accounts for his transformation of critique.

FROM EPISTEMOLOGY TO GENEALOGY

To transfer Kant's epistemological question to the realm of genealogy requires a twofold account: firstly, Nietzsche must explain how it is possible that this question comes to be posed as an epistemological issue, and secondly, he must illustrate that this question belongs not in the arena of epistemology but in that of genealogy.[4] We can initiate this discussion by citing a comment of Nietzsche's on Kant's belief in morality:

> Kant was, like every good German of the old stamp, a pessimist; he believed in morality, not because it is demonstrated in nature and history, but in spite of the fact that nature and history continually contradict it.
>
> (D Preface 3 pp. 3–4)

A synthetic *a priori* judgement such as the categorical imperative (in which Kant expresses his faith in morality) is therefore a judgement prior to experience in the sense of being grounded in reason (albeit that such judgements always entail a relationship to experience through the understanding). A starting point for Nietzsche's analysis is, thus, to examine the presuppositions required for postulating the possibility of judgements which are prior to experience. Kant's critical philosophy is, for Nietzsche, an exemplary instance of these presuppositions in which a distinction between a realm of being, the 'real' world, and a realm of becoming, the 'apparent' world, is legitimated by reference to a transcendental ego, that is, an non-contingent, non-empirical 'I' analytically separable from its contingent, empirical manifestation in thoughts, actions and emotions. A synthetic *a priori* judgement is possible on Kant's account because such a judgement describes the immanent structure of the pure ego as consciousness (the synthetic *a priori* judgements of theoretical reason) or will (the synthetic *a priori* judgements of practical reason). Nietzsche's task, consequently, is to present an account which undermines this belief in an ahistorical ego while also explicating the conditions which make this belief possible: this account is structured about a philosophy of grammar.[5]

'A philosophical mythology is concealed in *language* . . .' (HAH II.2 11 p. 306): the structure of our language, Nietzsche argues, is itself by no means philosophically neutral; on the contrary, 'thanks to unconscious domination and directing by . . . grammatical functions' (BGE 20 p. 32), language serves as an advocate of certain kinds of world interpretation. This is specifically the case with respect to the belief in the transcendental ego and the concomitant belief in a realm of being:

> Language belongs in its origin to the age of the most rudimentary form of psychology: we find ourselves in the midst of a rude fetishism when we call to mind the basic presuppositions of the metaphysics of language – which is to say, of *reason*. It is *this* which sees everywhere deed and doer; this which believes in will as cause in general; this which believes in the 'ego', in the ego as being, in the ego as substance, and which *projects* its belief in ego-substance on to all things – only thus does it create the concept 'thing'. . . . Being is everywhere thought in, *foisted on*, as cause; it is only from the conception 'ego' that there follows, derivatively, the concept 'being'. . . .
>
> (TI II 5 p. 38)

Nietzsche's argument in this passage is that our belief in 'ego' and 'being' is made possible by the distinction between doer and deed that language imposes on us in the form of the subject–predicate distinction. We can illustrate this argument by initial reference to a straightforward example: 'Lightning flashes'. In this phrase, the subject–predicate distinction acts to double the event in that it 'separates the lightning from its flash and takes the latter for an *action*, for the operation of a subject called lightning' (GM I 13 p. 45). *The event* (lightning/flash) *is taken both as subject-cause* (lightning) *and action-effect* (flash). For Nietzsche, this grammatical reification pervades our use of language. For example, the proposition 'I think' in which an event 'thinking' is separated into an action-effect 'thinking' and a subject-cause 'I' – implied in this separation are the claims that 'it is *I* who think, . . . that thinking is an activity and operation on the part of an entity thought of as a cause' (BGE 16 p. 28), that is, the construction of ego as transcendental will, and that 'what is designated by "thinking" has already been determined – that I *know* what thinking is' (BGE 16 p. 28), that is, the construction of ego as transcendental consciousness.

The cogency of this account of the possibility of belief in 'ego' and 'being' as being predicated on the reification of a grammatical function is dependent for its critical force on the claim that there exists no necessary correspondence between language and the world. It is in this grounding of his critique of the possibility of synthetic *a priori* judgements that Nietzsche transforms this question from the realm of epistemology to that of genealogy. This grounding is articulated in two stages: firstly, an account of language as exhibiting an aesthetic instrumentality and, secondly, an account of consciousness as a historical phenomenon.

Nietzsche's account may be located as beginning with a transformation of themes developed in the Romantic reaction to Kant. It had been argued, for example, by Herder that metaphor was connected to the beginning of speech and by Schelling that language was essentially aesthetic in character. In appropriating these arguments, however, Nietzsche dramatically transforms their intent. Whereas the Romantic movement sought to highlight the primacy of the aesthetic as the immediate disclosure of reality, Nietzsche assigns priority to the aesthetic as the value-mediated construction of reality.[6] In other words, Nietzsche deploys the idea of metaphor to undermine the conception that there exists any correspondence between language and the world and to assert that language constitutes the aesthetic instrument by means of which we create the world. Our investigation begins by focusing on a psychological allegory that Nietzsche puts forward to account for this belief that in language we possess knowledge of the world:

> To trace something unknown back to something known is alleviating, soothing, gratifying and gives moreover a feeling of power. Danger, disquiet, anxiety attend the unknown – the first instinct is to *eliminate* these distressing states.

> (TI IV 5 p. 51)

Language is constituted by an aesthetic instrumentality, for Nietzsche, precisely because the device by which we most readily translate the unknown into the familiar is metaphor. This creative act of translation, however, does not in itself suffice to master the anxiety attendant on the unknown. On the contrary, in its recognition of the aesthetic character of the identity it establishes, metaphor preserves the non-identity of the unknown. Further, the uniqueness displayed by metaphors – 'each perceptual metaphor is individual and without equals and is therefore able to elude all classification' (PT IV pp. 84–5) – resists the logic of identity, of reification, pertinent to the construction of causal explanations and it is by means of such explanations – 'First principle: any explanation is better than none' (TI VI 5 p. 51) – that the fear of the unknown is conquered.[7] Thus, Nietzsche argues, the cause-creating drive 'conditioned and excited by the feeling of fear' (TI VI 5 p. 51) requires that metaphors be dissolved into concepts through a repression of their aesthetic status: 'Only by forgetting this primitive world of metaphor can one live with any repose, security and consistency' (PT IV p. 86). This rationalisation of language's charismatic moment represents, for Nietzsche, the realisation of a causal explanation whereby the fear of the unknown is mastered through the constitution of the unknown as an effect of the known. It is only through this forgetting, it is only through this reification, that humanity secures its mastery.

It is on the basis of this account of language that Nietzsche argues that knowing is 'nothing but working with the favourite metaphors' (PT I p. 51) – and truth? Truth is:

A moving army of metaphors, metonymies and anthropomorphisms, in short a summa of human relationships that are being poetically and rhetorically sublimated, transposed, and beautified until, after long and repeated use, a people considers them as solid, canonical, and unavoidable. Truths are illusions whose illusory nature has been forgotten, metaphors that have been used up and have lost their imprint and that now operate as mere metal, no longer as coins.

(PT IV p. 84)

As such, for Nietzsche, a synthetic *a priori* judgement represents simply a reified metaphor constitutive of a particular form of life. It is, no doubt, such metaphors that Nietzsche has in mind when he suggests that, in the social activity of constituting causal explanations, certain explanations are preferred, namely, 'the kind by means of which the strange, new, unexperienced is most speedily and readily abolished – the most common explanations' (TI VI 5 p. 51) such that:

a particular kind of cause-ascription comes to preponderate more and more, becomes concentrated into a system and finally comes to *dominate* over the rest, that is to say simply to exclude *other* causes and explanations.

(TI VI 5 p. 51)

21

In developing this account of language as an instrument, Nietzsche both grounds his claim that there is no reason to suppose that language corresponds with the world and accounts for the need for the belief that language does correspond to the world and 'could lift the rest of the world off its hinges and make itself master of it' (HAH I 11 p. 16). In the context of Nietzsche's critique of Kant, the significance of this is twofold: firstly, it grounds the claim that the subject 'I' and the predicate 'think', for example, are simply fictions which enable the construction of causal explanations and that Kant's dualism represents the reification of these metaphors, and secondly, it requires that Nietzsche present an alternative account of consciousness.

For Nietzsche, Kant's error in reifying consciousness is typical of the philosophers: 'They think they are doing a thing *honour* when they dehistoricise it, *sub specie aeterni* – when they make a mummy of it' (TI III 1 p. 35). Kant's critical writings represent the reification of a specific historical stage of consciousness into consciousness *per se*, into a trans- cendental consciousness.[8] Ironically, Nietzsche's criticism itself finds support in Kant's post-critical writings, for to pose, as Kant does, the question of enlightenment as a historical question is to acknowledge the historicity of consciousness and to suggest that Kant's critiques represent the reflexive conclusions of an enlightened consciousness rather than of consciousness as such. The account of consciousness Nietzsche offers, as one might expect, departs from Kant's 'critical' dehistoricising.

Nietzsche's starting point is a functional question: what is the purpose of consciousness? To indicate its reflexive character is insufficient for Nietzsche – 'The whole of life would be possible without, as it were, seeing itself in a mirror' (GS 354 p. 297). Rather he proposes that the purpose and development of consciousness is related to the need and capacity for communication. Articulating this hypothesis, Nietzsche claims that consciousness

> is really only a net of communication between human beings; it is only as such that it had to develop; a solitary human being who lived like a beast of prey would not have needed it. . . . As the most endangered animal, he [man] *needed* help and protection, he needed his peers, he had to learn to express his distress and to make himself understood; for all of this he needed 'consciousness' first of all, he needed to 'know' himself what distressed him, he needed to 'know' how he felt, he needed to 'know' what he thought.
>
> (GS 354 p. 298)

On this understanding, consciousness is not an innate feature of the individual; rather it is a social product whose historical development is co-extensive with the development of language: 'The human being inventing signs is at the same time the human being who becomes ever more keenly conscious of himself' (GS 354 p. 299). In setting forward this naturalistic account of consciousness Nietzsche has provided the final ground necessary for his transformation of Kant's epistemological question into a historical question, and consequently we can conclude this section by summarising Nietzsche's account of, firstly, how it is possible that the question of critique be posed as an epistemological issue and, secondly, why it is necessary to pose it as a historical issue.

Kant articulates his concept of critique, for Nietzsche, under the seduction of the metaphysics of language. It is this which leads him both to the question of how synthetic *a priori* judgements are possible and to the answer that their conditions of possibility lie in a transcendental ego. Nietzsche's transformation of the concept of critique is grounded on a critique of the metaphysics of language which culminates in a conception of language as the instrument by means of which consciousness develops. It is this which leads him to the question of why synthetic *a priori* judgements are necessary and the general answer that they represent the means by which consciousness abolishes its fear of the unknown, that psychological correlate of man's status as 'the most endangered animal' which itself engenders the need for consciousness. This question is historical since, for Nietzsche, consciousness is a historical phenomenon which constitutes (and is constituted by) the development and refinement of certain synthetic *a priori* truths to the exclusion of others. Nietzsche's question – why are synthetic *a priori* truths necessary? – does not, however, simply manifest a general dimension; rather, this general concern leads to a specific interest which is embodied in the question: why are *these* synthetic *a priori* truths necessary as opposed to others? It is at this juncture that the question of necessity becomes a question of value; for to raise the possibility of other synthetic *a priori* truths is to pose the question of the relative value of these different sets of truths. How then does Nietzsche ground and articulate this second moment to his transformation of critique?

FROM LEGISLATION TO EVALUATION

The fundamental faith of the metaphysicians is *the faith in antithetical values*. It has not occurred to even the most cautious of them to pause and doubt here on the threshold, where however it was most needful they should: . . . For it may be doubted, first whether there exist any antitheses at all, and secondly whether these popular evaluations and value-antitheses . . . are not perhaps merely foreground valuations, merely provisional perspectives, ...

(BGE 2 p. 16)

Two moments are indicated in this passage: a moment of transformation and a moment of scepticism. The claims involved here may be illustrated by reference to Kant's antinomy of causality. This antinomy, it will be recalled, describes a thesis according to which the adequate determination of causality requires the existence of a free causality, a causality of will, and an antithesis according to which the idea of a free causality is a contradiction in terms. The two moments of Nietzsche's argument are that, firstly, the thesis and antithesis embody value-commitments constitutive of, respectively, the perspectives of morality and science, and secondly, that these perspectives are not necessarily antithetical but may describe a continuum, that is, moments within the development of a single perspective. The concern of this section is with elaborating Nietzsche's grounds for the former of these claims (the latter claim will be taken up in the next chapter). This elucidation involves an analysis of Nietzsche's doctrine of perspectivism which can be facilitated by focusing initially on the arena of knowledge-claims and latterly on the question of value.[9]

Let us return for a moment to Kant's third antinomy. The thesis may be read here as describing the perspective of free will: the will as a faculty which can produce effects in the realm of experience, that is, initiate causal sequences. The antithesis, on the other hand, may be taken as describing the perspective of determinism: the individual as a part of nature is subject to scientific law, that is, our actions are always already themselves moments in a causal sequence defined by natural necessity. Nietzsche's contention is that these positions, far from characterising the respective realms of being and becoming, both simply describe interpretations of the world which are constitutive of how we experience it.[10] He states, for example, with regard to the idea of free will that 'we know only too well what it is – the most infamous of all the arts of the theologian for making mankind "accountable" in his sense of the word' (TI VI 7 p. 53), and in relation to the notion of scientific laws of nature that 'physics too is only an interpretation and arrangement of the world . . . and *not* an explanation of the world' (BGE 14 p. 26). How does Nietzsche ground this claim? We can approach this question by returning firstly to the issue of grammar and secondly to the issue of metaphor.

Kant, it will be recalled, resolves the antinomy of causality by distinguishing between a noumenal self – the transcendental ego constituted by the faculty of reason – and a phenomenal self – the empirical individual constituted by feelings and desires. As we have noted, however, Nietzsche argues that the idea of a pure ego is made possible by the illicit reification of a grammatical category onto the world. What then, for Nietzsche, are the features of the self? To begin:

'The subject' is the fiction that many similar states in us are the effect of one substratum: but it is we who first created the 'similarity' of these states; our adjusting and making them similar is the fact, not their similarity (– which ought rather be denied –).

(WP 485 p. 269)

The self, Nietzsche hypothesises, is not a unitary entity; rather it consists of a multiplicity of different states upon which one endows a certain similarity. We can elucidate this passage by examining what is involved for Nietzsche in the proposition 'I know'. As we have noted earlier, two claims are embodied in this form of proposition: a positing of a subject 'I' who effects the action 'knowing' and a positing of 'knowing' as a determinate and unitary operation. Given Nietzsche's critique of these claims as exemplifying the false metaphysics of language, it is unsurprising that in the account of the self he offers both claims are radically reversed. Firstly, it should be noted that in attacking the idea of the noumenal self Nietzsche is not attacking the idea of the self as such; rather he is involved in reconceptualising the relationship between self and world. In claiming that ' "the doer" is merely a fiction added to the deed – the deed is everything' (GM I 13 p. 45), Nietzsche's point is that the self does not effect an action 'knowing' but rather is constituted *qua* knower by the activity of knowing. Just as lightning is constituted by the flash, the knower is by the knowing – the doer by the deed. Secondly, Nietzsche does not regard the activity of knowing as the unitary operation of a faculty; on the contrary, he suggests that knowing is constituted by its relationship to that which is known. The issue here is that 'knowing' is always a 'knowing x' and we have no reason, for example, to suppose that 'knowing Fiona' is a qualitatively similar state to 'knowing $F = ma$'. How do these points relate to the passage cited above? Consider the following remark:

first, an act is imagined which simply does not occur, 'thinking,' and secondly, a subject-substratum in which every act of thinking, and nothing else, has its origin: that is to say, both the deed and the doer are fictions.

(WP 477 p. 264)

'Thinking' (like 'knowing') is an imaginary act in that there is no such unitary operation, only a 'thinking x' and 'thinking y', etc. However, under the aegis of language, we subsume a variety of different states under the generic concept 'thinking'. Conceptual language (the reification of metaphorical language) represents the means by which we 'adjust and make similar' different states. It is on this basis that there arises the seduction of grammar, the possibility of positing a subject-substratum which causes this similarity of states. The significance of this account of the self lies in the implications which emerge when we consider it in relation to Nietzsche's account of the aesthetic character of language. The central point here is that the self is constituted by the metaphors it creates to deal with experience. Since synthetic *a priori* judgements represent those metaphors by which the fear of the unknown is most speedily abolished, that is, those metaphors whose forgetting is most deeply entrenched within a cultural tradition, it follows that these judgements are centrally constitutive of our selfhood. Thus Nietzsche grounds his claim that the two sides of Kant's antinomy represent interpretations which govern how we experience the world through an account which demonstrates that such interpretations are constitutive of selfhood. Perspectivism, thus far, denotes the doctrine that the self and the world are constituted by means of an ongoing activity of interpretation articulated around a set of central metaphors. How though does this doctrine engage with the questions of value and evaluation?

The question of value is engaged for Nietzsche in so far as a perspective immanently involves a project of evaluation. Nietzsche's grounds for this claim are twofold: firstly, he argues that in constructing an aesthetic interpretation of experience one is engaging in a valuation of experience and, secondly, he claims that this valuation involves privileging certain forms of activity above others. Again Kant may serve as an example for Nietzsche's argument in that Kant's positing of the noumenal realm of the thing-in-itself exemplifies, on Nietzsche's account, the characteristic valuation of metaphysics; Nietzsche summarises this position as follows:

> How *could* something originate in its antithesis? Truth in error, for example? Or will to truth in will to deception? . . . Such origination is impossible; he who dreams of it is a fool, indeed worse than a fool; the things of the highest value must have another origin *of their own* – they cannot be derivable from this transitory, seductive, deceptive, mean little world, from this confusion of desire and illusion. In the womb of being, rather, in the intransitory, in the hidden god, in the 'thing in itself' – *that* is where their cause must lie and nowhere else!
>
> (BGE 2 pp. 15–16)

The metaphysical perspective within which Kant's project is defined begins with a devaluation of the realm of experience, of becoming, as against the (for Nietzsche, purely fictional) realm of being. This devaluation is the condition for grounding the values of this form of life as *the* values. In the case of the perspective of which Kant's work is an exemplar, the highest values are those embodied in the moral law (e.g. freedom, equality, reciprocity, etc.). This entails that moral action is privileged above all other forms of action, an instance of this being Kant's privileging of the public use of reason over the private use of reason. Indeed, Kant's project of enlightenment involves precisely the gradual transformation of the conditions of action such that all activities may be moral in character; the realm of experience is given value only in so far as it is increasingly transformed in a moral direction. However, in so far

26

as the realm of being is a fiction added onto the realm of becoming, the metaphysical operation of privileging certain values, that is, the values embedded in certain kinds of activity, is deprived of its ground. Nietzsche's question concerning the necessity of synthetic *a priori* truths thus becomes simultaneously a question concerning the necessity of the values embodied in these judgements.

In this context, Nietzsche's argument is that one cannot simply presuppose the value of the activities represented by the ideals of morality and knowledge as Kant does; rather, it is necessary to raise the question of value of these values. Why these values and not others? Why this form of life not another? Yet to raise this question is simultaneously to raise the questions of *how* one can articulate an evaluation of values and *why* one would want to. In other words, Nietzsche's deconstruction of Kant's critical enterprise as failing to substantiate its claim to construct a mode of critique which is *immanent* requires the reconstruction of the activity of critique under a principle adequate to this task, that is, a principle which operates at both the level of explanation and that of evaluation.

WILL TO POWER AS A PRINCIPLE OF EXPLANATION

Kant's critical enterprise, it will be recalled, is dependent for its force on the claim that a synthetic *a priori* judgement is possible because such a judgement describes the activity of the transcendental ego as consciousness (the synthetic *a priori* judgements of theoretical reason) or as will (the synthetic *a priori* judgements of practical reason). Indeed, it has been noted that Nietzsche's critique of the idea of a transcendental ego requires the elaboration of an alternative account of consciousness as a historical phenomenon. It has further been noted that Nietzsche accounts for subjectivity as constituted by both the form and content of our activities as agents. In so far, therefore, as Nietzsche is concerned to evaluate the values embodied in these activities, or rather the value-perspective which governs these activities, the principle of evaluation he elaborates must be capable of generating an account of the capacity of the individual to act as an agent which is consonant with his account of the development of consciousness. In other words, Nietzsche must delineate an account of willing as the ground of his principle of critique. We can initiate discussion of this account by contrasting Nietzsche's position with Kant's understanding of the will.[11]

'At the beginning stands the great fateful error that the will is something which *produces an effect* – that the will is a *faculty*. . . . Today we know it is merely a word' (TI III 5 p. 38). This remark, which occurs during Nietzsche's critique of the metaphysics of language, sets the tone for his approach to the question of willing and this tone is echoed in a further comment: 'Willing seems to me to be above all something *complicated*, something that is a unity only as a word' (BGE 19 p. 29). What then are the features Nietzsche assigns to 'willing'?[12]

Firstly, Nietzsche describes a 'plurality of sensations' which include a feeling of leaving, a feeling of that left, a feeling of going, and a feeling of that approached. 'Willing' is an ongoing activity involving both the feeling of states and states of feeling. Secondly, 'willing' involves thinking: 'in every act of will there is a commanding thought' (BGE 19 p. 30). 'Willing' is always a willing *x* where *x* is determined by the commanding thought. Thirdly, 'willing' involves an emotion correspondent with the commanding thought, namely 'the emotion of command': 'What is called "freedom of the will" is essentially the emotion of superiority over him who must obey' (BGE 19 p. 30). To summarise: 'willing' involves a becoming, an interpreting, and a feeling of power in the realisation of its goal.

To this complex of feeling, thought and emotion, one must add the further feature of action. Here again Nietzsche reverses Kant's position; whereas Kant as a metaphysician 'believes wholeheartedly that willing *suffices* for action' (BGE 19 p. 30), Nietzsche's position is that it is only in the actualisation of 'will' in action that 'will' determines itself as 'will'. This emerges in Nietzsche's consideration of the structure of subjectivity. He notes, for example, that the 'subject' consists of a multiplicity of drives, each one of which embodies 'a kind of lust to rule; each one has its perspective that it would like to compel all the other drives to accept as a norm' (WP 481 p. 267). This notion of the 'subject' as constituted by a cluster of competing drives leads Nietzsche to a distinction between 'weak' and 'strong' wills:

> *Weakness of the will*: that is a metaphor that can prove misleading. For there is no will and consequently neither a strong or weak will. The multitude and disggregation of the impulses and the lack of any systematic order among them result in a 'weak will'; their co-ordination under a single predominant impulse results in a 'strong will': in the first case it is the oscillation and lack of gravity; in the latter, the precision and clarity of direction.
>
> (WP 46 pp. 28–9)

The constitution of the 'will' as an organisational unity is articulated through the *labour* of self-overcoming. To put this slightly differently, the co-ordination of the drives under a commanding impulse is achieved through adherence to the *telos* of the leading drive, that is, through practical activity. Nietzsche's conception 'will to power' may thus be distinguished from Kant's concept of the will on two counts: firstly, the idea of the 'will' does not describe the metaphysical essence of the 'subject' as agent, as doer, but rather the diverse and conflicting historically conditioned impulses which constitute the individual, and secondly, the determination of the will (either as a unified will – that is the constitution of selfhood as *goal-directed agency* – or as an unorganised will – that is the constitution of selfhood as *goal-lacking agency*) is achieved only through the actualisation of the will as power in practical activity.[13]

In developing the idea of will to power as a principle of explanation, two features of the phenomenological reconstruction of 'willing' given here assume particular relevance: firstly, the necessity of thought, that is, of consciousness for 'willing', and secondly, the notion of a 'centre of gravity' whose presence or absence corresponds respectively to 'strong' and 'weak' wills. The former of these features requires an account of movement from instinctual behaviour to conscious action as providing the necessary condition of agency, while the latter demands an account of the constitution of a 'centre of gravity'. Both of these will be addressed in the next chapter, but we will just briefly sketch the ideas Nietzsche proposes.

Nietzsche's account of the development of consciousness has already been touched on in an earlier section; his premise is that '*consciousness has developed only under the pressure of the need for communication*'. Man, as 'the most endangered animal', required consciousness in order to communicate his distress, an instance of this distress being his instinctive fear of the unknown. The development of language is co-extensive with the development of consciousness in that it articulates the possibility of naming and communicating this distress, and also in that it provides the instruments, that is, concepts, by which this fear is sublimated. One might note here Nietzsche's comment that

> Everything which distinguishes man from the animals depends upon this ability to volatilize perceptual metaphors in a schema, and thus to dissolve an image into a concept. . . .
>
> (PT IV p. 86)

The second idea Nietzsche deploys relates to an account of the constitution of a 'centre of gravity' where this phrase refers to the organisation of the various impulses constitutive of the individual under the aegis of a commanding drive. Nietzsche argues, however, that the constitution of a given drive as the commanding drive may be facilitated by two distinct and opposed routes. The first route is structured about the construction of a perspective expressed as an affirmation of *becoming*. Thus, in the first essay of *On the Genealogy of Morals*, Nietzsche suggests that the noble's 'centre of gravity' is constituted pre-reflectively through an affirmation of the relationship of self and world predicated on the *pathos of distance*, that is, the internalisation of the social order of rank. The second route is based on the construction of a perspective expressed as an affirmation of *being*. Thus, in the essay already referred to, Nietzsche suggests that the slave's 'centre of gravity' is constituted reflectively through a denial of the relationship between self and world predicated on the positing of a fictional world, the realm of being, which reverses the social order of rank and thereby provides the slave with the *pathos of distance* requisite to the construction of a 'centre of gravity'.[14]

These accounts, it is suggested, ground Nietzsche's idea of will to power as a principle of explanation in so far as they account for the constitution of selfhood as agency as articulated through, firstly, the development of consciousness and, secondly, the construction of a 'centre of gravity', that is, the constitution of an interpretive evaluation of the world (i.e. a perspective). It is on this ground that Nietzsche makes the claim that

> The world seen from within, the world described and defined according to its 'intelligible character' – it would be 'will to power' and nothing else.
>
> (BGE 36 p. 49)

To legitimate this claim would require Nietzsche to demonstrate that the development of a perspective, the elaboration and alteration of its central metaphors, is directly related to changes in the worldly conditions informing its capacity to operate as a 'centre of gravity', that is, to enable the organisation of the will as unitary will (i.e. goal-directed agency) and its determination through the actualisation of will as power in practical activity. This legitimation is one the topics of the following chapter; however, for the present it is necessary to elucidate Nietzsche's grounding of the idea of will to power as a principle of evaluation.

WILL TO POWER AS A PRINCIPLE OF EVALUATION

In Kant's essay 'What is Enlightenment?', the activity of critique is facilitated by positing autonomy as a transcendental ideal which is to be realised in modernity by the gradual overcoming of the ambivalence of reason, that is, the withering away of the instrumental–private use of reason in the face of the critical–public use of reason. In this context, the grounding of the idea of will to power as a principle of genealogical evaluation may be facilitated by indicating Nietzsche's transformation of the vision of maturity which animates Kant's critique. As a preface to this account, however, it is useful to reflect on the relationship between the history of reason and empirical history in Nietzsche's account and the implications of this relationship for the activity of evaluation.

Kant's dilemma, it will be recalled, is that his project demands an account of the relationship between the history of reason and empirical history while his system rules out the possibility of any such account. Nietzsche's resolves this dilemma, as his account of consciousness intimates, through a transformation of critique in which the question of reason is displaced from the realm of metaphysics to the realm of history. It is thus no longer a question of bridging the gap between the history of reason and empirical history; rather, the two are co-extensive. An implication of this transformation, however, is that Nietzsche cannot ground the authority of his critique on a claim to complete the history of reason; rather Nietzsche's critical evaluation of perspectives must acknowledge its own specificity as a moment within the history of reason. Consequently, the idea of will to power as a principle of immanent critique must be treated as embodying a project of evaluation specific to modernity. The significance of the specificity of Nietzsche's critique immediately emerges in so far as it implies that the vision of autonomy immanent within the idea of will to power – the vision of maturity which defines its principle of evaluation – is *an ideal specific to modern culture*.[15] The question raised in this instance by Nietzsche's transformation of Kant's critical project thus concerns the transformation of the vision of autonomy attendant on the transformation of its status from transcendental to historically specific ideal.

This discussion may be initiated by noting the stark contrast between Nietzsche's and Kant's visions of maturity. For whereas Kant conceives of maturity as moral autonomy, that is, as self-legislated obedience to the moral law, Nietzsche delineates the mature individual – 'the ripest fruit' – as 'the *sovereign individual*, like only to himself, liberated again from the morality of custom, autonomous and supramoral (for "autonomous" and "moral" are mutually exclusive), in short, the man who has his own independent and protracted will and the *right to make promises*' (GM II 2 p. 59). The central moment in Nietzsche's critique of Kant's vision of maturity appears to be a reconceptualisation of autonomy which disconnects it from the idea of a universalisable moral law. To account for Nietzsche's critique requires further consideration of his distinction between the type of perspective whose centre of gravity is sited in the realm of becoming and the type whose centre of gravity is located in the fictional realm of being.

For Nietzsche, Kant's formulation of maturity is a manifestation of that type of perspective which – given the possibility of belief in a realm of being – enables the constitution of goal-directed agency through affirmation of the realm of being, the 'real world'. The significance of this type of perspective is that it facilitates the transformation of a 'weak will' into a 'strong will'. It was suggested in our earlier discussion that the inability to organise the diverse impulses under a leading drive, that is, to posit a goal, which defines the 'weak will' is predicated on a lack of distance which manifests itself as a denial of the relationship between the self and the world of experience. Why is it, though, that this denial entails this inability? Nietzsche's claim here is that this denial takes the form of a denial of responsibility for the relationship between self and world – the slave pre-reflectively denies responsibility for his position as a slave – and this eschewal of responsibility, consequently, rules out the organisation of the will which is, precisely, a taking on of the responsibility of positing a goal for the self. What is involved then in the construction of a centre of gravity sited in the fictional realm of being? The initial moment of this construction is a displacement of responsibility; unable to posit a goal for himself, the individual posits a fictional authority which commands obedience to a goal it legislates. Moreover, in so far as this authority is posited to facilitate the self-affirmation of the individual, the goal it legislates necessarily embodies those values which prize the form of individuality displayed by the weak individual and, consequently, describes a reversal of the order of rank which characterises the social world at this juncture. The positing of this authority thus endows the weak individual with a goal and, *pari passu*, the *pathos of distance* requisite to the constitution of goal-directed agency. In the case of Kant, this authority is expressed in the categorical imperative and the goal which attends it, namely, a 'kingdom of ends'. Nietzsche's critique of Kant may thus be accounted for by noting that, while Kant's vision of maturity may facilitate a 'strong will' (goal-directed agency), it does not facilitate an autonomous will, that is, goal-directed agency in which the self determines its own goal. On the contrary, it appears that only an individual who affirms the relationship between self and world is capable of positing a goal for himself, that is, of constituting himself as an autonomous individual.

The significance of this transformation of the idea of autonomy for the operation of the notion of will to power as a principle of genealogical evaluation lies in the implication that a perspective may be evaluated in terms of its historical role in constituting those moments of modern culture which facilitate the possibility of autonomy. Consequently, we can conclude our concern with Nietzsche's transformation of critique from the realm of metaphysical legislation to genealogical evaluation by noting that this transformation entails that an investigation of the value of the ideals of knowledge and morality requires a historical account of the implications of the perspective embodying these ideals for the possibility of 'breeding' mature individuals in modernity.

3

THE GENEALOGY OF MODERNITY
Nietzsche, asceticism and nihilism

If you are to venture to interpret the past you can do so only out of the fullest exertion of the vigour of the present: only when you put forward your noblest qualities in all their strength will you divine what is worth knowing and preserving in the past.

(UM II 6 p. 94)

A reiteration: genealogy as a mode of critique is concerned with articulating a history of the present and, specifically, those moments of the present which facilitate the 'breeding' of an autonomous human type.[1] The genealogical accounts with which we are here concerned thus represent reconstructions whose purpose is to provide the modern individual with 'a context of meaning' (Strong 1988: 38) by means of which the development of *Menschentum* may be understood and evaluated in terms of its implications for the fate of man in modernity. In thus transforming the form of critique, however, Nietzsche also develops and transforms thematic moments present in Kant's essay on enlightenment. These, notably, concern the question of the 'guardians' of humanity, the ambivalence of modern reason and, as already noted, the issue of autonomy.

In approaching this topic, however, it is necessary to begin by examining Nietzsche's account of how man becomes that rarest of creatures – a *historical* animal. Or, to put it slightly differently, how man develops consciousness. This question – which Nietzsche's addresses as the question of the *prehistory* of man – provides the initial context of meaning within which Nietzsche's account develops.

FROM INSTINCT TO AGENCY: CUSTOM AND CULTURE

It will be recalled that the emergence of consciousness is predicated, for Nietzsche, on man's status as 'the most endangered animal' and attends the need to overcome the fear of the unknown through the individual's communication of their distress. The question of the prehistory of man

33

may be read as addressing the development of consciousness as the overcoming of this distress. To explore this question requires the determination of the conditions through which this transformation of man from a creature of instinctive behaviour to one of conscious action is wrought and of the relationship between man's instinctive structure and his emergent consciousness. To facilitate this exploration, we can begin by focusing on Nietzsche's characterisation of the animal state:

> Consider the cattle grazing as they pass you by: they leap about, eat, rest, digest, leap about again, and so on from morn till night and from day to day, fettered to the moment and its pleasure or displeasure, and thus neither melancholy or bored. . . . Thus the animal lives *unhistorically*: for it is contained in the present, ...
>
> (UM II 1 p. 60)

The animal, constituted by its instincts, is purely reactive; it responds directly, automatically, to stimuli on the basis of its instinctual structure.[2] There is, in this form of being, no sense of time, of cause and effect, only the moment to which it is chained. The animal is constituted by the faculty of forgetting. It is in this context that one must address the opening of Nietzsche's second essay in *On the Genealogy of Morals* where he states:

> To breed an animal *with the right to make promises* – is not this the paradoxical task that nature has set itself in the case of man? is it not the real problem regarding man?
>
> (GM II 1 p. 57)[3]

Nietzsche's concern here is not with the institution of promising but rather with the conditions requisite for the idea of promising, that is, the development of a sense of time, a *'memory of the will'* which locates the individual in culture. The central moment to the development of this memory – which is nothing other than the development of consciousness itself, that is, the capacity to resist the stimuli of the moment – is the emergence of the capacity to think causally. Recalling Nietzsche's identification of the development of consciousness with the development of language, we can note that it is the reification of metaphors into concepts which constitutes the condition of possibility for the belief in causality and the generation of causal explanations. The question which arises for Nietzsche at this stage thus concerns the conditions which enable the reification of metaphors into concepts and, consequently, the development of the capacity for thinking causally.

What is involved in the reification of a metaphor into a concept? The notion of reification refers here to the process of *entrenchment* that indicates the constitution of a specific form of life, that is, a culture.[4] It is, it seems, through the activity of culture formation that the aesthetic status of a metaphor is *forgotten* and it is transformed into a concept. Two issues take on significance here: firstly, is it not paradoxical to speak of forgetting in the context of the development of memory? and, secondly, how is the activity of culture formation facilitated? We will address each of these in turn.

The first issue raises the question of the relationship between man's instinctual structure and the development of consciousness, for the former is associated with forgetting (a forgetting itself prior to memory) and the latter with the development of memory. The crucial point here is that Nietzsche does not appear to regard the development of consciousness within the prehistory of man as antagonistic to the instinctual structure of man; on the contrary, in so far as the impetus to the emergence and development of consciousness is provided by man's instinctive fear of the unknown, it seems there is a concordance of interests between the instincts and consciousness. This is reflected in Nietzsche's comment that

> Consciousness is the last and latest development of the organic and hence also what is most unfinished and unstrong. Consciousness gives rise to countless errors that lead an animal or man to perish sooner than necessary, 'exceeding destiny,' as Homer puts it. If the conserving association of the instincts were not so very much more powerful, and if it did not serve on the whole as a regulator, humanity would have to perish of its misjudgements and its fantasies with open eyes, of its lack of thoroughness and its credulity – in short, of its consciousness; rather, without the former, humanity would long have disappeared.
>
> (GS 11 p. 84)

The instincts which lead man to the formation of communities facilitate the development of consciousness. The forgetting of the aesthetic status of metaphors, their entrenchment through culture formation, is thus a product of the instincts' regulation of man during his prehistory. How then is the formation of a culture facilitated?

In accounting for the constitution of a form of life, the formation of a culture, Nietzsche focuses on the establishment and maintenance of customs. It is in this context that Nietzsche's discussion of the 'morality of mores' assumes its initial significance. Consider, for example, the following passage:

> *First proposition of civilisation.* – Among barbarous peoples there exists a species of customs whose purpose appears to be custom in general: minute and fundamentally superfluous stipulations ... which, however, keep continually in the consciousness the constant proximity of custom, the perpetual compulsion to practise customs: so as to strengthen the mighty proposition with which civilisation begins: any custom is better than no custom.
>
> (D 16 p. 15)

35

Culture begins with the establishment of customs, for Nietzsche, simply because the transformation of metaphors into concepts, that is, entrenchment, is dependent on making communal life regular and calculable, and this is achieved through the reification of communal life as custom. The 'morality of mores' precisely in so far as it is 'a hinderance to the acquisition of new experiences' (D 19 p. 18) renders behaviour regular and calculable, thus enabling the entrenchment of the metaphors constitutive of customs, that is, their transformation into concepts and, eventually, synthetic *a priori* judgements. The capacity to think causally, it appears, is a product of the morality of custom. It should be noted here that Nietzsche is not, in this instance, concerned with the character of the customs constitutive of a culture; rather his concern is simply with the existence of customs *per se*. To speak of the 'morality of mores', however, does require an account of *how* it is that the customs constitutive of a culture are maintained. In other words, in so far as the cogency of Nietzsche's account entails that it is through adherence to custom that man makes himself regular and calculable (which is the condition of thinking causally), it is entailed that Nietzsche must explicate the mechanism by which the 'morality of mores' achieves this effect.

The mechanism Nietzsche identifies is punishment: 'pain is the most powerful aid to mnemotechnics' (GM II 3 p. 61). The question posed by nature, it will be recalled, is:

> 'How can one create a memory for the human animal? How can one impress something upon this partly obtuse, partly flightly mind, attuned only to the passing moment, in such a way that it will stay there?'
>
> (GM II 3 p. 60)

The answer supplied by the instincts is this: ' "If something is to stay in the memory it must be burned in: only that which never ceases to *hurt* stays in the memory" ' (GM II 3 p. 61). Thus Nietzsche invites us to consider 'the old German punishments':

> for example, stoning . . . , breaking on the wheel . . . , piercing with stakes, tearing apart or trampling by horses . . . , boiling of the criminal in oil or wine . . . , the popular flaying alive . . . , cutting flesh from the chest, and also the practice of smearing the wrongdoer with honey and leaving him in the blazing sun for the flies.
>
> (GM II 3 p. 62)

Such carnivals of cruelty ensure the maintenance of customs by training the individual in the practice of following a rule:

> With the aid of such images and procedures one finally remembers five or six 'I will not's,' in regard to which one had given one's *promise*

so as to participate in the advantages of society – and it was indeed
with the aid of this kind of memory that one at last came 'to reason'!

(GM II 3 p. 62)

It is then through punishment that there is bred a 'real *memory of the will*',
that is, the capacity to 'ordain the future in advance' (GM II 1 p. 58). The
telos of this generic activity, for Nietzsche, is the *'sovereign individual'*. What
is signified by this phrase is the conjunction of *conscience* as the dominating
instinct and the sovereignty of consciousness; we can delineate this by
noting the relationship between these moments.

It has been argued that, for Nietzsche, as long as the metaphors
constitutive of a culture are vulnerable to disentrenchment, consciousness
cannot be disconnected from regulation by the instincts in so far as its
development is dependent on metaphor entrenchment. This suggests
that it is only when these metaphors have been constituted as synthetic *a
priori* judgements, that is, when they have been made instinctive, that
consciousness may become sovereign. Nietzsche's argument is that the
significant feature of the morality of custom in this instance is not the
arbitrary and brutal customs obedience to which is burnt into man but
rather that the very process of entrenchment consists in the breeding of
a human type which obeys 'the law of obeying laws' (Deleuze 1983: 133).
This is the generic activity of culture in prehistory.[5] The morality of
custom burns into man the necessity of obedience to law such that this
necessity has 'penetrated to the profoundest depths and become instinct,
the dominating instinct':

> What will he call this dominating instinct, supposing he feels the
> need to give it a name? The answer is beyond doubt: this sovereign
> man calls it his *conscience*.

(GM II 2 p. 60)

In terms of Nietzsche's idea of will to power, it may be argued that the
morality of custom breeds agency through positing arbitrary and brutal
goals via custom and enforcing action oriented to these goals through
punishment. However, the *telos* – the meaning and justification – of this
prehistory with all its inherent violence and cruelty is the individual who
has the capacity to creatively posit goals (the sovereignty of consciousness)
and who will obey without the necessity of threats (conscience), that is, the
individual with the capacity for autonomous agency. Nietzsche's *sovereign
individual* is the individual who actualises this capacity.

It will no doubt be noted that the preceding comments are careful to
argue that the sovereignty of consciousness indicates only the capacity to
posit goals. The significance of this point will emerge in our discussion of
the first essay of Nietzsche's *On the Genealogy of Morals*; however, in the
remainder of our discussion of prehistory, we may indicate the ground

37

upon which this significance is predicated, that is, we can explore the ambiguity inherent in prehistory. This ambiguity can be approached initially by focusing on the question of state formation and latterly on the emergence of the concept of guilt.[6]

We have noted that Nietzsche argues that it is through the morality of custom that man's fear of the unknown is overcome in so far as this form of morality hinders the acquisition of new experiences – custom renders the forms of relationship between members of the community repetitive. The customs of a community demarcate its self-definition and the identity of its members. In this context, it is unsurprising that Nietzsche should argue that contact between cultures in prehistory invariably takes the form of violence:

> the same men who are held so sternly in check *inter pares* by custom, respect, usage, gratitude, and even more by mutual suspicion and jealousy, and who on the other hand in their relations with one another show themselves so resourceful in consideration, self-control, delicacy, loyalty, pride, and friendship – once they go outside, where the strange, the *stranger* is found, they are not so much better than caged beasts of prey.
>
> (GM I 11 p. 40)

The destruction of the stranger and the destruction of the customs of the defeated culture by the imposition of the customs of the victors – these represent (at individual and social levels) the necessary response of a community to the threat of the Other, the Other whose manner of being calls into question not simply one's actions but one's very identity. The formation of a state, Nietzsche argues, 'was not only instituted by an act of violence but also carried to its conclusion by nothing but acts of violence':

> I employ the word 'state': it is obvious what is meant – some pack of blond beasts of prey, a conqueror and master race which, organised for war and with the ability to organise, unhesitatingly lays its terrible claws upon a populace perhaps tremendously superior in numbers but still formless and nomad.
>
> (GM II 17 p. 86)

The significance of state formation for Nietzsche lies in its establishment of a social order of rank, victors and vanquished, masters and slaves. The dilemma posed for the latter class, Nietzsche suggests, is that they possess within prehistory no means of accounting for their suffering in terms of the metaphors constitutive of their culture. We can explore the implications of this raw *ressentiment* by recourse to Nietzsche's discussion of the mode of legitimation of punishment within prehistory.

In our previous discussion of punishment, the focus was provided by the *act* of punishment; however, in accounting for the ambiguity of prehistory, Nietzsche develops a focus on the *meaning* of punishment which is of similar significance. Initially, Nietzsche is at pains to distinguish the meaning of punishment in prehistory from the idea of *guilt*, that is, the idea that the individual could have acted otherwise. This distinction is facilitated by a focus on the form of responsibility manifest in prehistory as predicated on the idea of *debt*. Far from involving the equation of responsibility and guilt, punishment as the responsibility for debt functions to impede the feeling of guilt. For whereas the idea of guilt presupposes, for Nietzsche, the separation of agent and acts, no such separation need be involved in the idea of debt and, indeed, a condition of such separation is the sovereignty of consciousness which is simply not present in prehistory, but rather demarcates its *telos*. Consequently, Nietzsche may state that:

> If we consider those millennia *before* the history of man, we may unhesitatingly assert that it was precisely through punishment that the development of the feeling of guilt was most powerfully *hindered* – at least in the victims upon whom the punitive force was vented.
>
> (GM II 14 p. 82)

Deploying the idea of debt responsibility, Nietzsche argues that the basic relation between a community and its members is isomorphic with relation between a creditor and his debtors. This leads him to pose a question: 'What will happen *if this pledge is broken?*' (GM II 9 p. 71). In its early stages, Nietzsche suggests, the reaction is extreme:

> The lawbreaker is debtor who has not merely failed to make good the advantages and advance payments bestowed upon him but has actually attacked his creditor: therefore he is not only deprived henceforth of all these advantages and benefits, as is fair – he is also reminded *what these benefits are really worth*. The wrath of the disappointed creditor, the community, throws him back again into the savage and outlaw state against which he has hitherto been protected: it thrusts him away – and now every kind of hostility may be vented upon him.
>
> (GM II 9 p. 71)

Here again one may sense the regulatory role of the instincts; for customs at this early stage are vulnerable, its metaphors are not deeply entrenched, and consequently to offend against a custom is to threaten both the very constitution of a culture and the development of consciousness which attends it. As the process of culture formation develops, however, that is, as the relevant metaphors grow increasingly entrenched, 'a community ceases to take the individual's transgressions so seriously, because they can no longer be considered as dangerous and destructive to the whole as they were formerly' (GM II 10 p. 72). In other words, as a culture grows stronger, as consciousness approaches the possibility of sovereignty, so too

39

emerges an 'increasingly definite will to treat every crime as in some sense *dischargeable*, and thus at least to a certain extent to *isolate* the criminal and his deed from one another' (GM II 10 p. 72). The development of *mercy*, the 'self-overcoming of justice', however, is ambiguous in its implications: on the one hand, it indicates the completion of man's prehistory in the emergence of a sovereign consciousness (and therefore the possibility of autonomy), yet on the other hand, it is this moment which signals the possibility of separating the agent from his acts and, thereby, admitting the concept of guilt – a concept by means of which, Nietzsche argues, *ressentiment* becomes creative.

The ambiguity engendered by the completion of the prehistory of man, engendered at the very moment that man becomes a historical animal, provides the context within which Nietzsche's account of the history of man emerges. Consequently, to trace Nietzsche's reconstruction of the history of the present requires that we explore the development of the relationship between the two moments of this ambiguity, that is, the possibility of autonomy and the possibility of guilt.

MASTERS AND SLAVES: AUTONOMY AND *RESSENTIMENT*

In the essay ' "Good and Bad," "Good and Evil" ' which opens *On the Genealogy of Morals* Nietzsche provides an ideal-type of the emergent historical community which delineates the 'context of meaning' within which his investigation of two discrete modes of morality takes on its significance for the history of the present. Nietzsche's concern in this essay is both to indicate the conditions which govern the emergence of these two types of morality and to indicate their respective relationships to the question of autonomy and the question of *ressentiment* before tracing the implications of the relationship between these forms of morality for the development of *Menschentum*.

Within prehistory, the individual's goals were determined by the customs constitutive of the community. The moment of history, however, signals the overcoming of the morality of custom; for in so far as the metaphors by which customs were constituted and legitimated have become entrenched as synthetic *a priori* judgements, there is no longer a need for customs to perform the role of entrenching these metaphors by positing and enforcing goals. The significance of this is twofold: firstly, it indicates the necessity of an alternative source of goals, and secondly, it implies the possibility of the individuals determining their own goals. It is in this context that Nietzsche's comments on the sovereignty of consciousness as the capacity to posit goals assumes its relevance for his investigation of noble morality as an 'art of superabundance' and slave morality as an 'art of hunger' (GS 370 p. 329).

40

To begin we may note that the origins of the two types of morality which Nietzsche locates emerging within the nascent historical community are located in the forms of experience which characterise noble and slave classes. The question which arises here concerns the relationship between these forms of experience and the possibility of actualising the capacity of consciousness to posit goals. Nietzsche approaches this question by focusing on the conditions requisite for this actualisation as involving the interaction of, on the one hand, the individual's experience of the world and self as a question of value and, on the other hand, the practical conditions governing goal realisation. Together these moments describe the form of experience characteristic of a class situation.[7]

For Nietzsche, the masters' experience of themselves in relation to the world is characterised by the *pathos of distance*, that is, their recognition of 'themselves and their actions as good, that is, of the first rank, in contradistinction to all the low, low-minded, common and plebian' (GM I 2 p. 26). The noble class 'accepts with a good conscience the sacrifice of the innumerable men who *for its sake* have to be suppressed and reduced to imperfect men, to slaves and instruments' (BGE 258 p. 174) since for them the meaning and value of the culture is co-extensive with the existence of the noble class. This *pathos of distance* and this good conscience are predicated for Nietzsche on the political power of the masters to command the slaves; it is the internalisation of this right of command which designates the noble's capacity for self-mastery. To support this Nietzsche notes that 'a concept denoting political superiority always resolves itself into a concept denoting superiority of the soul' (GM I 6 p. 31). The crucial point at stake for Nietzsche is that the nobles' unreflective experience of themselves as practically able to command actions relative to goals, and thus as representing the meaning and value of the culture itself, resolves itself into an affirmation of the relationship between world and self which enables them to take responsibility for positing goals for themselves. In other words, the noble's constitution of self as goal-directed agency is predicated on a pre-reflective affirmation of the relationship between self and world.

The type of morality which emerges as an expression of this form of experience is simply one in which the qualities deemed to ground the right to command – the very qualities (e.g. health, strength, beauty, cunning, passion and toughness) prized by 'the blond beasts' which enabled their victory by making them '*more complete* human beings' (BGE 257 p. 173) – are designated as 'good' (Bergmann 1988: 29–30). The practical ability of the noble to command the actions of slaves indicates to the noble his possession of these traits, while the slave's position as a slave, that is, as subject to command, implies for the noble – as an afterthought – the lack of these qualities in the slave and, consequently, the designation of the slave as 'bad'. Morality, for the masters, is simply an aesthetic ethics in which their abundant qualities are expressed through the joyful pursuit of self-determined goals.

The type of morality which emerges from the class experience of the slave contrasts fatally with the naiveté of the nobles. To begin we may recall that the dilemma of the slave in prehistory lies in an inability to account for their suffering, that is, to provide it with a meaning. The *ressentiment* of the slave is, as it were, formless. Within the historical community, this dilemma is exacerbated by the slave's pre-reflective experience of themselves as lacking value, as unable practically to determine goals for themselves. The moment of history, for Nietzsche, marks the possibility of the slave's overcoming these dilemmas, that is, the possibility of consciousness becoming reflective. This reflectivity manifests itself in two analytically distinct but practically related moments: firstly, an explanation of suffering through the concept of guilt, and secondly, the positing of a 'centre of gravity' located in a realm beyond experience. Together these moments delineate the slave's denial of the relationship between self and world.

In so far as history marks the moment at which the criminal and his deed are, at least to some extent, separated from each other, it raises the possibility (facilitated by grammar) of reifying consciousness, of entrenching the separation of agent and act, through the concept of guilt, that is, the idea that the agent could have acted otherwise. As such, *ressentiment* becomes articulatable in history as the designation of the noble as guilty; the slave's suffering becomes accountable through the concept of the master's guilt. The articulation of *ressentiment* as the spirit of revenge, however, locates the slave within a practical dilemma in so far as the slave's revenge is 'denied the true reaction, that of deeds' (GM I 10 p. 36). While the assignation of guilt to the noble through the reification of consciousness explains the slave's experience of suffering and enables the reflective overcoming of the lack of distance that characterises the slave's position in the social order of rank, that is, enables the valuing of the weakness as merit, it confronts its constitution of revenge as the goal which provides direction for agency yet is unrealisable, that is, the slave's revenge lacks the practical conditions requisite to its actualisation. In this context, Nietzsche argues, the unification of the 'will' requires the displacement of revenge from the realm of experience to the realm of imagination. The slave's overcoming of the inability to realise revenge in the world leads to the reflective positing of another world, the 'real world'. Moreover, while the nobles take responsibility for determining goals for themselves, the slave – habituated to obedience – displaces this responsibility by locating the source of moral legislation not in themselves but in the 'real world' they invent.

For Nietzsche, the consequence of this slave revolt in morality is expressed in the constitution of morality as a *universal code* in which the qualities characteristic of the noble (the natural qualities requisite for man's prehistorical survival) are condemned as intrinsically evil and the qualities of the slave are lauded as intrinsically good. The significance of this morality is its requirement of locating one's activity within a reflective regime; for whereas the noble's Yes is pre-reflective, the slave's No is necessarily reflective. It is in respect of this reflectivity that Nietzsche argues that, while slave morality is constituted by the privileging of anti-natural values, it is also 'only fair to add that it was on the soil of this *essentially dangerous* form of human existence . . . that man first became *an interesting animal*, that only here did the human soul in a higher sense acquire *depth* and become *evil*' (GM I 6 p. 33).

In presenting this archetypal contrast between the two modes of morality characteristic of the emergent historical community – a contrast between the pre-reflective autonomy of the noble and the reflective *ressentiment* of the slave – in terms of the forms of experience characteristic of the noble and slave classes, Nietzsche is able to generate an account of the conditions of emergence governing the construction of goal-directed agency as predicated on either an affirmation or a negation of the realm of experience. To develop this account in terms of its significance for the constitution of modernity, however, requires that Nietzsche trace the historical significance of the opposition between these two forms of morality.

FROM *RESSENTIMENT* TO *BAD CONSCIENCE*: THE JEWISH EXPERIENCE

To explore the significance of *ressentiment* for the constitution of modern culture requires that we trace Nietzsche's account of the development of *ressentiment* and its overcoming of the noble's pre-reflective autonomy in the generation of *bad conscience*.[8] This investigation, however, needs to be prefaced with some general remarks on myth and conscience.

Myth, on Nietzsche's account, may be credited with the performance of a variety of tasks integral to the formation and maintenance of a culture. Firstly, it functions as a system of explanation which legitimates the customs constitutive of a culture. Typically, the force of mythic explanation is predicated on the self-definition and self-affirmation of a culture. Thus, Nietzsche argues that it is initially through ancestral myths that a community defines itself and expresses the idea of debt responsibility – 'a juridical duty toward earlier generations, and especially the earliest, which founded the tribe' (GM II 19 p. 88) – which allows for the maintenance of the customs of the community through punishment. The consciousness of indebtedness to the ancestor – i.e. the force of ancestral myth as a system of explanation – increases 'in exactly the same measure as the power of the tribe itself increases' (GM II 19 p. 89). Secondly, myth in its festive embodiment provides a channel through which the communal re-affirmation of a culture is articulated. Nietzsche notes, for example, that it is through festival worship that two moments of a community's self-affirmation – namely, its sense of power and its good conscience – find expression. Myth, to summarise, may be read as the expression of the conscience of a culture, its perspective, its delimitation of the (type of) horizon by means of which it defines itself. As such, myth serves Nietzsche as an indicator as to the form of value-relationship which a culture embodies with respect to the world.

The significance of myth with respect to conscience and consciousness is thus predicated on the form of explanation and legitimation through which it maintains the self-definition of culture. In prehistory, conscience is constituted by the internalisation of the law of obeying laws; concomitant with this internalisation, however, is the internalisation of the form of legitimation (debt responsibility) which attends it. This double internalisation has consequences, Nietzsche argues, for the form of causal thinking by which consciousness defines itself. In the case of debt responsibility, this is expressed as natural causality, that is, causality defined by reference to the realm of experience. The slave revolt in morals, though, makes another form of legitimation and another form of causal thinking possible through the concept of guilt with correspondingly significant implications for the form of conscience and the constitution of consciousness. To explore the transformation wrought by the concept of guilt, we can examine that culture which for Nietzsche initiates the slave revolt in morals, namely, Jewish culture. To begin:

> The Jews are the most remarkable nation of world history because, faced with the question of being or not being, they preferred, with a perfectly uncanny conviction, being *at any price*: . . . .
>
> (AC 24 p. 134)

Jewish culture is, for Nietzsche, 'invaluable as a typical history of the *denaturalizing* of natural values' (AC 25 p. 135) in so far as it exemplifies a type of culture in which the relationship between the conditions of the culture and the explanatory force of its myths is, firstly, ruptured and, secondly, reconstituted in a radically distinct manner. The initial significance of this double movement lies, for Nietzsche, in a shift in both the type of conscience facilitated by Jewish culture and the type of causal thinking characteristic of Jewish consciousness.

'Originally, above all in the period of the Kingdom, Israel too stood in a *correct*, that is to say natural relationship to all things' (AC 25 p. 135). Jewish culture is defined by the idea of debt responsibility which finds positive expression as gratitude in festive celebration: 'it is grateful for the great destiny which has raised it on high, it is grateful towards the year's seasons and all its good fortune with livestock and husbandry' (AC 25 p. 136). This 'natural' relationship is summarised by Nietzsche thus:

44

Their Yaweh was the expression of their consciousness of power, of their delight in themselves, their hopes of themselves: in him they anticipated victory and salvation, with him they trusted that nature would provide what the people needed – above all rain. Yaweh is the God of Israel and *consequently* the God of justice: the logic of every nation which is in power and has a good conscience about it.

(AC 25 pp. 135–6)

This reconstruction of Jewish culture as an exemplar of a healthy culture thus demands that Nietzsche provide an account of the conditions under which it is transformed. Nietzsche's argument is that it is a combination of factors internal and external to Jewish culture which constitutes the grounds of this transformation: 'anarchy within, the Assyrian from without' (AC 25 p. 136). The consequence of the conjunction of these two threats to Jewish culture is simply that the mythic system of explanation embodied in this culture no longer functions as adequate to its conditions: 'The old God *could* no longer do what he formerly could' (AC 25 p. 136). In other words, Jewish culture – in the face of internal and external threats – is deprived of its 'consciousness of power'.

What precisely is the character of this crisis for Jewish culture? For Nietzsche, the dilemma attends the constitution of goal-directed agency. Yaweh as the God of justice constitutes the central 'explanatory' metaphor of Jewish culture. It is through this metaphor that the Jewish nobility expressed their affirmation of the relationship between self and world. The crisis of Jewish culture may thus be expressed as the disinterment of its central metaphor on the grounds of its explanatory inadequacy and, concomitantly, the collapse of the grounds requisite to the noble's pre-reflective autonomy.

In this context, 'placed in impossible circumstances', the Jewish nobility is compelled to 'voluntarily' make of themselves 'an antithesis to natural conditions' (AC 24 p. 134). To preserve Jewish culture 'the price they had to pay was the radical *falsification* of all nature, all naturalness, all reality, the entire inner world as well as the outer' (AC 24 p. 134). To put it slightly differently, to overcome the loss of their 'consciousness of power', the Jewish nobility had to transform the central metaphor constitutive of Jewish culture such that it is once more capable of enabling the feeling of power which attends goal-directed agency, yet the only path by which this could be accomplished is the reversal of the natural order of values in accordance with the explanatory scheme of guilt characteristic of the weak and the sickly, that is, those in whom the lack of the naturally valued qualities (strength, beauty, health, etc.) has resulted in *ressentiment*. These creatures of *ressentiment* in Jewish culture, Nietzsche argues, are the priests. The overcoming of the Jewish cultural crisis is accomplished by the creative genius of *ressentiment*. As Nietzsche puts it:

45

To be able to reject all that represents the ascending movement of life, well-constitutedness, power, beauty, self-affirmation on earth, the instinct of *ressentiment* here become genius had to invent another world from which that *life-affirmation* would appear evil, reprehensible as such.

(AC 24 p. 135)

The invention of this 'other world' is facilitated by demarcating the realm of God from the realm of man and thereby transforming the God of *justice* into the God of *judgement*: 'A God who *demands* – in place of a God who helps, who devises means, who is fundamentally a word for every happy inspiration of courage and self-reliance' (AC 25 p. 136). This 'falsification' of the concept of God provides the grounds of explanation required by Jewish culture for its self-preservation: 'The new conception of him becomes an instrument in the hands of priestly agitators who henceforth interpret all good fortune as reward, all misfortune as punishment for disobedience of God, for 'sin'' ' (AC 25 p. 136). The significance of this transformation, for Nietzsche, lies in its establishment of an *'anti-natural causality'*. Whereas both the God of justice and the God of judgement are located as exemplifying the error of imaginary causes, the former expresses 'the conditions under which a nation lives and grows' (AC 25 p. 136), while the latter expresses 'the antithesis of life' (AC 25 p. 136). To put it alternatively, the idea of debt responsibility is displaced in Jewish culture by the idea of guilt responsibility. In discussing the transformation which effects this displacement, however, Nietzsche recognises that the re-interpretation of its central metaphor by Jewish culture, the displacement of one paradigm of explanation by another, requires that the transformed metaphor be capable of accounting for the anomalous events which initiate the need for re-interpretation and, further, that it ground itself, entrench itself, by accounting for those non-anomalous events which had been explainable within the previous 'paradigm'.[9] Thus Nietzsche states:

The concept of God falsified; the concept of morality falsified – the Jewish priesthood did not stop there. The entire *history* of Israel was useless: away with it! – These priests perpetuated that miracle of falsification the documentation of which lies before us in a good part of the Bible: with unparalleled disdain of every tradition, every historical reality, they translated their own national past *into religious terms*, that is to say they made of it a stupid salvation-mechanism of guilt towards Yaweh and punishment, piety towards Yaweh and reward.

(AC 26 p. 137)

By setting out an explanation of the history of Israel in terms of guilt responsibility, the priest both grounds the transformation of God into a God of judgement and, as the mediator between man and God, legitimates his own position of power: 'Supreme law: "God forgives him who repents" – in plain language: *who subjects himself to the priest*' (AC 26 p. 139).

The re-interpretation of Jewish history by the priests, which results in the actualisation of the revenge of the weak, that is, the reversal of the order of rank in Jewish culture, signals the formation of cultural *bad conscience* in which the noble is domesticated, is reduced to the level of the herd, through the concept of guilt. The expression of man's naturally (i.e. instinctively) valued qualities is censured as 'sin'; consciousness is defined not in terms of the selective deployment and postponement of instinctive impulses but in terms of an absolute opposition to instinct, to the animal in man, to man as a part of nature. This 'declaration of war' against the instincts expressed in the qualities of the noble represents, for Nietzsche, 'the gravest and uncanniest illness, from which man has not yet recovered' (GM II 16 p. 85) in so far as he suggests that '[a]ll instincts that do not discharge themselves outwardly *turn inward*' (GM II 16 p. 84) and, consequently, 'all those instincts of wild, free, prowling man turn backward *against man himself*'. Finally enclosed not just within the walls of society but also within the walls of peace – that is, unable to exercise the qualities of command – the noble is enchained by *bad conscience*, that consciousness of guilt which itself 'would not have developed *without them*, . . . it would be lacking if a tremendous quantity of freedom had not been expelled from the world, or at least from the visible world, and made as it were *latent* under their hammer blows and artists violence' (GM II 17 p. 87).

Nietzsche's argument here is complex and consequently it may be useful to summarise the salient points which emerge from this discussion. The establishment of an order of rank grounded on the instincts' regulation of the qualities valued within prehistory creates the *ressentiment* of the weak and the slaves. This *ressentiment* becomes creative in history through a denial of the realm of experience, of nature, articulated by the concept of guilt and the attendant reification of consciousness. The reification of consciousness as supra-natural immanently involves its definition as opposed to instinct, to man as part of nature, and constitutes *bad conscience* which Nietzsche defines as 'the existence on earth of an animal soul turned against itself, taking sides against itself' (GM II 16 p. 85). The nobles are able to ward off *bad conscience* in so far as the central metaphors constitutive of the culture continue to account adequately for their experience and, concomitantly, to express their 'consciousness of power'. However, the explanatory failure of this metaphor renders the noble susceptible, and indeed welcoming, to the interpretation through which the weak constitute themselves as goal-directed agents (the need for this interpretation being itself based on the prehistorical noble's expulsion of a 'tremendous quantity of freedom' from the world) with its attendant *bad conscience*.

47

While this account would appear in Nietzsche's eyes to fit the Jewish experience of the culture as a whole desperately embracing the priest's anti-natural interpretation of the human condition as the condition of maintaining the culture in its capacity to enable the constitution of goal-directed agency, we can explore it further by continuing our exploration of the historical implications of the slave revolt in morality by reference to Greek culture.

FROM *RESSENTIMENT* TO *BAD CONSCIENCE*: THE GREEK EXPERIENCE

The Jewish path to *bad conscience* involves, as we have seen, a fundamental re-interpretation of the mythic core, the central metaphor, of Jewish culture. To grasp the contours of the Greek route to *bad conscience* similarly requires that we initiate discussion by sketching the way in which myth performed its explanatory and legitimatory role in Greek culture before indicating the grounds upon which the mythic legitimation of self is displaced by appeals to rational criteria, that is, dialectics.

This discussion may begin by noting that Nietzsche explicitly regards the Greek myths as enabling the nobles' avoidance of a consciousness of guilt. This is revealed, Nietzsche suggests, 'even by a mere glance at the *Greek gods*':

> those relections of noble and autocratic men, in whom *the animal* in man felt deified and did *not* lacerate itself, did *not* rage against itself! For the longest time these Greeks used their gods precisely so as to ward off the 'bad conscience,' so as to be able to rejoice in the freedom of soul.
>
> (GM II 23 pp. 93–4)

Misdeeds are represented not as 'sin' but as 'folly' and, moreover, even this capacity for foolishness is presented as a problem:

> 'how is it possible? how could it actually have happened to heads such as *we* have, we men of aristocratic descent, of the best society, happy, well-constituted, noble and virtuous?' – thus noble Greeks asked themselves for centuries in the face of every incomprehensible atrocity or wantonness with which one of their kind had polluted himself. 'He must have been deluded by a *god*,' they concluded finally, shaking their heads. . . . This expedient is *typical* of the Greeks. . . . In this way the gods served in those days to justify man to a certain extent even in his wickedness, they served as the originators of evil – in those days they took upon themselves, not the punishment but, what is *nobler*, the guilt.
>
> (GM II 23 p. 94)

In this context, it is appropriate to pose the question already posed to Jewish culture, namely, how it is that *bad conscience* developed in Greek, and specifically Athenian, society. Nietzsche's response is to locate both external and internal factors, namely, Athenian victory in the Persian wars and the displacement of the *agon* by dialectics.[10]

It has been noted that the moment of *bad conscience* for Jewish nobility is the moment of enclosure within the walls of both society and peace; to investigate the triumph of *bad conscience* in Athenian society requires a similar focus on this double enclosure. We can begin by noting that the deification of the animal in man expressed in Greek myth is adequate to Greek experience only in so far as the naturally (i.e. instinctively) valued qualities of nobility – which include strength, cunning, health and beauty – themselves articulate this experience both internally, as competition amongst the nobles, and externally, as cruelty, joy in war, arson, rape and torture (cf. GM I 11 p. 40; II 16 p. 85). The dilemma posed by the Athenian triumph in the Persian wars is that of its very completeness such that the nobles are unable to 'compensate themselves in the wilderness for the tension engendered by protracted enclosure within the peace of society' (GM I 11 p. 40) precisely because 'no external enemies remain on whom to fashion the aggressions that the inner contradiction of the state releases' (Strong 1988: 199). The acuteness of this dilemma is expressed in the inability of the mythic core of Greek society to account for this experience of a lack on the part of the nobility. This manifests itself initially in a transformation attendant on the reproduction of the mythic core of Greek culture, namely, the displacement of Aeschylus by Euripides.[11]

The distinction between Aeschylus and Euripides lies in the form of relation their plays embody with respect to the synthetic *a priori* judgements which, expressed as myth, are constitutive of Greek culture. In the dramatic tragedies presented by Aeschylus, these judgements are *embodied* in the drama as the unquestioned presuppositions of the drama itself. The spectator's experience of the drama is grounded in the unconscious affirmation and re-affirmation of the foundations of Greek culture. Significantly, this includes the reproduction of Homer's identification of character and destiny: 'There can be no separation . . . of a person and his acts' (Strong 1988: 167). In contrast, Euripides' tragedies mark the disinterment of the Greek's synthetic *a priori* judgements; the horizon of Greek culture becomes a matter of conscious reflection in which tragedy and heroic destiny are displaced by dialectical reason and the separation of the agent from his acts. As Strong notes: 'In Homer or Aeschylus there is no obvious, point by point relation between the choices an individual makes, and the outcome to which he submits. . . . If, as with Euripides, one tries to makes choices on the basis of the accurate knowledge of the prudential consequences of one's actions, heroics and the tragic are impossible' (Strong 1988: 176). In Euripides, noble actions are no longer simply any actions performed pre-reflectively by noble persons (literally, the nobility) but rather actions performed reflectively in accordance with noble principles. The significance of Euripides is that his tragedies represent the movement of Greek myth from the realm of the unquestioned to the realm of the questionable and, thereby, set the scene for the displacement of myth by reason, that is to say that Euripidian drama is the partner of Socratic dialogue. Indeed, as Nietzsche puts it: 'Even Euripides was, in a sense, only a mask: the deity that spoke through him was . . . an altogether newborn demon, called *Socrates*' (BT 12 p. 82; cf. also BT 13 p. 86).

For Nietzsche, this demon named Socrates represents the *ressentiment* of the rabble (TI I 3 p. 30); however, whereas in Jewish culture *ressentiment* is articulated through a theological dialectic of sin, in Greek culture it is articulated through a philosophical dialectic of truth. The Socratic philosopher has an elective affinity with the Judaic priest. As Nietzsche puts it in a note from 1888: 'when Socrates and Plato took up the cause of virtue and justice, they were *Jews* or I know not what' (WP 429 p. 234). However, while Jewish culture developed *bad conscience* through a dialectical re-interpretation of its mythic core, Socratic philosophy represents the dialectical exorcism of myth as such. How is this accomplished?

It is necessary to note initially that the *ressentiment* expressed by the Socratic philosopher manifests the same structural concerns as that which animates the Judaic priest, namely, the delineation of a supersensory realm capable of serving a centre of gravity for the weak, the sick and the slaves by reference to which they can construct themselves as goal-directed agents. A central feature of this creative act of imagination on the part of the Socratic philosopher is that 'moral judgements are torn from their conditionality, in which they have grown and alone possess any meaning, from their Greek and Greek-political ground and soil, to be denaturalised under the pretence of sublimation. The great concepts "good" and "just" are severed from the presuppositions to which they belong and, as liberated "ideas, " become objects of dialectic' (WP 430 pp. 234–5). Prior to Socrates, as Nietzsche notes, 'the dialectical manner was repudiated in good society: it was regarded as a form of bad manners, one was compromised by it' (TI I 5 p. 31), yet in the context of the failure of Greek myth to account for the experience of the nobility after the Persian wars, dialectics defeats the *nobler* taste because it offers 'a *last-ditch weapon* in the hands of those who have no other weapon left' (TI I 6 pp. 31–2). Dialectics offers a route for the cultural construction of goal-directed agency in a context in which the creative–affirmative force of the instincts has been undermined by the double enclosure of the noble within the walls of society and peace precisely because this creative role is taken on by consciousness. The collapse of the mythic ground which legitimised the order of rank and established the good conscience manifest in the nobles' pre-reflective affirmation of the realm of becoming leads to the entrenchment of a reflective affirmation of a fictional realm of being as the condition for the preservation of the culture and its capacity for enabling the construction of goal-directed agency. In another note from 1888, Nietzsche expresses this by suggesting that the Socratic philosopher 'desires the ideal *polis* after the concept *"polis"* has had its day (approximately as the Jews held firm as a "people" after they had fallen into slavery)' (WP 427 p. 231). As in the Jewish case, this was not a matter of choice for the Greeks but rather a *necessity* for the preservation of the culture:

> Rationality was at that time divined as a *saviour*; neither Socrates nor his 'invalids' were free to be rational or not, as they wished – it was *de rigueur*, it was their *last* expedient. The fanaticism with which the whole of Greek thought throws itself at rationality betrays a state of emergency: one was in peril, one had only *one* choice: either to perish or – be *absurdly rational*.
>
> (TI I 10 p. 33)

Philosophical dialectics as the Greek mode of *bad conscience* manifests itself as that consciousness of guilt which is articulated not through the concept of sin (as in Jewish theological dialectics) but through the concept of ignorance.[12]

JEW–GREEK, GREEK–JEW: CHRISTIANITY AND THE WILL TO TRUTH

The development of *bad conscience* as theological dialectics in Jewish culture and philosophical dialectics in Greek culture already intimates an *elective affinity* between the priest and the philosopher in that they have 'set the bad conscience of the noble soul against its self-sufficiency; they have led astray, to the point of self-destruction, the brave, magnanimous, daring, excessive inclinations of the strong soul' (WP 205 p. 122). In articulating the guilt of the noble, *ressentiment* (in both Judaic and Greek forms) makes possible both the self-affirmation of the slave, the reflexive valuation of self which is a condition of goal-directed agency, and – as *bad conscience* – the reduction of noble to the herd, the transformation of the noble into one who *suffers from guilt*. However, Nietzsche claims, 'Christianity raised all this to the second power' (WP 182 p. 111). This claim can be explored by focusing on (Pauline) Christianity as the perspective in which guilt becomes *universal*.[13]

We can initiate discussion by noting that, despite their affinity, the Jewish priest and the Greek (Socratic) philosopher represent distinct, culturally specific, modes of *ressentiment*, that is, theological dialectics and philosophical dialectics. This emerges, moreover, in the distinct concepts through which each articulates guilt (irrationality as 'sin' or as 'ignorance'). Christianity, however, raises this to a further level of abstraction by divorcing the unconditionality of moral judgement from its culturally specific modes of representation. On the one hand, Nietzsche suggests that while Christianity grows out of the soil of Jewish experience 'as *Christianity* it negated the last remaining form of reality, the "holy people", the "chosen people", the *Jewish* reality itself' (AC 27 p. 139):

> once the chasm between Jews and Jewish Christians opened up, the latter were left with no alternative but to employ *against* the Jews the very self-preservation procedures counselled by the Jewish instinct, while the Jews had previously employed them only against every-thing *non*-Jewish. The Christian is only a Jew of '*freer*' confession.
>
> (AC 44 p. 159)

On the other hand, in thus negating its cultural specificity, Christianity institutes itself as neither theological nor philosophical dialectics but as dialectics as such, as universal dialectics. The specificity of the theological Idea of God and the philosophical (Platonic) Idea of Good is overcome in Christianity's abstraction from 'Jews' and 'Greeks' to 'Man'. In this overcoming, Christianity constitutes itself as the universal moment of *ressentiment*, a moment whose universality as theory is intimately related to a certain universality in practice. We can approach this issue through Nietzsche's reading of the universalisation of the consciousness of guilt.

This analysis may begin with Nietzsche's account of the 'physiological cause' of *ressentiment*:

> every sufferer instinctively seeks a cause for his suffering; more exactly, an agent; still more specifically, a *guilt* agent who is susceptible to suffering – in short, some living thing upon which he can, on some pretext or other, vent his affects, actually or in effigy: for the venting of his affects represents the greatest attempt on the part of the suffering to win relief, *anaesthesia* – the narcotic he cannot help desiring to deaden pain of any kind.
>
> (GM III 15 p. 127)

In the case of the slave, as we have noted, this guilty agent is the noble, the 'bird of prey', and it is in venting revenge on the noble through the concept of guilt, the separation of agent and act, the reification of consciousness – in short, the construction of *bad conscience* – that the slave grounds his self-affirmation in the suffering of the noble. For whereas the slave revolt in morals begins with the displacement of a non-actualisable revenge into the realm of the imaginary, it develops with the actualisation of a revenge articulated by this imaginary realm. However, in so far as this revenge is successful, in so far as the noble is reconstituted as a suffering agent, to that degree also the philosopher-priest – as the artist of *ressentiment* – is confronted with a dilemma: the reduction of the noble to the herd initiated by Jewish theology and Socratic philosophy threatens to undermine the adequacy of the explanations of suffering upon which the authority of the philosopher-priest is grounded. Under the regime of Jewish and Greek *bad conscience*, the suffering of the slave is explained as the guilt of the Other (the noble) and the suffering of the noble as the guilt of the Self (the instincts); however, in so far as the noble is driven to displace the creativity of instinct with a creativity grounded in consciousness, so too is the noble becoming sick, becoming weak, becoming a slave. In this context, the Christian abstraction from the culturally specific categories 'Jew' and 'Greek' to the universal category 'Man' allows for a double overcoming in which *ressentiment* is redirected onto the Other within the Self.

In our discussion of the constitution of *bad conscience* in Jewish and Greek culture, it was noted that the grounding of the guilt of the noble within the judgements of the culture is predicated on both external and internal threats: externally, the threat posed to the cultural identity as such by the non-Jew or the non-Greek, and internally, the threat posed by the slave revolt in morals – the 'choice' posed to the noble being the destruction of cultural identity on the one hand, and the transformation of cultural identity on the other hand. Placed in these impossible circumstances, the latter option is adopted as a 'last expedient'. In displacing the question of cultural identity by a question of human identity, that is, in abstracting from the specific to the universal, however, Christianity also allows for the abstraction from the specificity of guilt to the universality of guilt, the displacement of the guilt of Other or Self by the guilt of the Other in/as Self. In other words, the 'synthetic' universalisation of the Idea of God and the Idea of Good simultaneously involves the universalisation of the concepts of 'sin' and 'ignorance' – of sin as ignorance and ignorance as sin – such that the reification of consciousness, that is, the self-delimitation of consciousness contra instinct, assumes the form of an ongoing injunction for the domination of instinct by consciousness. The division of man – as natural and supra-natural being – instituted by Jewish and Greek *bad conscience* here assumes its logical end as the active and universal suppression of the natural in the name of the supra-natural on the part of man as such. Nietzsche describes this redirecting of *ressentiment* which fulfils the logic of *bad conscience* thus:

> 'I suffer: someone must be to blame for it' – thus thinks every sickly sheep. But his shepherd, the ascetic priest, tells him: 'Quite so, my sheep! someone must be to blame for it: but you yourself are this someone, you alone are to blame for it – *you alone are to blame for yourself*!'
> (GM III 15 p. 128)

The philosopher-priest as shepherd – as 'guardian of humanity' to recall Kant's phrase – preserves the explanatory force of Christianity, that is, its capacity to enable the constitution of goal-directed agency, by relocating the cause of the sufferer's suffering within the sufferer as the failure of consciousness's domination of instinct, as the failure of spirit (soul/mind) in the face of flesh (body/instinct).

It is in this context that the identification of virtue with knowledge established by the Christian 'synthesis' of theological and philosophical dialectics assumes its significance. It has been suggested by one commentator that for Nietzsche 'the Western manipulative conception of truth . . . begins with the Socratic maxim that "Virtue is knowledge, man sins only from ignorance, " ' (Ansell-Pearson 1986: 501), the implication being that knowledge provides the resources by which man masters his nature or, more specifically, by which consciousness develops mastery of the instincts. The Western conception of science as the mastery of man over nature thus emerges, for Nietzsche, in the reification of consciousness as man's supra-natural being and of instinct as man's natural being and from the need of mind to master instinct. Thus enclosed within a regime of interpretation which emphasises the need for perpetual supervision and suspicion over the self, the *factum brutum* provides a secure foundation for action. In other words, the 'eternal vigilance' required with respect to the self finds its relief in a will to truth which 'enslaves man to positivism, to seeking the facts about the world at any cost' (Ansell-Pearson 1986: 501). Christian morality finds its meaning and ground for Nietzsche in the will to truth – which is to say in science – while this will to truth secures its legitimacy through its service to morality. To explore this further requires an examination of the character and consequences of this will to truth; however, prior to this it may be useful to focus on the development of Christianity in terms of the implications for modern culture of the type of individual bred under its aegis.

CHRISTIANITY, 'BREEDING' AND SELF-REFLECTION

[The] existence on earth of an animal soul turned against itself, taking sides against itself, was something so new, profound, unheard of, enigmatic, contradictory, *and pregnant with a future* that the aspect of the earth was essentially altered.

(GM II 16 p. 84)

How is 'the aspect of the earth' altered? Nietzsche's argument is that *bad conscience* enables the formation of 'second nature' as the repression of 'first nature' – what does this mean? It was noted earlier that the moment of history is that moment at which consciousness secures its sovereignty in that this moment marks the rendering instinctive of the synthetic *a priori* judgements of a culture, these judgements being constitutive of 'second nature'. *Bad conscience* as an analytical concept signals the opposition of consciousness to instinct which is articulated through the predication of such judgements on a devaluation of the realm of experience through the creative positing of a realm beyond experience, the 'real' world. Christianity as the universalisation of *bad conscience* represents the entrenchment of the judgement that morality and science (or, rather, moral purity and scientific truth) are interdependent. The initial consequences of this entrenchment are twofold: firstly, the philosopher-priest secures his role as 'guardian of humanity' as the symbol of a truth (grounded on purity) and of a purity (grounded on truth), and secondly, the individual is inscribed within a regime of reflection, of interrogation, of confession, which requires the judgement of the priest. The implication of this grounding of the authority of the divine, the supra-natural, in the figure of the priest is that it is the priest's judgement which articulates the labour of self-overcoming on the part of the individual. In other words, while the synthetic *a priori* judgements of a culture are constitutive of 'second nature', it is through the mechanism of the priest's judgement that this constitution of 'second nature' is articulated. It is in this context that Nietzsche sets out the psychology of the believer: 'The man of faith, the "believer" of every sort is necessarily a dependent man – such as cannot out of himself posit ends at all. The 'believer' does not belong to *himself*, he can only be a means, he has to be *used*, he needs someone who will use him' (AC 54 p. 172). This 'someone' is God; the Christian exists simply as an instrument of the divine in which the 'use-value' of the believer is determined by priestly judgement.

This initial form adopted by the Christian Church to facilitate the preservation and breeding of the type of man characterised by the inability to posit goals is displaced, however, by an alternative form with significant implications for the possibility of breeding autonomous individuals in modernity. To examine this displacement requires an exploration of Nietzsche's view of the meaning of both the Renaissance and the Reformation.

Nietzsche's fragmentary and scattered comments on the Renaissance are almost entirely positive – why is this? The laudable feature of Renaissance man lies, for Nietzsche, in his attempt to overcome Christian morality through the concept of *virtù* conceived of as 'moraline-free virtue' (cf. WP 317, 327, 740). Nietzsche – like Machiavelli to whom he refers – sees the attributes of *virtù* exemplified in the figure of Cesare Borgia. The meaning of this Renaissance, for Nietzsche, is simply this: 'The *revaluation of Christian values*, the attempt, undertaken with every expedient, with every instinct, with genius of every kind, to bring about the victory of the opposing values, the *noble* values' (AC 61 p. 184). How though is this possible within a culture defined by the synthetic *a priori* judgements of Christianity?

While Nietzsche does not explicitly address this question, the implication of the comments he does make is that – for historically contingent reasons – the period of the Renaissance and the Reformation represents the recognition of the independence or autonomy of scientific practices and moral practices, this recognition involving a displacement of the dialectic of identity by a dialectic of difference. In other words, the idea of scientific truth is separated from that of moral purity. The dilemma which emerges from this divorcing of science and morality is simply this: in so far as science and morality are non-identical, which commands? The non-identity of science and morality requires the constitution of their relationship as one of hierarchy, of master and slave; Nietzsche's interpretation of the significance of the Renaissance and the Reformation is grounded in their antithetical constructions of this hierarchy.

The Renaissance is marked by the dominance of a scientific consciousness displayed in the following characteristics:

> liberation of thought, disrespect for authorities, victory of education over the arrogance of ancestry, enthusiasm for science and the scientific past of mankind, unfettering of the individual, a passion for truthfulness and an aversion to appearance and mere effect.
>
> (HAH I.237 p. 113)

By contrast, the Reformation is marked by the dominance of a moral consciousness which similarly expresses itself as an individualism, as an abolition of the authority of the priest, but one which represents not an overcoming of *bad conscience* but a heightening of *bad conscience*. That this is not an overcoming is manifest in Luther's re-affirmation of the unconditionality of moral judgements; that it is a heightening of *bad conscience* is apparent in the abolition of the mediating role of the priest in that this constitutes the individual *as the 'judge and avenger and victim' of himself with respect to the moral law*.[14] In other words, the reflexivity instituted by the shift in direction of *ressentiment* from the noble to the self is hereby deepened in so far as the judgement of the self is displaced from the realm of a priestly judgement to an ongoing regime of self-judgement and is thereby reconstituted as a hermeneutics of self-suspicion.

The confrontation between Renaissance and Reformation worldviews appears to represent, for Nietzsche, a re-confrontation between master and slave moralities; yet again, however, it is the latter which triumphs. Nietzsche suggests two contingent historical reasons for this result. The first is political:

> It was an extraordinary chance political constellation that preserved Luther and lent force to [his] protestation: for the Emperor protected him so as to employ his innovation as an instrument of pressure against the Pope, while the Pope likewise secretly befriended him so as to employ the Protestant princes of the Holy Roman Empire as a counterweight to the Emperor.
>
> (HAH I.237 p. 114)

The second reason, suggested in a note from 1888, is grounded in a characterisation of the Renaissance as a time 'when everything is *spent*, when the very strength is spent with which one collects, capitalizes, and piles riches upon riches' (WP 93). The Renaissance exhausts itself, squanders itself, because its strength lacks the capacity to reproduce itself.[15] What then are the implications of the triumph of the Reformation?

These are basically fourfold: two relating to the psychology of the believer and two relating to the question of politics. Firstly, Protestant asceticism represents a heightening of the pyschological need to overcome inner nature (instinct); only a consciousness fully present to itself is capable of undistorted self-judgement – a morality of truthfulness. Secondly, it represents a heightening of the pyschological need to overcome external nature in so far as this functions as a sign of the overcoming of internal nature; the development of scientific consciousness is required by moral consciousness. Thirdly, in so far as the individual's self-reflection is no longer mediated by the priest but requires self-judgement in terms of the moral law, this is expressed politically as individualism. Fourthly, in so far as morality is grounded on the values of freedom and equality, this is expressed politically in the impetus to liberal democratic forms of government.

From the perspective of modern culture, these implications for the breeding of man under Protestant asceticism have profound consequences which can be explored by reference to, on the one hand, the emergence of nihilism and the psychology of modern man and, on the other hand, the pathos of distance and the capacities of modern man.

THE EMERGENCE OF NIHILISM AND THE PSYCHOLOGY OF MODERN MAN

You see what it was that really triumphed over the Christian God: Christian morality itself, the concept of truthfulness that was understood ever more rigorously, the father confessor's refinement of the Christian conscience, translated and sublimated into a scientific conscience, into intellectual cleanliness at any price.

(GS 357 p. 307)

Protestant asceticism as a hermeneutics of self-suspicion is predicated on the pyschological need for a morality of truthfulness requiring the development of science and of the scientific conscience, yet paradoxically, Nietzsche claims, this will to truth facilitates the undermining of faith in the Christian God. The argument Nietzsche develops can be examined by reference to his claim that the invention of a realm of being which articulates the slave revolt in morals institutes an *anti-natural* (or supernatural) interpretation of causality. The implication of this is that, in so far as supernatural forms of explanation are displaced by scientific forms of explanation, the God-hypothesis becomes increasingly redundant. Certainly, as Nietzsche notes, 'physics too is only an interpretation' (BGE 14 p. 26) – yet one demanded by Christian morality itself, the depth of the pyschological need for the absolute repression of instinct by consciousness being exhibited precisely in the development of a scientific conscience even at the cost of displacing the figure of God: 'it is the awe-inspiring *catastrophe* of two thousand years of training in truthfulness that finally forbids itself the *lie involved in belief in God*' (GM III 27 p. 160).

This morality of truthfulness, this will to truth, this scientific conscience, does *not* however represent, for Nietzsche, the overcoming of asceticism, that is, the overcoming of the dichotomy of 'real' and 'apparent' worlds; on the contrary, 'this will [to truth], this *remnant* of an ideal, is, if you will believe me, this ideal itself in its strictest, most spiritual formulation, esoteric through and through, with all external additions abolished, and thus not so much its remnant as its *kernel*' (GM III 27 p. 160). In other words, the scientist is still a metaphysician:

> That which *constrains* these men, however, this unconditional will to truth, is *faith in the ascetic ideal itself*, even if as an unconscious imperative – don't be deceived about that – it is the faith in a *metaphysical* value, the absolute value of *truth*, sanctioned and guaranteed by this ideal alone (it stands or falls with this ideal).
>
> (GM III 24 p. 151)

To put this slightly differently, one might say that the belief in the 'real world' is still a necessary condition of goal-directed agency or, as Nietzsche puts it, '[t]hey have got rid of the Christian God, and now feel obliged to cling all the more firmly to Christian morality' (TI IX 5 p. 69). At a literal level, however, as Nietzsche goes on to point out, Christian morality 'possesses truth only if God is truth – it stands or falls with the belief in God' (TI IX 5 p. 70). This is exemplified in Kant's philosophy in which the grounding of morality is ultimately only possible given the postulation of the figure of God as a *matter of faith*. The pyschological consequence of the repudiation of God which is not yet a repudiation of the 'real world' is the emergence of a culture of *pessimism*, 'an expression of the uselessness of the *modern* world – not of the world of existence' (WP 34 p. 23).

Pessimism – as the preliminary form of nihilism – is an ambivalent phenomenon; it can manifest itself both as strength and as decline (cf. WP 8–9 p. 11). In the latter form, it represents the quest for a God-substitute, that is, '*another* authority that can *speak unconditionally* and *command* goals and tasks' (WP 20 p. 16); Nietzsche instances in this context eschatological visions of history, for example (cf. WP 20 p. 17). As decline, pessimism represents the habituation to obedience which is expressed as a need 'to get around the will, the willing of a goal, the risk of positing a goal *for oneself*; one wants to rid oneself of the responsibility (one would accept fatalism)' (WP 20 p. 17). In the former form, however, that is as strength, pessimism manifests itself as resolutely energetic in positing for itself the goal of following through the logic of truthfulness, that is, reflexively questioning the value of science, and of confronting the meaninglessness of the modern world through a reflexive questioning of the meaning of the world of existence as such. Nihilism – the devaluation of the highest values – emerges through this active pessimism when this remorseless will to truth subjects itself to scrutiny; nihilism, in this sense, represents the coming to self-consciousness of universal dialectics.

What is the nature of the dilemma confronted by the will to truth? Simply this: science as the will to truth cannot itself articulate a ground on which to assert the value of truth. As Nietzsche puts it: 'there is no such thing as science "without any presuppositions"' (GM III 24 p. 151); or again: '[science] requires in every respect an ideal of value, a value-creating power, in the *service* of which it could *believe* in itself – it never creates values' (GM III 25 p. 153). Nihilism emerges in that moment in which the will to truth abolishes the ground of its own value and becomes conscious of itself as a problem.

This cultural moment expresses itself as a pyschological dilemma: 'we discover in ourselves needs implanted by centuries of moral interpretation – needs that now appear to us as needs for untruth; on the other hand, the value for which we endure life seems to hinge on these needs' (WP 5 p. 10). Again, however, this is ambivalent in terms of its possibilities for the development of *Menschentum*. On the one hand, the abolition of the 'real world', that is, the abolition of any transcendental ground of value, expresses itself as decline in a feeling of valuelessness and the impulse to retreat into self-narcotisation (cf. WP 29 p. 20): 'one grants the reality of becoming as the *only* reality, forbids oneself every kind of clandestine access to afterworlds and false divinities – but *cannot endure this world though one does not want to deny it*' (WP 12 p. 13). This is the moment of a resigned fatalism. On the other hand, nihilism as strength represents the recognition of the possibility of overcoming slave morality, of positing values for oneself, of commanding oneself, that is, of autonomy. Nietzsche's task – the overcoming of nihilism – is to facilitate the actualisation of this possibility of autonomy and thereby overcome the ambivalence of modern culture: 'A doctrine is needed powerful enough to work as a breeding agent: strengthening the strong, paralyzing and destructive for the world-weary' (WP 862 p. 458).

In this delineation of Nietzsche's conception of the ambivalence of modern culture, however, it has been presupposed that modern man has the capacity for strength requisite to the task of confronting and overcoming nihilism. To indicate the possibilities immanent in modern culture is not, after all, the same as indicating the possibility of actualising these possibilities. What is required here is an account which grounds the actuality of the possibility of realising these cultural potentials.

THE PATHOS OF DISTANCE AND THE CAPACITIES OF MODERN MAN

Overcoming nihilism – what is required for the actualisation of this possibility? Nietzsche's discussion of 'master-morality' intimates the answer to this question, namely, a self-affirmation predicated on an affirmation of the realm of experience, of becoming. Yet this affirmation of self and world is grounded, it will be recalled, on the *pathos of distance*, that is, the place of noble at the summit of a social order of rank, whereas, for Nietzsche, modern (democratic) culture is structured about precisely the absence of such an order of rank. It is in this context that the question of the possibility of actualising the potential for overcoming nihilism assumes its significance. To explore this question requires an analysis of Nietzsche's account of the construction of 'inner distance'.

In Nietzsche's account of the emergence of master morality, the pathos of *social* distance is intrinsically tied to that of *inner* distance: 'Without the *pathos of distance* such as develops from the incarnate differences of classes . . . that other, more mysterious pathos could not have developed either, that longing for an ever-increasing widening of distance within the soul itself' (BGE 257 p. 173). The pathos of inner distance manifest as the ability of the noble to command goals and tasks for himself is grounded on the pathos of social distance exhibited as the power to command goals and tasks for the slave. The self-determining goal-directed agency (autonomy) of the noble is grounded on an *unreflective* internalisation of the social order of rank. By contrast, the slave revolt in morals is predicated on the *reflective* positing of a metaphysical beyond charac- terised by a pathos based on the inversion of the social order of rank. The pathos of inner distance is tied to a pathos of metaphysical distance as the ground of the slave's goal-directed agency. It is the reflective character of this morality, however, which constitutes the soil upon which 'man first became *an interesting animal*, . . . only here did the human soul in a higher sense acquire *depth* and become *evil*' (GM I 6 p. 33).

What is the nature of this acquisition of depth? In its initial form as Jewish theological dialectics and Greek philosophical dialectics, this depth is that capacity for reflection which is generated through the need to articulate a self-affirmation grounded on reflection on the other. The capacity for self-reflection, in other words, is founded on an other-reflection structured about the concept of guilt, that is, the constitution of *bad conscience*. Recall Nietzsche's characterisation of man 'finally enclosed within the walls of society and of peace':

The situation that faced sea animals when they were compelled to become land animals or perish was the same as that which faced these semi-animals, well adapted to the wilderness, to war, to prowling, to adventure: suddenly all their instincts were disvalued and 'suspended.' From now on they had to walk on their feet and 'bear themselves' whereas hitherto they had been borne by water: a dreadful heaviness lay upon them. They felt unable to cope with the simplest undertakings; in this new world they no longer possessed their former guides, their regulating, unconscious and infallible drives: they were reduced to thinking, inferring, reckoning, co-ordinating cause and effect, these unfortunate creatures; they were reduced to their 'consciousness,' their weakest and most fallible organ!

(GM II 16 p. 84)

Bad conscience as the opposition of consciousness to instinct which reduces man to reliance on consciousness is '*pregnant with a future*' (GM II 16 p. 85), for Nietzsche, precisely because this reduction demands the development of self-consciousness, the capacity for self-reflection, which is initiated by the slave revolt in morals. With the emergence of Christianity as universal dialectics, this need is raised to a higher power.

The central feature here is the redirecting of *ressentiment* which displaces the other-directed assignation of guilt characteristic of the emergence of slave morality with a self-directed assignation of guilt. Thus while the emergence of the capacity for self-reflection is predicated on a needful reflection on the other, the development of this capacity is articulated through an imperative need for reflection on the self (or, more specifically, the other in/as self). The individual is thus inscribed within a confessional regime of self-interrogation. However, this regime of self-reflection, this deepening of the human soul, is manifestly not a regime of self-judgement; on the contrary, the self-reflection initiated by redirecting of *ressentiment* is facilitated by the priest and it is the priest – the figure of an authority grounded in purity and truth – who articulates the judgement attendant on this self-reflection and who commands the penance. The individual is, if you like, the victim of the moral law but neither judge nor avenger. It is the Reformation's abolition of the priest which constitutes this regime of self-reflection as a regime of a self-judgement in which the individual determines and commands his own penance, in which the individual is constituted as 'judge and avenger and victim' of the moral law. What then are the implications of this for the question of the pathos of distance?

It was noted earlier that the slave's constitution of the pathos of *inner* distance was predicated on the reflective positing of a pathos of *metaphysical* distance which, in so far as it represents a reversal of the social order of rank, is tied to the pathos of *social* distance. However, the redirecting of *ressentiment* which attends Christianity as universal dialectics signals the separation of the pathos of metaphysical distance from that of social distance in the idea of 'the equality of all souls before God'. Indeed, the reduction of the noble to the herd which instances the requirement of this redirecting of *ressentiment* logically entails such a separation. The pathos of metaphysical distance, at this stage then, is constituted in relation not to social position but to the embodiment of the values of slave morality. Concomitant with this restructuring of metaphysical distance, however, is a restructuring of the nature of moral judgement. Whereas this judgement initially requires simply a location of the social position of the judged, it now requires an examination of the integration of slave values within the structure of the self – it requires, in other words, a hermeneutics of suspicion in which the manifest actions and intentions of the individual are interrogated to reveal the values embodied in the structure of the self. Prior to the Reformation, this judgement is articulated by the priest. The constitution of inner distance – the individuals' ability to command themselves in relation to a goal – is grounded on the pathos of metaphysical distance as articulated through the priest's judgements and commands. To command oneself is to obey the commands of the priest. With the Reformation, however, the activity of interpreting, judging and commmanding the self is displaced onto the individual. What is the implication of this? Christian asceticism breeds an individual with the capacity for the self-reflexive constitution of inner distance – 'that other, more mysterious pathos' (BGE 257 p. 173) – which is not dependent on the pathos of social distance but rather is constituted through reflexive adherence to a goal defined by a set of values.

The significance of this asceticism, for Nietzsche, emerges in relation to the ambivalence of modern culture. On the one hand, nihilism signals the collapse of the pathos of metaphysical distance, the destruction of the Christian *telos*, that is, the devaluation of the values through which inner distance was constituted. On the other hand, modern individuals bred under the aegis of Christian asceticism have the capacity to constitute inner distance, to command themselves, and thereby the potential for autonomy, for a self-determining goal-directed agency. To realise this potential, however, requires that individuals not merely command themselves in relation to a set of values but that they determine the values which define *their* goal.

Consequently, what is needful, Nietzsche argues, for modern culture is a thought which *enables* the self-affirmation requisite to this goal-positing activity – a pathos of neither social nor metaphysical distance but of *artistic* distance. The name of this thought which is both to lift up and to crush, to enable and disable? Eternal recurrence.[16]

4

THE POLITICS OF THE *ÜBERMENSCH*
Nietzsche, maturity and modernity

The problem I raise here is not what ought to succeed mankind in the sequence of species (– the human being is an *end* –): but what type of human being one ought to *breed*, ought to *will*, as more valuable, more worthy of life, more certain of the future.

(AC 3 p. 116)

One recognises the superiority of the Greek man and the Renaissance man – but one would like to have them without the causes and conditions that made them possible.

(WP 882 p. 471)

Nietzsche's transformation of critique, it will be recalled, is structured around a displacement of the question of legislation by one of evaluation. The purpose of this transformation emerges in Nietzsche's investigation of the ambivalent implications for modern culture of the ideals of knowledge and morality, or, more specifically, of a morality tied to a will to truth. The concept of nihilism – as the self-overcoming of this will to truth – signals the fulfilment of the negative moment of this project of evaluation; the positive moment, however, remains to be articulated. If Nietzsche's project is, as has been argued, to evaluate ideals from the perspective of breeding an autonomous human type in modernity, then the positive moment of his critique requires the articulation of an ideal which facilitates this possibility. This ideal may be located, I suggest, in the doctrine of eternal recurrence. Before focusing on this doctrine, however, it is necessary to specify further the depth of the crisis which Nietzsche argues is posed for modern individuals and communities by nihilism. In other words, it is only by making clear the fundamental ambivalence of modern culture that we can take up Nietzsche's attempt to address this ambivalence.

CULTURE, COMMUNITY AND NIHILISM

In our discussion of the triumph of slave morality in Jewish and Greek culture, it was noted that, in each case, this triumph is predicated on the

63

loss of a 'consciousness of power', that is, the capacity of the synthetic *a priori* judgements constitutive of a culture to enable the formation of goal-directed agency. To put this slightly differently, one might suggest that, for Nietzsche, the synthetic *a priori* judgements of a culture are constitutive of the *structures of recognition* which both make possible the possession of an identity and articulate the type of identity possessed.[1] These judgements, thus, become problematic when the type of identity articulated constrains rather than enables individuals in their practical experience of themselves as goal-directed agents, that is, when these judgements lose their capacity to explain the individual's experience of themselves. The implication of this is that what is at stake when the synthetic *a priori* judgements of a culture lose their legitimacy (i.e. their capacity to enable the formation of goal-directed agency) is the possibility of having a self, a cultural identity, at all – and only then does the question of the character of this self, the nature of this cultural identity, the form of this goal-directed agency, arise.[2] As Nietzsche expresses this: 'man would rather will *nothingness* than *not* will' (GM III 28 p. 163). Nihilism viewed formally represents a repetition of the type of crisis of legitimation and identity confronted by Greek and Jewish cultures; viewed substantively, however, it represents a transformation of this crisis in that it is the synthetic *a priori* judgements of slave morality in its Christian form which have been deconstructed. It is this, after all, which Nietzsche signals with the idea of the death of God. In this context, it is possible to specify the dimensions of the crisis posed by nihilism for modern culture.

At one level, this crisis is one of community; the destruction of the *particular* public structures of recognition through which individuals relate to each other in terms of agreement in form of life.[3] The death of God in this respect signals the self-overcoming of the synthetic *a priori* judgements of Christian culture and thereby of the ground through which the ethical life (*Sittlichkeit*) of a community is articulated.[4] This is the crisis of the self as goal-directed agent. At another level, however, the crisis posed by nihilism is one of selfhood as such: the collapse of the grounds of cultural identity signifying the paralysis of 'willing' *per se*. The will to truth in overcoming itself abolishes the fictional realm of being posited by the philosopher-priest, yet an abjuration of the realm of becoming is deeply entrenched within the psyche of modern man – this 'historical animal' weighed down by his past – which results, Nietzsche argues, in 'a process of dissolution' (WP 5 p. 10), that is, the dissolution of the will. The ambivalence of modern culture can, consequently, be expressed as the recognition that while modern individuals have the capacity for constituting themselves as autonomous selves, as goal-determining agents, the conditions requisite to the realisation of this potential are lacking and the possibility of constituting them is being progressively undermined.[5]

What are the implications of this for the positive moment of Nietzsche's critique embodied in the attempt to overcome nihilism? Firstly, it requires that Nietzsche articulate a ground for the constitution of cultural identity which is not subject to the ravaging logic of nihilism. This is the condition requisite for the formation of selfhood as such. Secondly, it requires that this ground is constitutive of structures of recognition which facilitate the affirmation of the realm of becoming. This is the condition requisite to the formation of autonomous selves. To put these points another way, we might say that Nietzsche needs to articulate an overcoming of both *bad conscience* as the articulation of *ressentiment* and the feeling of *ressentiment* as such.

OVERCOMING *BAD CONSCIENCE:* BECOMING WHAT ONE IS

Ressentiment, it will be recalled, becomes creative through the separation of agent and act which enables the emergence of the idea of guilt, that is, the idea that the agent could have acted otherwise. *Bad conscience* manifest as consciousness of guilt represents the rendering instinctive of the reification of consciousness exhibited in the idea of guilt – that is, the displacement of debt responsibility by guilt responsibility articulated in the transformation of the synthetic *a priori* judgements constitutive of a culture – a reification of consciousness which, as we have noted, requires the active suppression of the instincts. To put it slightly paradoxically, we might say that the *telos* of *bad conscience* is the production of an instinctive repression of instinct. In this respect, the death of God as the disentrenchment of the synthetic *a priori* judgements of modern culture represents a becoming conscious of this reification of consciousness, while nihilism as the delegitimation of these constitutive metaphors signals the possibility of overcoming the idea of guilt articulated through this reification.

The critical modern awareness of this reification of consciousness is itself manifest in Nietzsche's critique of Kant which we examined earlier; there, it will be recalled, Nietzsche is at pains to indicate that Kant's philosophy operates under the seduction of the metaphysics of language in which the grammatical structure of language (in particular, the subject–predicate distinction) is taken as corresponding to the structure of the world. By contrast, Nietzsche's argument is that the doer is constituted by the deed(s) or, to put this in terms of its implications, the 'I' is not unitary and static but multiple and dynamic. What is needful for our account, therefore, is to explore this view of the self and to trace its consequences for the overcoming of *bad conscience*.

'*What does your conscience say?* – "You shall become the person you are" ' (GS 270 p. 219): this aphorism, which embodies Nietzsche's dynamic view of selfhood, provides a route into our discussion through the apparently paradoxical conjunction of becoming and being; we can indicate the resolution of this paradox, however, by viewing the self metaphorically as a narrative.[6] Under this trope, Nietzsche's argument is that our selfhood is constituted by the totality of actions and events undergone where this totality consists precisely in the story of our life, that is, our biography. What one is at a given moment is thus determined by the narrative of our past as defined by this moment. In other words, one is always 'becoming what one is' simply because the narrative constitutive of 'what one is' (the self) is always already ongoing. How does this relate though to the overcoming of *bad conscience*?

We can explicate this relation by referring to the Kantian antinomy of freedom and necessity. In Kant, it will be recalled, this antinomy is resolved through the positing of the noumenal realm of freedom and the phenomenal realm of necessity, or, in Nietzsche's terms, the 'real' world and the 'apparent' world. In articulating his critique of this dualism, however, Nietzsche does not abolish the antinomy of freedom and necessity; rather he transforms it by locating the relationship of freedom and necessity as a temporal relationship – the realm of necessity is the past and the realm of freedom is the future. The peculiar double nature of man as both free and determined is preserved as the self's existence in the *moment* of the present as both becoming (freedom) and being (necessity). While retaining the double nature of man, however, this resolution of the antinomy radically transforms its implications; the expression of this resolution in the idea of becoming what one is captures this transformation in that it expresses the overcoming of this separation of agent and act – the reification of consciousness – thereby signifying the abolition of the conditions of possibility of the idea of guilt. The implications of this are twofold: firstly, it displaces an idea of responsibility grounded on what one does as being distinct from what one is (guilt responsibility) by an idea of responsibility grounded on what one is as inseparable from what one does – that is, a *tragic* understanding of responsibility;[7] and secondly, in displacing the idea of guilt, it displaces the necessity of a self-understanding based on the opposition of consciousness and instinct for the determination of the 'will', that is, goal-directed agency.[8] The crucial question with respect to the latter point is not that of the recognition of the *fateful* character of life, where the idea of fate expresses the conjunction of freedom and necessity, but rather whether this fate which is authored in the relationship of self and world can be affirmed. In other words, we confront at this moment Nietzsche's idea of *amor fati*.

We can conclude this section by expressing these points in relation to our characterisation of modern man. Viewed as a synthetic *a priori* judgement for modern culture, Nietzsche's temporalisation of Kant's antinomy of freedom and necessity provides a ground which enables the articulation of identity, of selfhood as such, in so far as it provides a structure of recognition – the idea of fate – through which the ethical life of the community can be articulated. It is by no means apparent, however, that this resolves the problem posed for the cultural formation of autonomous agents; on the contrary, in the absence of the pathos of social distance, with the collapse of the pathos of metaphysical distance, and despite the capacity of modern man to reflexively constitute the pathos of inner distance through adherence to a set of values, Nietzsche has not provided a ground through which self-affirmation (and thereby the positing of values) may be articulated. As we noted in the previous chapter, the noble exhibited an unreflective affirmation of self grounded on the pathos of social distance and the slave manifested an affirmation of self grounded on the pathos of metaphysical distance; Nietzsche's transposition of Kant's third antinomy does not articulate a pathos of distance of any type. In other words, to enable the formation of self-determining goal-directed agents Nietzsche needs to provide a ground of meaning, of justification, in terms of which existence takes on value. That such a ground is not present in his formulations at this stage is evident in the ambivalence which attends the idea of fate, for while this idea in displacing the concept of guilt renders this expression of *ressentiment* inarticulate, it does not thereby overcome *ressentiment* as such.

OVERCOMING *RESSENTIMENT* 1: ETERNAL RECURRENCE AS PATHOS OF DISTANCE

The question of overcoming *ressentiment* through the construction of a ground of value, that is, a pathos of distance, assumes its pertinence in relation to the dual features of man in modernity: on the one hand, the modern individual has a capacity for self-reflection which rules out the unreflective grounding of value in social position characteristic of the classical noble; on the other hand, the modern individual is confronted by the death of God as the inability authentically to accept a transcendental ground of value in the manner of the Christian.[9] The dilemma Nietzsche faces is thus that of providing a ground of value which demands neither an unreflective internalisation of the social order of rank nor an acceptance of transcendental fictions. Nietzsche's resolution of this dilemma is predicated on the claim made in *The Birth of Tragedy* that 'it is only as an *aesthetic phenomenon* that existence and the world are eternally *justified*' (BT 5 p. 52; cf. also BT 24 p. 141), or, more precisely, on the latter version of this claim expressed in *The Gay Science* that as 'an aesthetic phenomenon existence is still *bearable* for us' (GS 107 p. 163). To explore the character and coherence of this resolution requires an exploration of Nietzsche's doctrine of eternal recurrence; we can enter this arena, however, by focusing on the question of style and the determination of the will.

In a well-known passage from *The Gay Science*, Nietzsche argues that what is needful is to ' "give style' to one's character – a great and rare art!' (GS 290 p. 232). Two questions arise in this context: firstly, what is involved in giving style to one's character? and secondly, what is signified by this claim that Nietzsche makes? Both of these questions appear relatively straightforward in that Nietzsche goes on to specify the idea of giving style to one's character as self-formation under the 'constraint of a single taste' (GS 290 p. 232) and to indicate, at least implicitly, that stylistic coherency of character is exclusive to autonomous agents, sovereign individuals. To trace in adequate detail what is involved here and what its significance is, however, requires that we return to the question of the will.

In our discussion of Nietzsche's conception of the self, it was noted that the self is seen as both dynamic and multiple, and it was argued that we could grasp the dynamic character of the self expressed in Nietzsche's notion of *becoming what you are* by viewing the self as the narrative of the actions performed and events undergone by the individual. To give this alternative expression, we might say that the self is constituted by the individual's will as it is determined and expressed in the world, that is, the narrative of the individual's will to power. However, it will be recalled that the 'will' is, for Nietzsche, 'merely a word' (TI III 5 p. 38) which bestows an unwarranted unity on the multiple drives constitutive of the self; drives, moreover, which are in conflict – each one embodies 'a kind of lust to rule; each one has its perspective that it would like to compel all the other drives to accept as a norm' (WP 481 p. 267). It is on this basis, as already noted, that Nietzsche distinguishes strength and weakness of the will. In terms of our narrative metaphor, we can express this by suggesting that a 'strong will' – a will which unifies itself under the aegis of a 'single predominant impulse' which is expressed in adherence to the values embodied in this drive (its perspective) – represents the imposition of a stylistic unity over the narrative constitutive of the self. The appropriateness of this metaphor is clear if we consider the centrality to slave morality of the idea of soul (cf. GM I 13 p. 46); the positing of the soul as the creative moment of *ressentiment* representing the subversion of the constraint of style – which the weak hate (cf. GS 290 p. 233) – in that the slave, unable to unify the will under a leading drive, that is, to give stylistic coherency to the narrative of his life, posits the soul as *underlying* the disparate impulses of the 'will', that is, invents a *narrator* as a device for endowing the slave's selfhood with a distinct form of unity – the unity of an author's *oeuvre*.[10] In terms of our discussion of agency, we can say that while both stylistic unity and authorial unity denote the formation of goal-directed agency, it is only in the former case that this agency is autonomous in the sense of determining its own goals. Why though does Nietzsche engage in this redescription of will to power from an aesthetic perspective, this redescription of existence and the world as an aesthetic phenomenon? – and what is the significance of this activity of redescription for the question of a ground of value, a pathos of distance?

The *raison d'être* for this strategy on Nietzsche's part emerges with his understanding of a work of art as self-referential, as containing its own criteria of legitimation. In other words, the value of a work of art is constituted in and through an internal reflexivity in which the whole and the parts articulate a mutual affirmation, or, rather, the justification of the whole is constituted through the willing of the totality of the parts of the whole. In so far as this model indicates a ground of value, therefore, Nietzsche's redescription of existence as an aesthetic phenomenon signals an attempt to provide a form of synthetic *a priori* judgement which will enable the formation of autonomous agents in modern culture. This 'regulative principle' is his doctrine of eternal recurrence as becomes clear by noting the allegorical reduplication of the self-legitimation characteristic of a work of art which is posed as a thought-experiment in an early version of eternal recurrence:

> *The greatest weight* – What, if some day or night a demon were to steal after you into your loneliest loneliness and say to you: 'This life as you now live it and have lived it, you will have to live once more and innumerable times more; and there will be nothing new in it, but every pain and every joy and every thought and sigh and everything unutterably small or great in your life will have to return to you, all in the same succession and sequence – . . . .'
>
> Would you not throw yourself down and gnash your teeth and curse the demon who spoke thus? Or have you once experienced a tremendous moment when you would have answered him: 'You are a god and never have I heard anything more divine.' . . . how well disposed would you have to become to yourself and your life *to crave nothing more fervently* than this ultimate eternal confirmation and seal?
>
> (GS 341 pp. 273–4)

This thought, with its emphasis on the affirmation of every moment of one's life as having its highest form in the 'willing' of the eternal recurrence of one's life as it has been and is, exemplifies the internal reflexivity which constitutes an aesthetic grounding of the value of existence. The doctrine of eternal recurrence, thus, provides a pathos of artistic distance which is dependent for its possibility on precisely that capacity for the self-reflexive unification of the will bred under the aegis of Christian asceticism – it is, in this sense, a specifically *modern* ideal.[11] To express this another way, we may say that the idea of eternal recurrence constructs a reflexive relationship between a ground of value for existence (a pathos of distance) and the capacity for positing values for oneself (autonomous agency) in

69

so far as it is precisely through positing and adhering to a set of values (the constraint of style) that one grounds the value of one's existence (as work of art) in an affirmation of the relationship between self and world.[12]

The reading of eternal recurrence developed here suggests that it articulates an overcoming of *ressentiment* through the constitution of a set of synthetic *a priori* judgements which elaborate an artistic perspective that enables the formation of autonomous agents in so far as it constructs a reflexive relationship between the pathos of (artistic) distance and the self-determination of values. However, given the complexity of Nietzsche's position and to determine the precise character of this reflexive relationship, it is useful to provide a complementary reading of eternal recurrence to supplement that set out here.

OVERCOMING *RESSENTIMENT* 2: THE TIME OF ETERNAL RECURRENCE

To explore this reading of eternal recurrence, we can begin by returning again to the question of the will. It was argued in our discussion of overcoming *bad conscience* that the displacement of the idea of guilt by that of fate renders this expression of *ressentiment* inarticulate; as was noted, however, this does not indicate an overcoming of *ressentiment* – the recognition that one becomes what one is does not entail that one wants to become what one is. The idea of fate is ambivalent in that its recognition may take the form of either an active pursuit of destiny or a retreat into 'Turkish fatalism'. It is in the latter form that the spirit of revenge still resides. What is the character of this *ressentiment* and how can it be overcome? We can begin by noting that while Nietzsche's temporalised resolution of Kant's third antinomy displaces the articulation of *ressentiment* through the positing of another world, it thereby transforms the direction of *ressentiment* from a need to negate existence from the perspective of a fictional realm of being into a need to negate existence from the perspective of an alternative past. *Ressentiment* could only be articulated as transformative re-invention of the past.[13] Yet the form of Nietzsche's resolution of Kant's antinomy rules out this possibility – the past has the character of necessity – and *ressentiment* rendered inarticulate can only exist as an ethos of passive fatalism. Indeed it is this recognition of the temporal character of the will which is expressed in Nietzsche's idea of will to power, that is, the will only determines itself as will (freedom) in so far as it determines itself as power (necessity), or, alternatively, 'free will' is only manifest in its actualisation of itself as 'determined will'. It is notable in this context that it is precisely this realisation of the temporal character of the will which prompts Zarathustra to abandon his initial attempt to teach the *Übermensch* directly and take up the abysmal thought of eternal recurrence. As Zarathustra recognises: 'The will cannot will backwards; that it cannot break time and time's desire – that is the will's most lonely affliction' (Z Of Redemption p. 161). The implication which strikes Zarathustra such that he 'suddenly broke off and looked exactly like a man seized by extremest terror' (Z Of Redemption p. 163) is that to authentically will one's will, to overcome *ressentiment*, requires that one also will the temporality of the will.[14] It is with respect to this requirement that we return to eternal recurrence.

In our earlier discussion, the doctrine of eternal recurrence was treated as constituting an enabling perspective for the formation of autonomous agents in so far as it constructs a reflexive relationship between a ground of value for existence and a self-determining positing of values. At this stage, it is necessary to specify the nature of this reflexivity by focusing on the transformation of the experience of time induced by Nietzsche's doctrine.

Within the doctrine of eternal recurrence, this experience is explored through a focus on the moment (*Augenblick*) as the site of both a liberation from the seriality of time, the seriality which imprisons the will, and an affirmation of the seriality of time and thereby of the temporality of the will.[15] How does this operate? We should note to begin with that the idea of eternal recurrence does not describe a cosmological version of time; it does not, in other words, embody the cosmological claim that time is cyclical.[16] This is made clear both by Zarathustra's angry rebuke to the Spirit of Gravity when such a claim is made (Z Of the Vision and the Riddle p. 178) and by the passive fatalism which would necessarily attend such a cosmology.[17] Rather eternal recurrence functions as a regulative idea, an enabling fiction, which represents an existential vision of time that transforms our experience of the relationship between past, present and future. This emerges if we consider that, for Nietzsche, the moment (the present) does not exist between past and future but as the site of the conjunction of past and future, as the gateway from which an eternal lane runs back and an eternal lane runs forward – *the moment is the site of eternity* (cf. Z Of the Vision and the Riddle pp. 178–9).[18] As such the eternal return of the moment in time signals nothing less than the eternal return of the totality of time – and this is to say that the value of the moment, any moment, is equal to the value of the totality of time. Time, in other words, is an aesthetic phenomenon and to experience time under the existential aegis of the thought of eternal recurrence is thus to experience one's existence as of intrinsic, and self-generating, value and it is this experience which creates the pathos of artistic-existential distance which enables the willing of the will as the willing of the temporality of the will, that is, the affirmation of the relationship of self and world which is constitutive of autonomous agency.[19]

The complementary arguments developed in the two readings of eternal recurrence offered suggest that Nietzsche's doctrine functions as a counter-ideal to the spirit of asceticism and represents an attempt to construct synthetic *a priori* judgements for modern culture which articulate the overcoming of both *bad conscience* and *ressentiment*, thereby enabling the realisation of that capacity possessed by modern man for autonomy through the construction of a pathos of artistic-existential distance.[20] Two questions arise at this moment: firstly, what are the politics of eternal recurrence? and secondly, what are the politics of entrenching eternal recurrence as a synthetic *a priori* judgement? As a preface to the exploration of these questions and as a conclusion to our clarification of the doctrine of eternal recurrence, however, it may be useful briefly to contrast Nietzsche's imperative of eternal return with Kant's categorical imperative.

AUTONOMY AND ETERNAL RECURRENCE

Our question is perhaps this: in so far as Nietzsche's idea of eternal recurrence involves the displacement of Kant's dualist 'spatial' resolution of the antinomy of freedom and necessity by a non-dualist 'temporal' resolution, this implies that the law governing autonomous subjectivity is isomorphically transformed from the Kantian rule 'act always according to that maxim you can at the same time will as universal law' to the Nietzschean rule 'act always according to that maxim you can at the same time will as eternally returning', but what are the implications of this transformation?

In his description of the sovereign individual, Nietzsche writes of this man with the right to make promises that he is 'autonomous and supramoral (for "autonomous" and "moral" are mutually exclusive)' (GM II 2 p. 59). This claim becomes clear once we understand that, for Nietzsche, morality (by which he means slave morality) involves precisely the claim to universality which entails the subordination of self to a superhuman authority (cf. WP 20 pp. 16–17) and, moreover, thereby engages in an abstraction of values from the conditions which gave them meaning, that is, the conditions in which they preserved life. Thus Nietzsche writes, for example:

> A word against Kant as *moralist*. A virtue has to be *our* invention, *our* most personal defence and necessity: in any other sense it is merely a danger. . . . The profoundest laws of preservation and growth demand . . . this: that each one of us should devise *his own* virtue, *his own* categorical imperative. A people perishes if it mistakes *its own* duty for the concept of duty in general. Nothing works more profound ruin than any 'impersonal' duty, any sacrifice to the Moloch of abstraction. – Kant's categorical imperative should have been felt as *mortally dangerous*!
>
> (AC 11 p. 122)

In other words, not only does Kant's identification of autonomy with willing the categorical imperative misdescribe what it means to will one's own will but further it does so in a manner which legislates obedience to certain values without respect for the conditions under which willing occurs and is thereby actually constitutive of conditions in which the will becomes subject to a process of dissolution, that is, nihilism. Indeed, it becomes apparent in Kant's essay 'What is Enlightenment?' that he cannot hold to the absolute rule of the categorical imperative under the conditions of an age of enlightenment in so far as this age requires that members of the state, for example, are treated and treat themselves in this capacity as 'things', as beings without purposes. Kant's paradoxical position in this essay involves the claim that the movement to an age in which the categorical imperative rules requires for its achievement the suspension of the categorical imperative at least with respect to civic posts. In this respect, Nietzsche's critique appears to be well-grounded; it needs to be asked, however, whether the rule of eternal recurrence is entirely successful in avoiding 'the Moloch of abstraction'. Does not Nietzsche's rule of eternal return in so far as it has a universal form also involve a commitment to a certain unconditional value – namely, probity (*Redlichkeit*)?[21]

Consider Nietzsche's rule as we have formulated it: 'act always in accordance with that maxim you can at the same time will as eternally returning'. To will the eternal return of the moment – does this not presuppose a certain integrity, a certain honesty, in one's relationship with oneself? Indeed, Nietzsche presents us with confirmation of the centrality of this value when Zarathustra announces to the Higher Men that he counts nothing more valuable and rare than honesty (cf. Z IV 'Of the Higher Men' 8 p. 300). Consider, moreover, the following passage:

> We . . . *want to become those we are* – beings who are new, unique, incomparable, who give themselves laws, who create themselves. To that end we must become the best learners and discoverers of everything that is lawful and necessary in the world: we must become *physicists* in order to be able to be *creators* in this sense – . . . . Therefore long live physics! and even more so that which compels us to turn to physics – our honesty (*unsere Redlichkeit*)!

> (GS 335 p. 266)

The significance of this passage lies not simply in its signalling of the necessity of probity for the *amor fati* embodied in the idea of eternal recurrence nor in its intimation that probity is a dynamic moment in the culture of modernity (it is after all this probity which leads the will to truth to undermine itself) but in its recognition that this probity of which Nietzsche speaks is not a *moral* value, it is not the will to truth cultivated by Christianity (though it would not be possible without this will to truth);

rather, it is that moment within the will to truth which both exceeds and undermines the will to truth, it is the voice not of our moral (bad) conscience but of our intellectual conscience, the conscience behind our conscience (cf. GS 335 pp. 263–6).

In this context, recall Zarathustra's claim that the individual 'must become judge and avenger and victim of his own law' (Z II Of Self-Overcoming p. 137), Nietzsche's suggestion being that the *Übermensch* must rule himself in accordance with the values he posits for himself – must, in other words, subject himself to the constraint of style – yet it is apparent that probity is prior to the values through which the labour of self-overcoming is articulated in so far as it is probity which makes the reflexive rule of the self possible. This is not to say, however, that probity is prior to self-legislation but rather that probity is constitutive of the structure of self-legislation; it is the value which attends the *becoming* of what one is as opposed to the *what one is* that one becomes in that it articulates not the values to be posited and adhered to but rather the process of positing and adhering which is precisely a taking of responsibility for oneself (and therefore also the heteronomous manifold constitutive of oneself).[22] The implication of this for the question of whether the thought of eternal recurrence may be said to avoid the problem of unconditionality and abstraction is that, in so far as probity describes a self-reflexive relation, it does entail a certain unconditionality but does not entail an abstraction from the conditionality of willing; on the contrary, it is the very condition of autonomous willing. The crucial difference between Kant's doctrine and Nietzsche's that emerges here has been well expressed by Ansell-Pearson:

> Like the categorical imperative, the thought of eternal return has a universal character or form, but unlike the categorical imperative it does not posit a universal content. However, it might be argued in response that the categorical imperative too is a purely formal doctrine, for it has no determinate content. But the key point is that, although the categorical imperative is indeed formalistic, its willing does *presuppose* that the actions the autonomous will is to will are universal in content: . . . . The eternal return, however, provides the form of universality only in the act of returning, whereas what returns (the actual content) and is willed to be returned cannot be universal, since each life (each becoming) is unique.
>
> (Ansell-Pearson 1991b: 198)

Thus the doctrine of eternal return transforms Kant's account of autonomy by relocating the relationship of autonomy and morality as one of opposition. To put this slightly differently, one might say that moral autonomy is displaced by aesthetic autonomy as the understanding of maturity in so far as the constraint of universality embodied in the categorical imperative is replaced by the constraint of probity embodied in eternal recurrence. At this stage, it becomes pertinent to pose a question to Nietzsche's account of autonomy, namely, what are the political implications of this understanding?

THE POLITICS OF ETERNAL RECURRENCE

The political dimension of Kant's vision of autonomy emerges via the 'historical' imperative in the idea of a kingdom of ends, this idea representing Kant's solution to the Rousseauian problem of reconciling individual and collective autonomy. Nietzsche, despite (or perhaps because of) his critiques of both Rousseau's and Kant's moralism, is similarly concerned with this issue. Thus, in a passage from *Daybreak*, he speaks of a possible future lawgiving, 'one founded on the idea "I submit only to the law which I myself have given, in great things and small." ' (D 187 p. 110). This, however, introduces a dilemma – for in so far as Nietzsche's account of autonomy is radically individualistic it is difficult to see how he might attempt to reconcile individual and collective autonomy having ruled out the possibility of recourse to those 'moral' ideas such as the general will and the categorical imperative which attempt to mediate between the individual and the collectivity. To explore Nietzsche's resolution of this dilemma requires that we take up the question of individualism.

We can begin with a revealing comment that Nietzsche makes concerning the relationship between individuals and society in modernity:

> To say it briefly (for a long time people will still keep silent about it):
> What will not any more henceforth, and *cannot* be built any more, is
> – a society [*Gesellschaft*] in the old sense of that word; to build that
> everything is lacking, above all the material. *All of us are no longer
> material for a society*; this is a truth for which the time has come.
> (GS 356 p. 304; cf. also TI IX 39 p. 93)[23]

What is Nietzsche signifying here? Simply this: in so far as the death of God represents the collapse of the grounds of any unconditional extra-human authority, nihilism breeds a culture of individualism; there is not, and cannot be, any universally accepted authority or set of moral values – rather we are plunged into a polytheism of values.[24] Nietzsche's account of autonomy embodies the recognition that to overcome nihilism requires the individual to become the authority for himself which is also to say to become responsible for himself. If, however, this is indeed the case, does it not simply imply an anarchic politics, an extreme individualism of the type described in Hobbes's vision of the state of nature in which life is a war of all against all?[25] If we are no longer material for a society, how can communal life be possible?

75

The doctrine of eternal recurrence represents Nietzsche's response to this dilemma in so far as it is viewed not as an individual thought-experiment but as a proposed synthetic *a priori* judgement for modern culture. Let us begin with a remark from Nietzsche's essay on the uses and disadvantages of history for life: 'And this is a universal law: a living thing can be healthy, strong and fruitful only when bounded by a horizon' (UM II 1 p. 63). In the case of a culture, the horizon is constituted by its synthetic *a priori* judgements, the unquestioned (and, while it is adequate, unquestionable) unconscious of the collectivity that is agreement in a form of life. It is, after all, these judgements which we have forgotten are judgements that articulate our identities. The challenge posed by nihilism is that it deconstructs the synthetic *a priori* judgements of European culture and, moreover, delegitimates any such judgement which attempts to articulate cultural identity by reference to any collective, even if purely formal, mode (e.g. Kant's categorical imperative). How does the doctrine of eternal recurrence overcome this? The central point is that, in so far as it does not presuppose universality of content with respect to our identities, eternal recurrence articulates the possession of a cultural identity by reference to an individualistic mode. We can clarify this by suggesting that the constitution of a community requires, at least minimally, a *public value* which can articulate communal identity. For Nietzsche (and this is exhibited in his account of Zarathustra's down-going), [26] probity – the 'becoming' of becoming what one is – is a public value since it exhibits itself in the sphere of public testing and recognition or, rather, because it is constitutive of the sphere of public testing and recognition. To put this another way, we may say that eternal recurrence as a ground of culture, as a synthetic *a priori* judgement, provides *the structure of recognition* through which we create our own identity in the context of a recognition of the identities of others and which thereby articulates the ethical life of the community.

Recall to begin with that under the aegis of eternal recurrence one experiences one's life as of intrinsic value, that is, one recognises oneself as a being with a purpose, as an end in oneself. The implication of this, however, is that one must also recognise that the other who exhibits probity, whatever the difference (in content) he also exhibits, is similarly of intrinsic value and constitutes a being who is an end in himself. Eternal recurrence, one might say, involves the recognition of the individual who manifests probity as possessing dignity and as thereby requiring respect. Two points should be noted here. Firstly, the dignity of the individual is recognised only in so far as he exhibits probity within the sphere of public testing. Secondly, the manifestation of probity (which is, in actuality, to say *nobility*) is an always already ongoing requirement. In this respect, ethical life is constituted as an arena within which one perpetually manifests one's *right* to respect not on the basis of what one is but rather on the basis of *becoming* what one is. In so far as eternal recurrence is constituted as the ground of culture, that is, in so far as probity is rendered instinctive as *conscience*, this implies a type of Nietzschean correlate to Kant's kingdom of ends. This apparent equality, however, becomes more complex when we move to the question of the type of political life articulated in the doctrine of eternal recurrence in so far as this shift brings into play, for Nietzsche, the question of *rank*.

This, indeed, is the seemingly paradoxical character of Nietzsche's thought, his question being how one can reconcile the idea of equality between those who earn the right to respect and the idea of an ordering or ranking of those who are formally equal. We can explicate this feature of Nietzsche's thought by introducing a distinction between judgements of style and judgements of taste. This distinction can be put thus: a judgement of style is a judgement of probity in that it relates to the *becoming* of what one is, that is, the stylistic unity of the will in its formal aspect, whereas a judgement of taste is a judgement of value in that it relates to the *what one is* one becomes, that is, the stylistic unity of the will in its substantive aspect. A remark of Max Weber's may clarify this a little:

> A work of art which is genuine 'fulfilment' is never surpassed; it will never be antiquated. Individuals may differ in appreciating the personal significance of works of art, but no one will ever be able to say of such a work that it is 'outstripped' by another work which is also 'fulfilment'.
>
> (SV p. 138)

A judgement of style, in the sense deployed above, is the judgement that a work of art is genuine 'fulfilment' (i.e. that an individual has given style to their character). A judgement of taste, by contrast, refers to 'the personal significance of works of art' (i.e. the responses of others to the particular style an individual's character exhibits). But what governs this response, what is its law? For Nietzsche, I suggest, the significance of a work of art lies in the degree to which it discloses an understanding that we find in ourselves.[27] Thus the 'personal' ranking of works of art, the degree of authority with which they speak to us, is a ranking in terms of the degrees to which they disclose understandings we find in ourselves and the significance of these understandings to our selves. In political terms, this describes nothing other than an agonistic vision of politics in which the judgement that one's character has style grounds one's right to enter the arena of contest while the *agon* itself consists of the ranking of individuals according to the authority they manifest which is grounded in the degree to which the understanding they disclose is found within the other individuals constitutive of the collectivity. The *agon* is constituted through the ongoing construction, destruction and reconstruction of 'communities of judgement' (Strong 1988: 158). It is perhaps for this reason that Nietzsche describes the wisest man as 'the one richest in contradictions, who has, as it were, antennae for all types of men' (WP 259 p. 150). It is important to recognise here that individuals remain the *source* of authority for themselves in that the political authority of a given individual is grounded in his expression of what others find in themselves.

The conclusion which emerges from this is that Nietzsche's doctrine of eternal recurrence appears to provide a vision which reconciles individual and collective autonomy through the articulation of agonistic politics. Of course, all of this is to presuppose the entrenchment of eternal recurrence as the ground of culture, to presuppose the entrenchment of probity as instinct, that is, the formation of a sovereign conscience. The question which must therefore be posed is how Nietzsche grounds the possibility of this 'sovereign culture'.

THE AMBIVALENCE OF THE *ÜBERMENSCH*: 'NAPOLEON' AND 'GOETHE'

The problem Nietzsche confronts at this juncture is the same dilemma which required Kant to present an account of the dynamics of moving from an age of enlightenment to an enlightened age, a dynamics in which the ambivalence of modern reason erupts fatally for the coherence of Kant's account. It has been suggested that a similar ambivalence attends Nietzsche's position in so far as 'the Nietzschean stance turns out not to be a mode of escape from or an alternative to the conceptual scheme of liberal individualist modernity, but rather one more representative moment in its internal unfolding' (MacIntyre 1984: 259). Yet such a reading may elide the complexity and antinomies of Nietzsche's thought; to explore this we can examine two distinct versions of the *Übermensch* presented, implicitly or explicitly, by Nietzsche. Daniel Conway has termed these two models the 'world-historical' *Übermensch* and the 'quiet' *Übermensch*;[28] we shall address each in turn.

The figure of the world-historical *Übermensch* arises in relation to the foundational dimension of Nietzsche's politics, that is, as the agency of establishing a 'sovereign culture'. This aspect of Nietzsche's project emerges in considering the following passage:

> there are cases of individual success constantly appearing in the most various parts of the earth and from the most various cultures in which a *higher type* does manifest itself: something which in relation to collective mankind is a sort of superman [*Übermensch*]. Such chance occurrences of great success have always been possible and perhaps will always be possible. And even entire races, tribes, nations, can under certain circumstances represent such a *lucky hit*.
> (AC 4 p. 116)

The crucial point for Nietzsche is that the appearance of these autonomous individuals has always been more or less a matter of chance; if, however, eternal recurrence can be instituted as the ground of culture, this would *secure* the existence of this higher type of man. Suspending for the moment an examination of the ambivalence attendant on this account, let us turn to the question of the characteristics and politics of this world-historical *Übermensch*, that is, to the question of entrenching eternal recurrence.

Nietzsche's most consistent exemplar of this type of *Übermensch* is provided by Napoleon 'this synthesis of the *inhuman* and *superhuman*' (GM I 16 p. 54; cf. also WP 1017 pp. 525–6, 1027 p. 531). What are the features of this type? One may note initially that Nietzsche conceives of the political leader as an artist who is 'objective, hard, firm, severe in carrying through an idea – . . . whatever the cost in men' (WP 975 p. 511). Nietzsche approvingly cites in this context Taine's characterisation of Napoleon as 'the posthumous brother of Dante and Michelangelo' (WP 1018 p. 526).[29] Moreover, as an artist, the leader embodies the capacity of dissimulation (cf. WP 544 pp. 292–3). This point is significant not merely in itself but further because it already indicates the similarity which marks Nietzsche's notion of the world-historical *Übermensch* and Machiavelli's conception of the Prince. Not only are both 'beyond good and evil' but further markedly similar functions are ascribed to them. For Machiavelli, the role of the Prince is to create the conditions within which civic *virtù* can develop as a prelude to the establishment of a republic, that is, to overcome the conditions which make the Prince necessary by generating, through a politics of domination, the political stability which allows for the entrenching of a culture of civic *virtù*.[30] For Nietzsche, the role of the world-historical *Übermensch* is to create the conditions within which extra-moral autonomy can develop as a prelude to the establishment of a 'sovereign culture', that is again, to overcome the conditions which make this type of *Übermensch* necessary by generating, through a politics of domination, the regime of probity which allows for the entrenching of eternal recurrence as the ground of culture. The pertinence of this comparison – which is consonant with the predication of Nietzsche's admiration for the Renaissance on the Machiavellian idea of *virtù* (cf. for example WP 317, 327, 740; AC 61) – is not simply that it indicates the type of politics of domination instituted by the world-historical *Übermensch*, that is, entrenching of eternal recurrence through the establishment of a regime of probity, but that it indicates that, with respect to this ground of overcoming nihilism, Nietzsche elides (as Machiavelli does) the question of legitimation. In other words, it is not a question of *right* addressed here for Nietzsche but one of *power*. The establishment of a 'sovereign culture' appears to involve an unlimited economy of violence in which the world-historical *Übermensch* serves as the hammer which tests the mettle of individuals on the anvil of eternal recurrence, reworking the strong into autonomous individuals and crushing the weak.[31]

Having encountered the features of the world-historical *Übermensch* and the form of politics this type embodies, we can return to the question we left suspended concerning the ambivalence of this conception. It is not here a question of 'rescuing' Nietzsche from his politics by arguing that he did not seriously engage in positing this model (whatever status one gives to his notebooks) but of examining the antinomies and incoherencies which attend this idea. Three related dilemmas may be seen as emerging here: the problem of chance, the problem of authority and the problem of redemption.

The problem of chance concerns an immediately visible ambivalence in Nietzsche's position which is simply this: the world-historical *Übermensch* is required to secure the existence of an *übermenschlich* culture, yet by this token the existence of the world-historical *Übermensch* can only itself be a matter of chance. In other words, if the existence of this higher type of humanity has been a matter of 'lucky strikes', then this implies that the world-historical *Übermensch* who is to generate the overcoming of this dependence on chance must himself be a lucky hit. Consequently, when Nietzsche writes of this figure that '*he must come someday*' (GM II 24 p. 96), either he is being incoherent in that this 'must' has no force or, alternatively, he is being disingenuous in that this figure must have already come and, perhaps, be none other than Nietzsche himself.[32] This ambivalence, however, is by no means the least to infect Nietzsche's account.

The second dilemma, that of authority, may also be simply put: in so far as the world-historical *Übermensch* acts as legislator, as commander, it is difficult to see how this may produce individuals who legislate for themselves – rather, being subject to command surely habituates individuals to obedience. This ambivalence, which is akin to that of legality and morality in Kant, may at first sight appear to be illusory in that it could be argued that the trainability of modern man upon which Nietzsche pins his hopes for the success of the mission of the world-historical *Übermensch* as legislator (cf. WP 128 p. 79) relates to his capacity to acquire the habit of probity upon which the possibility of autonomy is grounded. This is a vision of the world-historical *Übermensch* as a kind of Jacob's ladder. Yet the dilemma remains: how can the individual recognise himself as his own source of authority if this recognition is predicated on obedience to the authority of another? The ambivalence which emerges here may be read as a specific instance of the final dilemma in the idea of a world-historical *Übermensch*, that is, the problem of redemption.

Consider again Nietzsche's characterisation of the world-historical *Übermensch* as 'the *redeeming* man of great love and contempt . . . who will redeem us not only from the hitherto reigning ideal but also from that which was bound to grow out of it, the great nausea, the will to nothingness, nihilism' (GM II 24 p. 96). As Daniel Conway has acutely indicated, this 'vivid portrayal of the modernity-crushing *Übermensch* betrays a nihilistic commitment to the deficiency of the human condition' (Conway 1989: 212) in that it implies that humanity requires a redeemer in order to actualise its potential for autonomy and affirmation. The dilemma which confronts Nietzsche's thought here is that it is his specific contribution to articulate a teaching grounded on the idea of the sufficiency of the human condition, it is the self-sufficiency which is the condition of the idea of eternal recurrence and which is celebrated in the affirmation of this thought, yet the conception of the *Übermensch* as redeemer undermines this teaching in that this conception plays a role analogous with the role of God in Kant's account of the possibility of a kingdom of ends. Conway again makes the point neatly: 'If the *Übermensch* is presented as a potential redeemer of modernity, as a *diabolus ex machina*, then does not Nietzsche in fact exacerbate the disease he intends to cure?' (Conway 1989: 213). Given these ambivalences which plague the ideal of the world-historical *Übermensch*, it might seem reasonable to dismiss Nietzsche (as so many have done) as a politically disastrous thinker. Yet to do justice to Nietzsche's thought demands that firstly we turn to the other conception of the *Übermensch* which emerges in his work, the quiet *Übermensch* characterised by the figure of Goethe.

In contrast to the world-historical *Übermensch*, the quiet *Übermensch* does not manifest any necessary connection with political life; on the contrary, Nietzsche's model here is the artist rather than the prince, the characteristic features of figure being that excess, abundance, surfeit of creative energy exemplified by Goethe:

> he did not sever himself from life, he placed himself within it; nothing could discourage him and he took as much as possible upon himself, above himself, within himself. What he aspired to was *totality*; he strove against the separation of reason, sensuality, feeling, will . . . ; he disciplined himself to a whole, he *created* himself. . . . a man of tolerance, not out of weakness, but out of strength. . . .
>
> (TI IX 49 p. 102)

As a genius, Goethe's greatness 'lies in the fact that *he expends himself*' (TI IX 44 p. 98) and it is in the *squandering* of themselves by such 'explosive beings' that they create themselves as works of art. It is this sense of overflowingness which characterises Zarathustra in the opening chapter of the last book of *Thus Spake Zarathustra* (after his affirmation of eternal recurrence at the end of the third book) when he describes himself as 'a squanderer with a thousand hands' (Z The Honey Offering p. 252; cf. also Conway 1989: 218–19). This vision of the *Übermensch*, however, does appear to involve a dilemma in so far as the central feature of this self-creation is its monological character; the artistic *Übermensch* is not concerned with the world-historical or otherwise effects of his self-creation because this superabundant self-creation involves precisely a forgetting of the world (cf. GS 367 p. 324). How then does this fit with the project of entrenching eternal recurrence as the ground of culture?[33]

The straightforward answer appears to be that this version of the *Übermensch* does not fit neatly into the project of constructing an '*agora* of ends' but, on the contrary, represents the problematisation of any such utopian vision, the 'global' or 'totalistic' overcoming of nihilism which is the project of the world-historical *Übermensch* being displaced by an individualistic ideal which Conway has termed 'local rebellion'; the politics of the hammer, that is, of legislating probity through an economy of violence, being displaced by a politics of seduction – the recommendation of probity which operates through an economy of exemplification. The quiet *Übermensch* is not a world-redeemer but rather exemplifies in his life the overcoming of the need for redemption and by virtue of his example encourages adoption of this quiet ideal of self-creation. Thus Nietzsche states of Zarathustra that he is no prophet or fanatic demanding faith (cf. EH Preface 4 pp. 219–20) and, indeed, Zarathustra's journey of self-discovery involves precisely an abandonment of any such role in favour of an aesthetic of self-cultivation, this politics of exemplification being, as the subtitle of *Thus Spake Zarathustra* tells us, 'for all and none' in that the life of the quiet *Übermensch* is offered as an example of probity to all but the content, and the journey of this life is necessarily open to none as we must each undertake our own down-going and fashion ourselves according to our own 'unique and incomparable' taste.[34] Within this ideal then Nietzsche may resolve the ambivalences which plague the world-historical conception of the *Übermensch* but only at the cost of abandoning the utopian ideal of an '*agora* of ends'.

What emerges here in Nietzsche's apparently antinomical images of the *Übermensch* is a confrontation between ambivalences analogous to those which plague Kant's modernist utopianism and a postmodernist abandonment of such ideas as constituting the ground of political critique. In this respect (if few others), Habermas is surely correct to locate Nietzsche as signalling the entrance to a path in which the enlightenment ideal of a collective achievement of maturity celebrated by Kant is rendered deeply problematic.

CONCLUSION: THE AUTHORITY OF NIETZSCHE

We can begin to conclude our examination of Nietzsche by noting that his historicisation of Kant's notion of immanent critique operates a transformation of the ambivalent character of modern thought in so far as it signals both the re-emergence and heightening of ambivalences which attend Kant's political utopianism *and* the emergence of the double of these ambivalences in the perpetual postponement of the utopian moment which marks Nietzsche's ethic of exemplarity. Given this ambivalence, with what authority does Nietzsche's critique of modernity speak?

To address this final question we begin by noting that the issue of authority is necessarily preceded by that of relevance. This is entailed by Nietzsche's reflexive recognition of the historical specificity of his critique in both its negative and positive dimensions. If Nietzsche is to speak to us with authority, it can only be because *his* questions and concerns remain *our* questions and concerns. Nietzsche's authority, in this context, is not grounded in any claim to complete the history of reason nor is it appealing to a pre-constituted community, but rather it is grounded in a *seduction*, that is, in the community of judgement which his work brings into being. Nietzsche, in other words, is prepared to enter the philosophical *agon* and be ranked in terms of the nobility of his thought while reserving his disdain for those who attempt to stand above the contest. The dilemma which attends the legitimation of his thought is that its very ambivalence has produced two opposed styles of politics. The first relates to the extent to which his texts function successfully in constructing an 'epical' vision of politics, that is, in so far as they fuse theory and practice in a potentially world-transforming gesture.[35] In other words, Nietzsche's ground of legitimation (like that of Marx) would be dependent on the capacity of his critique to initiate a utopian politics. Noting those who have appropriated Nietzsche in this world-historical mode might lead us to conclude that Nietzsche's voice has little to offer. The second potential source of authority is markedly different; here Nietzsche's legacy lies in the degree to which his thought enables individuals to confront and overcome nihilism in their everyday lives, to mount 'local rebellions' against nihilism, and to achieve a measure of maturity. Merleau-Ponty remarks that both the politician and the artist aim to bring new publics into being; the tragic fate of Nietzsche's thought is to oscillate between the two.[36]

5

GENEALOGY AS CULTURAL SCIENCE

Weber, methodology and critique

Weber's 'methodological' question as to the value of science is basically the same question that Nietzsche posed in regard to *philosophy* when he inquired after the meaning and value of 'truth' – for 'what sense could *our* existence have, if not the sense that within us this urge toward truth has become conscious of itself *as a problem*?'

(Löwith 1982: 30)

by the road of reason, Weber reached a point which was not that different from that reached by another humanist, Nietzsche, who pursued the road of unreason. God, even Rickert's God, was dead now. History ceased to be a meaningful process and became the scene of insoluble value conflicts. Man, confronted by the ethical meaninglessness of the universe, found nothing left but the will to power.

(Iggers 1968: 173)

To place the scholarly figure of Max Weber in relation to Nietzsche, an author who scorned the constraints of academic discourse, may still seem a curious conjunction despite compelling contemporary arguments.[1] In elaborating Weber's scientific project as involving a political dimension, however, this relationship is central. Indeed, it will be argued that Weber's account of modernity is precisely structured about Nietzsche's question concerning the 'type of human being one ought to *breed*, ought to *will*, as more valuable, more worthy of life, more certain of the future' (AC 3 p. 116).[2] To facilitate this argument, however, requires both an examination of Weber's methodological reflections as embodying Nietzschean commitments and a delineation of the transformations wrought by Weber on Nietzsche's critical principles. The former of the tasks is particularly needful given the orthodox location of Weber as a marginal member of the neo-Kantian school of which Rickert stands as an exemplary exponent.[3] If we are to uncover the Nietzschean Weber to whom both Löwith and Iggers gesture, it would seem that a necessary starting point is the establishment of Weber's critique of Rickert's neo-Kantianism and an account of Weber's own methodology. Only then will we be in a position both to locate the critical principles of explanation and evaluation which inform Weber's cultural science and to specify the relation of these principles to those deployed by Nietzsche.

HISTORY, CULTURE, VALUES: THE CRITIQUE OF RICKERT

In *Science and History*, Rickert develops Windelband's distinction between the natural and cultural sciences in terms of their respective interests:

> only a concept which is likewise logical can constitute the opposite of the *logical* concept of nature as the existence of things as far as it is determined according to universal laws. But this, I believe, is the concept of *history* in the broadest formal sense of the word, i.e., the concept of the *nonrepeatable event* in its particularity and individuality, which stands in formal opposition to the concept of a universal law.
>
> (Rickert 1962: 15)

This distinction provides the starting point for Rickert's analysis of the possibility of objectivity in historical investigation. Rickert's claim is that what guides the selection of the data of history and thus ultimately determines the foundation of all historical concepts is *values*. In making this claim, however, Rickert is immediately confronted with the spectre of relativism: if 'subjective' values govern the selection of data, how can historical investigation be meaningfully said to be 'objective'? Rickert, however, is sensitive to this problem; he notes, for example, that a 'representation of events that makes reference to values is only valid for those who belong to the same culture' (Rickert 1962: 133). The implications of this are specified shortly afterwards:

> if the objectivity of a representation of events that makes reference to values is always confined to a more or less large circle of men with a common cultural background, it is an *historically limited objectivity*.
>
> (Rickert 1962: 136)

To address this problem, Rickert raises the question of universal values; before moving to this topic, however, it is useful to note that even at this stage Rickert is committed to the idea of cultural science as a 'value-free' activity.

The ground for this claim is located in a distinction between a *value-relation* and a *valuation*. The latter of these indicates a value-judgement, while the former implies only that a particular phenomenon is 'worth knowing'. For example, the socialist and the conservative make very different kinds of value-judgement in the political sphere, yet both hold that 'politics' as an area of human activity is worth knowing about. Both have, in other words, a value-relation to politics as a theoretical value (Aron 1970: 78). In so far, Rickert argues, as it is logically possible for a cultural scientific account to rest purely on theoretical values which are common to a particular community, then this account may be said to be 'value-free' in the sense of having 'empirical objectivity', that is, being valid for all members of the community whatever the differences they exhibit at the level of practical values. An integral component of this is that, if the account has validity across a community, the account cannot in itself be utilised to justify one particular valuation as opposed to another (Rickert 1986: 200).

This specification of the nature of the 'empirical objectivity' of the cultural sciences still leaves open, however, the problem of cultural relativism. For, as Rickert recognises, even if some theoretical values appear to be common across cultures, it could still be claimed that

> from a purely scientific point of view, the entire development of human history may be regarded as a completely indifferent and meaningless chaos of individual events, the representation of which must be far inferior in scientific importance to the search for general laws. In general, the relating of reality to values is always a matter of human caprice. The consensus of the many or the all makes no difference.
>
> (Rickert 1986: 205)

The implication of this claim, Rickert argues, is that 'if historical science claims that its problem is a scientific necessity, it must assume that in the domain of value as well, it is not *only* a question of the caprice of many or all persons' (Rickert 1986: 205). This assumption involves the meta-empirical claim that the possibility of a non-contingent objectivity implies that there must be 'some values that are *unconditionally* valid and that all human value positions stand in a more or less proximate *relation* to them that is defined as more than capricious' (Rickert 1986: 205). In other words:

> We must, in fact, assume, if not the existence of an already definite body of knowledge of what values are valid, then the validity of objective values and the possibility that we can approach knowledge of it ever more closely.
>
> (Rickert 1962: 139)

The objectivity of the cultural sciences, thus, is ultimately to be legitimated by the claim that there are certain objective values. On this point, Aron has noted that for Rickert 'there is at least one value which must be admitted by any science, namely truth. This is sufficient to justify theoretically the idea of a universal theory of values, and therefore the possibility of a universal history' (Aron 1970: 78).

It is manifestly apparent that Rickert's position is considerably divorced from that taken up by Nietzsche. In so far as Rickert remains necessarily committed at least to the objectivity of truth as a value, he simply manifests, from Nietzsche's perspective, the latest form of the ascetic ideal, that is, science as a means of self-narcosis (cf. GM III 23 p. 147). Rickert was himself aware of the distance between his position and that of Nietzsche; indeed he acknowledged the force of Nietzsche's position but argued against the costs of adopting a Nietzschean standpoint:

> This [Nietzsche's] point of view is, if one will, indeed consistent. But its consistency destroys the objectivity of *every* science, that of the natural sciences as well as of the cultural sciences. . . . The scientist is the very one who must assume the *absolute* validity of theoretical values if he does not wish to cease to be a scientist.
>
> (Rickert 1962: 144)[4]

Indeed, Nietzsche's perspectivism – and his attendant understanding of 'objectivity' 'not as "contemplation without interest" (which is a nonsensical absurdity), but as the ability *to control* one's Pro and Con and to dispose of them, so that one knows how to employ a *variety* of perspectives and affective interpretation in the service of knowledge' (GM III 12 p. 119) – must necessarily appear destructive of objectivity from the standpoint of Rickert's epistemology in so far as this epistemology entails a commitment to the dualist ontology (i.e. a realm of ruling values divorced from the realm of experience) which was precisely the target of Nietzsche's critique of Kant. The question which must be addressed at this stage concerns the location of Weber within this debate. Is it the case, as Löwith argues, that Weber's methodology draws on Nietzschean insights and specifically that 'Weber's methodological treatises spring ultimately from his awareness of this particular situation, that "after a thousand years of allegedly or supposedly exclusive orientation to the magnificent pathos of the Christian ethic, our eyes have become blinded to it" ' (Löwith 1982: 34)?

An initial entry into this discussion is provided by Rickert's acknowledgement that 'Weber was convinced that there was no way theoretical research could deal with the question of the validity of values' (Rickert 1989: 79). Indeed, Weber reminds the reader during his essay on ' "Objectivity" in Social Science and Social Policy' that even 'the belief in the value of scientific truth is the product of certain cultures and is not a product of man's original nature' (MSS p. 110). Such a comment appears to provide *prima facie* evidence for suggesting that Weber is concerned to distance himself from Rickert's meta-empirical claim concerning the unconditional validity of certain objective values. This view receives support from both Weber's justification of his engagement in methodological reflection and the account of the meaning of scientific activity which he offers in 'Science as a Vocation'; we shall consider these in turn.

That Weber should feel the need to provide a justification of his engagement in methodological analysis is itself indicative of a certain distance between himself and Rickert. This is not just because Weber did not consider himself a logician; rather it is a comment on the conditions under which methodological activity becomes justifiable.[5] Whereas Rickert's studies are self-legitimating in that they assume the necessity of epistemology to the clarification of the nature of *the* method of the cultural sciences, Weber stresses the *historicity* of scientific method:

> All research in the cultural sciences in an age of specialisation, once it is orientated towards a given subject matter through particular settings of problems and has established its methodological principles, will consider the analysis of data as an end in itself. It will discontinue assessing the value of the individual facts in terms of their relationships to ultimate value-ideas. Indeed, it will lose its awareness of its ultimate rootedness in value-ideas in general. And it is well this should be so. But there comes a moment when the atmosphere changes. The significance of the unreflectively utilized viewpoints becomes uncertain and the road is lost in twilight. The light of the great cultural problems moves on. Then science too prepares to change its standpoint and its analytical apparatus and to view the streams of events from the heights of thought.
>
> (MSS p. 112)

Methodological reflection is justified in so far as it is made necessary by the transformation of the cultural problems that science addresses. The central point here, for Weber, is the shift from one set of cultural problems to another as the defining problems of an age requires not simply a shift in the gaze of science but further a transformation of the 'analytical apparatus' of science.[6] Weber stresses this point again in his critique of Meyer:[7]

> Only by laying bare and solving *substantive problems* can sciences be established and their methods developed. On the other hand, purely epistemological and methodological reflections have never played the crucial role in such developments. Such discussions can become important for the enterprise of science only when, as a result of considerable shift of the 'viewpoint' from which a datum becomes the object of analysis, the idea emerges that the new 'viewpoint' also requires a revision of the logical forms in which the 'enterprise' has hitherto operated, and when, accordingly, uncertainty about the 'nature' of one's own work arises. This situation is unambiguously the case at present as regards history. . . .
>
> (MSS p. 116)

Weber's claim, contra Rickert, is that cultural science as a *reflection on culture* operates in terms of thorough-going reflexivity in relation to itself as a *product of culture*.[8] It may be recalled at this stage that Nietzsche's critique of Kant operates on similar grounds and, indeed, Nietzsche's philosophical interrogation of modernity is explicit in its acknowledgement of its own historico-cultural specificity. This parallel is not enough in itself, however, to ascribe a Nietzschean position to Weber; to take this step requires a focus on the implications of the transformation of the cultural problems of the age for scientific activity. This theme is taken up in Weber's essay on 'Science as a Vocation'.

Weber's topic in this essay is that of the meaning of scientific activity in modernity; as part of this discussion, he focuses on the history of science's understanding of its own activity and it is this which is our immediate concern. Weber's suggestion is that science, in various historical periods, has understood itself as 'the "way to true being," the "way to true art," the "way to true nature," the "way to true God," the "way to true happiness" ' (SV p. 143). Scientific knowledge is granted under each of these understandings a certain (instrumental) value which provides the meaning of science as a vocation. As Nietzsche put it in his essay on ascetic ideals: '[science] requires in every respect an ideal of value, a value-creating power, in the *service* of which it could *believe* in itself' (GM III 25 p. 153). Weber's question concerns the meaning of scientific activity 'now after all the former illusions . . . have been dispelled' (SV p. 143); his response is that science is meaningless because, as Nietzsche argued, 'it never creates values' (GM III 25 p. 153), that is, it cannot itself provide us an answer to the Tolstoyan question of how we should live. Indeed, science cannot even ground its own value:

> Science . . . presupposes that what is yielded by scientific work is important in the sense that it is 'worth being known'. In this obviously are contained all our problems. For this presupposition cannot be proved by scientific means.
>
> (SV p. 143)

Weber, as this passage makes clear, recognises with Nietzsche that 'there is no such thing as science "without any presuppositions" ' (GM III 24 p. 151). The implication of this is that Weber accepts Nietzsche's diagnosis of modern culture as one in which the value of truth is called into question and therefore one in which science requires justification.[9] In the light of Weber's remarks on the historicity of scientific method, it seems reasonable to suggest that Weber's methodological essays are concerned precisely with developing a method for investigating culture which is not itself dependent on the ascetic assumption of the objective value of truth which is exemplified by Rickert. To ground this Nietzschean reading of Weber's methodological reflections consequently requires that we turn to the philosophical character of the methodology that results from these reflections.

'VALUE-FREEDOM', INTELLECTUAL INTEGRITY AND IDEAL-TYPES

Science can neither create values nor ground the presupposition of its own value: these two dimensions of the fate of modern science are integral to Weber's methodological considerations. Yet, as Weber's contemporaries recognised, this tragic vision of knowledge in modernity places the question of politics at the heart of Weber's philosophical reflections.[10] Landshut, for example, locates Weber within an intellectual tradition whose central concern is with the 'progressive destruction of any generally binding force in the public sphere' (Landshut 1989: 101), an interest which similarly animated Nietzsche's confrontation with the question of nihilism. In addressing the philosophical character of Weber's methodology as grounded in a fundamentally Nietzschean vision of the modern world, this question of politics assumes an ongoing significance.

A route into this topic is provided by Weber's stress on the centrality of the postulate of 'value-freedom' to modern cultural science and his call for intellectual integrity (*intellektuelle Redlichkeit*) on the part of the scholar. It is in situating these dimensions of Weber's methodology in the context of his account of the fate of modern science that the outlines of Weber's Nietzschean fusion of political and epistemic themes emerges.[11] Certainly such an account provides the context within which Weber's conception of cultural science may be examined.

In highlighting the inability of science to tell us how we should live, Weber may be read as making the philosophical claim that an explanation of the world in terms of causality necessarily excludes from itself the categories of meaning and value. It would be a serious error, however, simply to locate Weber at this neo-Kantian level; for Weber's point is essentially Nietzsche's that in 'the same measure as the sense for causality increases, the domain of morality decreases' (D 9 p. 10). This historical development, moreover, has a tragic quality in its signalling of the disenchantment of the world, that is, the recognition that in the face of science 'the ultimate and sublime values have retreated from public life' (SV p. 155).[12] It is this political vision which underlies Weber's demand for 'value-freedom'; thus Löwith argues that Weber is impelled to this position because of his insight into the fact that

> *we here today* live in a world that has become reified through scientific technology while, at the same time, the objectivist rationality of science has liberated us from an adherence to universally binding moral and religious norms. Since the progress of science is unstoppable, it must be seen as a force which destroys the authority of tradition. The value-judgements we ultimately make can therefore neither find support in tradition, nor claim scientific foundation; they are, whether we like it or not, a matter of personal decision.
>
> (Löwith 1989: 145)

Similarly, Landshut notes that whereas classical social theories 'start from the presupposition that the principle of binding force itself, the criterion of legality, can be discovered and derived from man's existence in the world', the radical dismantling of all received public values at the end of the nineteenth century makes such a presupposition, for Weber, an intellectual absurdity (Landshut 1989: 102). The postulate of 'value-freedom' emerges from this recognition of the tragic fate of modern science.

It is in this relation that Weber's call for probity on the part of the scholar assumes its initial significance, his point here being simply that, in so far as science cannot legislate values, the scholar as scientist must surrender the right to propagate any political position. Thus Weber writes in 'Science as a Vocation':

> Now one cannot demonstrate scientifically what the duty of an academic teacher is. One can only demand of the teacher that he have the intellectual integrity to see that it is one thing to state facts, to determine mathematical or logical relations or the internal structure of cultural values, while it is another thing to answer questions of the *value* of culture and its individual contents and the question of how one should act in the cultural community and in political associations. These are quite heterogeneous problems.
>
> (SV p. 146)[13]

Were this the only ground for Weber's call for intellectual integrity, however, this aspect of his methodology would be simply subsumable under the doctrine of 'value-freedom'; there is though a more significant ground for this demand which emerges in relation to science's inability to ground the presupposition of its own value. For Rickert, as we have noted, the possibility of scientific activity requires the positing of the objective value of truth; only this can avoid what he sees as the Nietzschean undermining of science as such. The dilemma this poses for Weber is that while he agrees with Rickert that scientific activity immanently involves the presupposition that what it generates is worth knowing, he also accepts Nietzsche's point that the value of truth cannot be scientifically grounded. Weber's resolution of this dilemma is to root the possibility of scientific activity in the 'personality' of the scientist, that is to say, in the integrity of the scientist's 'irrational' commitment to truth as the ultimate value. In other words, Weber argues that the modern scholar is he who recognises that the value of truth cannot be rationally grounded and yet chooses to legislate this value for himself and to affirm its value as a matter of faith.[14] Weber's emphasis on the probity of the scholar is an instance of his more general claim that 'personality' is constituted through 'a constant and intrinsic relation to certain ultimate "values" and "meanings" of life' (RK p. 192); the significant point here, however, is that in adopting this position Weber is able to ground the possibility of scientific activity as meaningful activity in a Nietzschean age.

To the extent that Weber's postulate of 'value-freedom' and his call for intellectual integrity emerge on the basis of a recognition of the disenchanted character of the modern age, it seems reasonable to conclude that his methodology exemplifies a Nietzschean reflexivity at least with respect to the conditions of meaningful scientific activity. In particular, it appears that Weber's reflections are similarly animated by a political concern with the withdrawal of the highest values from the public sphere and a philosophical concern with the inability of knowledge to ground its own value. In this context, it may be useful to finish this section by raising the question of the philosophical character of the ideal-type as the device for investigating culture that emerges from Weber's methodological reflections.[15]

We can begin by noting Weber's argument that 'cultural science in our sense involves "subjective" presuppositions in so far as it concerns itself only with those components of reality which have some relationship, however indirect, to events to which we attach cultural *significance*' (MSS p. 82). Here Weber appears to be adopting Rickert's position concerning the selection of the data of history and the formation of historical concepts as guided by values. Yet, as we have already noted, Weber rejects the idea of objective values on which Rickert grounds the objectivity of scientific accounts; the question which arises from this concerns the 'objectivity' of Weber's cultural science. Let us recall that for Weber the specificity of modernity lies in the withdrawal of ultimate values from the public sphere. The implication of this is that the selection of the subject matter of cultural science cannot be guided by 'inter-subjective' values, let alone 'objective' values, but rather is dependent on the particular evaluative ideas of specific researchers concerning both the determination of cultural significance and the ranking of phenomena in terms of their cultural significance. It is on this basis that Weber argues that all cultural knowledge 'is always knowledge *from particular points of view*' (MSS p. 81). In indicating the interested character of knowledge, Weber is echoing Nietzsche's claim that 'objectivity' depends on neither disinterestedness nor objective universal interests but consists rather 'in the ability *to control* one's Pro and Con and to dispose of them, so that one knows how to employ a *variety* of perspectives and effective interpretations in the service of knowledge' (GM III 12 p. 119). Weber's emphasis on the perspectival character of knowledge attends this notion of 'objectivity' as Nietzsche made clear with respect to himself:

> There is *only* a perspective seeing, *only* a perspective 'knowing'; and the *more* affects we will allow to speak about one thing, the more complete will our 'concept' of this thing, our 'objectivity, ' be.
>
> (GM III 12 p. 119)

It is in this context that Weber's notion of an ideal-type assumes its significance in that it is in the construction of ideal-types that Weber locates the concrete manifestation of the evaluative ideas of the researcher. This emerges clearly in Weber's description of the characteristics of an ideal-typical construct:

> Substantively, this construct is in itself like a *utopia* which has been arrived at through the analytical accentuation of certain elements of reality. . . . It is not a *description* of reality but aims to give unambiguous means of expression to such a description. . . . An ideal-type is formed by the one-sided *accentuation* of one or more points of view and by the synthesis of a great many diffuse, discrete, more or less present and occasionally absent *concrete individual* phenomena, which are arranged according to those one-sidedly emphasised viewpoints into a unified *analytical* construct. In its conceptual purity, this mental construct cannot be found anywhere in reality. It is a *utopia*.
>
> (MSS p. 90)

The one-sided accentuation embodied in an ideal-typical construct is determined by the value-perspective of the researcher, that is, the aspect of the phenomena that the investigator sees as culturally significant – worth knowing about. The consequences of this account of knowledge are twofold: firstly, Weber is able to 'emphasise to a greater extent the important and positive role of the personality of the scholar' (Bruun 1972: 138) and secondly, the realm of knowledge is constituted as *agonistic* in that the construction of ideal-typical accounts always already involves conflict with other such accounts embodying distinct value-perspectives. The struggle of worldviews which Weber locates as a consequence of the withdrawal of the ultimate values from the public sphere thus extends into the nature of scientific method itself. As Löwith notes:

> The ideal-typical 'construct' is based upon a human being who is specifically 'free of illusions', thrown back upon itself by a world that has become objectively meaningless and sober and to this extent emphatically 'realistic'.
>
> (Löwith 1982: 38)

It is the objective meaninglessness of the world which leads Weber to reject as Nietzsche does 'the *confusion* of theory and history stemming from naturalistic prejudices' (MSS p. 94) and to embrace perspectivism through the idea of ideal-types. For, as Löwith acutely indicates, the basic philosophical character of the ideal-type 'lies in the fact that it lays open reality while at the same time constructing it' (Löwith 1982: 62 fn.36) and this constructivist and nominalist account of knowledge is nothing but the product of Weber's philosophical recognition of the death of God.

The concern of this section has been to illustrate both the features of Weber's methodology and their Nietzschean character. It has been shown that, for Weber, the postulates of value-freedom and intellectual integrity are the political and philosophical conditions of scientific activity in a culture characterised by the withdrawal of the highest values from the public sphere and the inability of science to ground its own value. This vision of modern culture similarly informs Weber's account of knowledge and the idea of the ideal-type. Having thus established the Nietzschean character of Weber's project at the levels of philosophy and methodology, we are in a position to take up the question of the character of Weber's cultural science through a specification of his critical principles of explanation and evaluation.

EXPLANATION AND CULTURAL SCIENCE

Weber's conception of cultural science finds its starting point in the argument that culture 'is a finite segment of the meaningless infinity of the world process, a segment on which *human beings* confer meaning and significance' (MSS p. 81). Culture, for Weber, is constituted through the specifically human activity of creating value-perspectives. The implication of this notion of culture for the idea of a cultural science is as follows:

> The transcendental presupposition of every *cultural science* lies not in our finding a certain culture or any 'culture' in general to be *valuable* but rather in the fact that we are *cultural beings*, endowed with the capacity and will to take a deliberative attitude towards the world and lend it *significance*. Whatever this significance may be, it will lead us to judge certain phenomena of human existence in its light and to respond to them as being (positively or negatively) meaningful. Whatever may be the content of this attitude – these phenomena have cultural significance for us and on this significance alone rests its scientific interest.

> (MSS p. 81)

The concern of modern cultural science is, thus, the historical determination of *how we have become what are*, namely, beings for whom certain aspects of social reality (and not others) have cultural significance. The site of explanation in Weber's work is similarly derived from this presupposition in that accounting for cultural change entails a principle which articulates the relationship between the value-perspectives which are constitutive of culture and the conditions of social life.[16] To specify this further, what is required by Weber's cultural science is a principle of explanation through which he can examine conditions governing the dynamics of creating and transforming the value-perspectives through which we constitute ourselves as selves, that is, as particular types of cultural being (such as, for example, cultural beings for whom the will to truth is conscious of itself as a problem).

This principle is stated formally in Weber's 'switchmen' metaphor in which he elaborates a conception of the relationship between ideas (i.e. value-perspectives) and social interests:

> Not ideas, but material and ideal interests, directly govern men's conduct. Yet very frequently the 'world images' that have been created by 'ideas' have, like switchmen, determined the tracks along which action has been pushed by the dynamic of interest.
>
> (SPWR p. 280)[17]

The direction of this passage is towards a notion of the 'world image' as the context which governs the form in which ideal and material interests are expressed. Indeed, the switchmen metaphor occurs in the context of an example which makes precisely this point:

> The conception of the idea of redemption, as such, is very old, if one understands by it a liberation from distress, hunger, drought, sickness, and ultimately from suffering and death. Yet redemption attained a specific significance only where it expressed a systematic and rationalised 'image of the world' and represented a stand in the face of the world. For the meaning as well as the intended and actual psychological quality of redemption has depended on such a world image and such a stand. . . . 'From what' and 'for what' one wished to be redeemed and, let us not forget, 'could be' redeemed, depended on one's image of the world.
>
> (SPWR p. 280)

In other words, the value-perspective expresses itself in the form of a 'world image' which is constitutive of the ground of social life – it constructs the *structures of recognition* through which our cultural identities are articulated and thus the form in which our material and ideal interests manifest themselves. In adopting this principle of explanation, Weber is taking up a recognisably Nietzschean position; after all, it is precisely Nietzsche's argument that the will to power expresses itself through an evaluative interpretation of the world which governs the character of the goal-directed agency exhibited by members of the culture in question. This interpretation of Weber's switchmen metaphor can be further grounded by examining his mode of accounting for cultural change.[18]

What is required here is a capacity to account for, firstly, the creation and entrenchment of the value-perspective constitutive of a culture, secondly, the conditions governing the potential for change within a culture, and thirdly, the actual development of change within a culture. For Nietzsche, each of these aspects is subsumed under the principle of will to power; Weber, however, seeks to specify the particularity of each of these analytically distinct moments. The three dimensions of Weber's analytical apparatus corresponding to these explanatory requirements can be identified as, firstly, the dynamic of charisma and routinisation, secondly, the differentiation between the spheres of life, and thirdly, the inner logic of worldviews. Each of these aspects can be briefly illuminated.

The dynamic of charisma and routinisation represents Weber's attempt to account for the emergence and entrenchment of a value-perspective. The concept of charisma attends to the emergence of a value-perspective in terms of its capacity to confront and displace the prevailing ground of cultural life through a reconstruction of the criteria of authority operant within social life. The idea of routinisation signals the entrenchment of a value-perspective within social life. The central features here are expressed in two related dimensions of routinisation: firstly, the systematic elaboration and interpretation of the worldview through which a value-perspective manifests itself on the part of those endowed with authority 'so that it constitutes a coherent whole and its tenets are extended to apply to various aspects of social life' (Schroeder 1992: 10); secondly, the grounding of this authority through an accommodation of the worldview to the interests of, initially, those strata who are predisposed to this type of value-perspective and, latterly, the strata of believers.[19] Together these features, on Weber's argument, account for the entrenchment of a value-perspective as the ground of culture, that is, the entrenchment of a worldview within social life.

While the dynamic of charisma and routinisation accounts for the emergence and entrenchment of a value-perspective within social life, Weber attempts to account for the conditions governing the potential for change within a culture in terms of the differentiation of life-spheres. By 'life-spheres' Weber is referring to analytically distinct modes of human activity which each involve their own criteria concerning meaningful social action. He identifies six such modes: the economic, political, religious, intellectual, aesthetic and erotic spheres. Weber's idea here is that the potential for cultural change – by which he is referring to the degree of ease with which a value-perspective may be subject to either re-interpretation or delegitimation – is dependent on the degree of reinforcement or conflict between particular spheres of life. This notion is predicated on the claim that 'each sphere of life makes certain demands on the individual's practical and ethical conduct which may reinforce or conflict with the demands of another sphere' (Schroeder 1992: 23). Why though should the relationship between the demands of the different life-spheres act to resist or promote social change? To account for this presupposes that underlying Weber's idea of the individual as a social agent is the idea of will to power, that is, individuals' need to experience themselves as goal-directed agents, possessing a unified 'will'. The dilemma posed to individuals confronted by the demands of conflicting life-spheres is that this differentiation threatens their experience of themselves as a coherent self, whereas the mutual reinforcement of life-spheres sustains their sense of an integrated identity. The implication of this is that to the degree to which life-spheres reinforce each other so too to that degree is the need for cultural change obviated; while, in contrast, to the degree to which life-spheres conflict to that degree also is cultural change promoted in that a re-interpretation (or ultimately replacement) of the value-perspective is required which re-integrates the identity of the individual, that is, his experience of himself as a goal-directed agent. With the idea of the differentiation of life-spheres, Weber can consequently account for the potential for change in a culture – what though of the actual direction and development of cultural change?

This final dimension of Weber's analytical apparatus is intimately related with the question of the differentiation of life-spheres in that the direction of cultural change is dependent on the particular life-spheres that come into conflict at a given time. What then governs the specificity of these sites of conflict? Weber gestures here towards a notion of the 'inner logic' of a worldview by which he means the relationship between a value-perspective and the worldly conditions informing its capacity to articulate goal-directed agency. A value-perspective, as we have noted, manifests itself as an attempt to provide a complete and coherent explanation of the place of the individual within the world. In so far as it is successful, this value-perspective facilitates the individual's experience of himself as a goal-directed agent. However, as we also noted in relation to Nietzsche, the very success of a value-perspective in constituting itself as the ground of culture and promoting a particular form of goal-directed agency transforms the conditions of social life which may in turn require a re-interpretation of the value-perspective if it is to retain its explanatory power. The central point here is that the entrenchment of a value-perspective through an interpretation that is also an accommodation to interests of particular strata may as an unintended consequence, precisely because of this interested character, create conflict between particular life-spheres, the specificity of the conflict being dependent on the *content* of the worldview through which the value-perspective manifests itself. The resolution of this conflict through re-interpretation may then in turn create further unintended consequences requiring further re-inter-pretation, etc. The implication of this, for Weber, is that one can analyse the process and direction of cultural development by attending to the transformations wrought on the value-perspective, that is, the foundation of cultural life.[20]

In so far as the explanatory purpose of cultural science is to account for how we have become what we are, Weber's threefold scheme of analysis (with all its Nietzschean overtones) is central to his project. The legitimation of this apparatus, however, does require a substantive analysis of cultural development; this is particularly the case given the reflexivity exhibited by Weber's cultural science. At this stage, however, we can note that the explanatory purpose of cultural science immanently involves another purpose, that is to say that to ask how we have become what we are is also to ask what possibilities for cultural development are open to us as we are. Weber's explanation of the genealogy of modern culture cannot but also address the implications of modern culture for our future becoming. It is here that the question of evaluation arises.

CULTURAL SCIENCE AS CRITIQUE

It may seem paradoxical to pose the question of evaluation for Weber's cultural science; after all, Weber explicitly rejects the idea that such a science could tell an individual what he should do in making 'value-freedom' a condition of scientific activity. Consequently, before we can address the issue of the principle of evaluation Weber deploys, it is necessary to demonstrate that Weber's cultural science involves an implicit politics. A starting point for this discussion is provided by the following remarks from Weber's inaugural address at Freiburg:

> The question which leads us beyond the grave of our own generation is not 'how will human beings feel in the future', but 'how will they be'. . . . We do not want to train up feelings of well-being in people, but those characteristics we think constitute the greatness and nobility of our human nature.
>
> (NSEP p. 437, cited in Hennis 1988: 53)

Our question can thus be expressed as this: how can we reconcile this evaluative statement with the idea of a 'value-free' cultural science? To address this issue requires that we engage with the question of the presuppositions of scientific activity in modernity.

It was argued earlier that two fundamental presuppositions are involved in the activity of science in a disenchanted age, namely, intellectual integrity and 'value-freedom'. In choosing science as a vocation, Weber argues, the scholar is immanently committed both to the value of truth and the refusal of politics. These obligations, in other words, are intrinsic to modern science as a distinct life-sphere and the 'personality' of the scholar exhibits itself by steadfast adherence to these duties. What though does Weber mean by this idea of 'personality'? Consider the following definition:

> 'personality,' a concept which entails a constant and intrinsic relation to certain ultimate 'values' and 'meanings' of life, 'values' and 'meanings' which are forged into purposes and thereby translated into rational-teleological action.
>
> (RK p. 192)[21]

Weber's argument in this passage is that 'personality' consists of goal-directed agency. The significance of this emerges when we note that modernity, for Weber, is characterised by the differentiation of the life-spheres (most notably those of science and politics) such that these distinct modes of human activity involve value-commitments which are irreconcilable, that is, the conditions of meaningful (i.e. goal-directed) action within the different life-spheres are incommensurable with each other. Weber spells out the implications of this quite clearly in 'Science as a Vocation': 'the ultimately possible attitudes toward life are irreconcilable, and hence their struggle can never be brought to conclusion. Thus it is necessary to make a decisive choice' (SV p. 152). What Weber appears to be claiming here is that 'personality' in modernity consists of goal-directed agency where the goal is determined by the individual's calling. This, however, is nothing but the conception of autonomy which Nietzsche constructs through the idea of will to power. To return to our starting point then, it seems as if the fundamental presupposition underlying the possibility of scientific activity is the possibility of individual autonomy. Indeed, as one commentator has noted in relation to Weber's substantive studies, it appears that Weber's very concept of the individual 'presupposes a certain conception of the self to which the attributes of autonomy and self-expression are somehow essential' (Schroeder 1991: 62).

It is at this stage that Weber's implicit politics become apparent; for while his project does not attempt to posit a universal moral principle capable of reconstituting the binding character of the public sphere, it is nonetheless concerned with a project of evaluation. The suggestion to be developed here is that Weber's project may be outlined as an interrogation of modern culture in terms of its capacity for 'breeding' autonomous individuals and that concomitant with this evaluation is a political activity which is manifest through the specification of the conditions of autonomy in the different life-spheres. Evidence for the first of these moments is provided by the following comment:

> Without exception every order of social relations (however constituted) is, if one wishes to *evaluate* it, ultimately to be examined in terms of the human type (*menschlichen Typus*) to which it, by way of external or internal (motivational) selection, provides the optimal chances of becoming the dominant type. For without it empirical research is neither really exhaustive, nor is there the necessary real foundation for such an evaluation, be it consciously subjective, or an evaluation claiming objective validity.
>
> (GAW p. 517, cited in Hennis 1988: 59)

Given that Weber's science presupposes the possibility of individual autonomy, this passage suggests that the evaluation of modern culture must be in terms of the chances it provides for autonomous individuals to become the dominant human type. The political correlate of this evaluative project for science, that is, its specification of the conditions of autonomy, is addressed in 'Science as a Vocation':

> [I]f we are competent in our pursuit (which must be presupposed here) we can force the individual, or at least we can help him, to give himself an *account of the ultimate meaning of his own conduct*. This appears to me as not so trifling a thing to do, even for one's own personal life. Again, I am tempted to say of a teacher who succeeds in this: he stands in the service of 'moral' forces; he fulfills the duty of bringing about self- clarification and a sense of responsibility.
>
> (SV p. 152)

As this passage makes clear, the scholar is engaged in a form of political activity in specifying for individuals who are committed to a given life-sphere (or, implicitly, those who are engaged in making this decision) what the consequences of this commitment are with respect to the conditions of meaningful action, the political character of this scientific activity lying precisely in the fostering of self-responsibility.[22] Again the echoes of Nietzsche's similar concern with autonomy as self-responsibility resonate through Weber's work. Indeed, it seems difficult not to agree with Scaff that 'the entire meaning of Weber's melancholy meditations on the "modern soul" presupposes the paths in thought traversed by Nietzsche' (Scaff 1989: 133).

We can conclude by noting that this project of evaluation does, of course, require a genealogy of modern culture, that is to say that it is only by addressing how we have become what we are that Weber can evaluate modern culture in relation to its capacity for 'breeding' autonomous individuals. This task, however, is *the* task of cultural science; it is the task that 'leads us beyond the grave of our own generation' and in addressing our historical fate takes up 'those characteristics we think constitute the greatness and nobility of our human nature' (NSPE p. 437, cited in Hennis 1988: 53).

6

THE GENEALOGY OF MODERNITY
Weber, asceticism and disenchantment

For Weber, cultural science is concerned with how we have become what we are, that is to say, with articulating a history of the present. It will be recalled, however, that to engage in this activity requires an 'evaluative' interest which constitutes the perspective from which the cultural significance of phenomena are determined and ranked. To address Weber's substantive writings requires that we identify the 'central question' which animates his investigations.[1] This interest has already – at least implicitly – emerged through our discussion of Weber's methodological writings, being nothing other than his concern with, firstly, modern culture as one in which the highest values have withdrawn from the public sphere and the will to truth has become conscious of itself as a problem, and secondly, the capacity of this culture to facilitate the emergence of autonomous individuals. Expressed conventionally, Weber's central question is, thus, with the character of Western rationalism and the potential consequences of this form of rationalism for the development of *Menschentum*. In other words, the purpose of Weber's accounts is the same as Nietzsche's, namely, to provide a 'context of meaning' within which the development of *Menschentum* may be understood and evaluated in terms of the fate of man in modernity.[2]

In contrast to Nietzsche, though, Weber develops this interest in two complementary directions: firstly, through a reconstruction of the development of Western rationalism, and secondly, through differential comparison of this development with that characteristic of other cultures. Despite Weber's broadening of the approach to this topic, however, our concern will be exclusively with the former, that is, his genealogy of Western rationalism.[3] In approaching this topic, we can begin by noting that Weber, in common with Nietzsche, constructs this genealogy in terms of two major transitions in culture. In Weber's sociology of religion, the first transition is from a prehistorical stage characterised by localised beliefs to the realm of history and the development of universalist religions, while the second is from universal religion to modern secular culture. This examination can proceed by focusing on ancient Judaism and Protestantism in that it is these two religious worldviews that Weber locates in relation to the two transitions in Western culture. We can begin with the initial transition focusing on Weber's study of ancient Judaism.

FROM PRIMITIVE TO UNIVERSAL RELIGION: ANCIENT JUDAISM

For Weber, the analysis of ancient Judaism may be approached by distinguishing between four stages of development: firstly, the period of the political confederacy; secondly, the period of the kingdom; thirdly, the pre-exilic period; and finally, the post-exilic period.[4] In terms of the movement from primitive to universal religion, it is the first three periods which are directly relevant. With respect to the question of the development of rationalism, however, the post-exilic period also assumes significance. In tracing the development of ancient Judaism, therefore, we can begin by outlining the characteristics of this religion in its primitive stage, that is, at the period of the confederacy.

The emergence of the figure of Yahweh as the Jewish God is tied by Weber to the development of a political association, the confederation of the tribes of Israel (SR p. 16). It should be noted here that this relationship between a god and a political association is characteristic of the development of primitive religion in general and, moreover, is indicative of the *this-worldly* orientation of religious action in its initial form (SR pp. 1–19). The specificity of Judaism lies rather in the form of the relationship between Yahweh and the Israelites:

> His relationship to the people of Israel, who had accepted him under oath, together with the political confederation and the sacred order of their social relationships, took the form of a covenant (*berith*), a contractual relationship imposed by Yahweh and accepted submissively by Israel. . . . This is the primary root of what is most distinctive in the Israelite religion: the trait of mutual promise which despite various analogues is found nowhere else in such intensity.
>
> (SR p. 16)

In the period of the confederacy, as Schroeder has noted, 'the strength of the covenant was assured only because it coincided with the political needs of the Israelites' (Schroeder 1992: 77). In other words, Judaism served to provide a common cultural identity to the different tribes within the confederation, yet the strength of this identity and the authority of Yahweh and his representatives was dependent on their success in preserving the security of the confederation against external threat.[5] As such 'political and military leaders were not always clearly distinguished from magicians and prophets' (AJ p. 224) in so far as the sign of charismatic authority, that is, of direct communication with Yahweh, was ultimately a question of political or military success. To examine the movement from this period of Judaism (in which Yahweh is seen a warrior-god and in which culture is characterised by the 'unity' of religion and politics) to the pre-exilic period (in which Yahweh takes on a universal character) requires that we focus on the conflict that arises in the development of the Judaic worldview between privileged and dis-privileged classes, and the role of prophets and priests in resolving this conflict in the context of the internal and external position of Israel, during the period of the kingdom.[6]

We can begin by noting that the role religion plays in Weber's account is akin to that played by morality in Nietzsche's genealogy, namely, to provide an explanation of the relationship between individuals and the world as a 'meaningful' ordered totality. The conflicting interpretations of Judaism which arise are between the this-worldly interpretation which characterises the period of the confederacy and an other-worldly interpretation in which the meaning of the covenant is transformed, these interpretations mediating the interests of the privileged and disprivileged classes respectively. This emerges initially in a point Weber makes about religion in general:

> Their [the nobles'] sense of self-esteem is an expression of their underived, ultimate, and qualitatively distinctive *being*; indeed, it is in the very nature of the case that this should be the basis of the elite's feeling of worth. On the other hand, the sense of honor of disprivileged classes rests on some concealed promise for the future which implies the assignment of some function, mission, or vocation to them. What they cannot claim to *be*, they replace by the worth of what they will one day *become*, ... Their hunger for a worthiness that has not fallen to their lot, they and the world being what it is, provides this conception from which is derived the rationalistic idea of a provi-dence, a significance in the eyes of some divine authority possessing a scale of values different from the one operating in the world of man.
>
> (SR p. 106)[7]

What Weber has set up here clearly corresponds to Nietzsche's distinction between master and slave moralities. In the case of the nobles, they 'assign to religion the primary function of legitimizing their own life pattern and situation in the world' (SR p. 107). By contrast, the disprivileged's 'particular need is for release from suffering' (SR p. 108). The specificity of Judaism, for Weber, is that it is the only major religion in which 'the religion of suffering acquires the specific character of *ressentiment* (in Nietzsche's use of this term): the Jew expected of the participation of his descendants in a messianic kingdom which would redeem the entire pariah community from its inferior position and in fact raise it to a position of mastery in the world' (SR p. 110):

In this theodicy of the disprivileged, the moralistic quest serves as a device for compensating a conscious or unconscious desire for vengeance. This is connected in its origin with the faith in compensation, since once a religious conception of compensation has arisen, suffering may take on the quality of the religiously meritorious, in view of the belief that it brings in its wake great hopes of future compensation.

(SR pp. 110–11)

What Weber is describing here is the transformation of the figure of Yahweh from the warrior-god of the confederacy and the local god of Jerusalem into a god 'who took on the prophetic and universalistic traits of a transcendently sacred omnipotence and inscrutability' (SR p. 24). In this context, the meaning of the covenant is transformed from that of a political agreement into that of an ethical relationship which entailed 'relating the people's life as a whole and the life of each individual to the fulfillment of Yahweh's positive commandments' (AJ p. 255, cited in Schroeder 1992: 78). The question which arises for us is how this transformation comes about.

The initial point to note is that the movement from the period of the confederacy to that of the kingdom is characterised by the localisation of Yahweh as the god of the city of Jerusalem which attends the growth of an urban population. Indeed, the emergence of the theodicy of misfortune is tied by Weber to the movement from a militarised peasantry to demilitarised plebeian strata: 'Here and only here plebeian strata became exponents of a rational religious ethic' (AJ p. 224). The development of this theodicy, however, must be addressed in terms of the role of the priests and prophets in the context of the internal and external situation of the kingdom. Firstly, the internal situation was characterised by 'social upheaval, political crises and competition amongst cults' and 'the establishment of a mostly disliked kingly court' (Schroeder 1992: 79). In this context, the prophets were able to develop 'a theodicy of misfortune in which obedience to Yahweh's commands was the only way to secure a better future' (Schroeder 1992: 79), this theodicy being grounded in a retrospective idealisation of the period of the confederacy. This prophetic development was supported by the rationalism of the priests and their interest in securing their authority over the masses. Secondly, the external situation was characterised by political and military threats which required explanation. As Weber points out:

In this case, universalism was a product of international politics, of which the pragmatic interpreters were the prophetic protagonists of the cult of Yahweh and the ethics enjoined by him. As a consequence of their preaching, the deeds of the other nations that were profoundly affecting Israel's vital interests also came to be regarded as wrought by Yahweh. At this point one sees clearly the distinctively and eminently *historical* character of the Hebrew prophets, ... Equally striking is the ineluctable obligation resulting from Yahweh's promises: the necessity of interpreting the entire history of the Hebrew nation as consisting of the deeds of Yahweh, and hence as constituting a pattern of world history.

(SR pp. 23–3)

The emergence of the theodicy of misfortune in the pre-exilic period can thus be seen as a combination of factors: the emergence of a plebeian mass predisposed to such an interpretation and the interest of the priesthood in preserving their authority over the masses, and the grounding of the charismatic authority of the prophets in the development of an interpretation capable of explaining the internal and external events affecting Israel.[8] The issue which now arises concerns the implications of this development for Western rationalism.

We can begin by noting that the emergence of Yahweh as a universal god is constitutive of the idea of world history as an ordered meaningful totality. Since Yahweh's actions are themselves bound by his covenant with the Jewish people, the systematic elaboration and rationalisation of the ethical relationship involved here provides a grid of intelligibility in terms of which history can be interpreted and institutes a will to truth in the form of a desire to uncover the meaning of historical events (SR p. 112); the intellectual-religious sphere is thus constituted about the activity of historico-theological dialectics. In its practical form, that is, in the spheres of politics and economics, this rationalism manifests itself in terms of the responsibility of the collectivity:

The virtues enjoined by God are practiced for the sake of the hoped for compensation. Moreover, this was originally a collective hope that the people as a whole would live to see the day of restoration, and that only in this way would the individual be able to regain his own worth.

(SR p. 112)

It is 'the unshakeable strength of the doctrine of collective compensation in the Jewish religion' which prevents the development of a theodicy oriented specifically to the individual in the form of the doctrine of predestination, despite the prefiguring of this doctrine in the Book of Job (SR p. 112). In this context, Weber argues that 'for the Jew the theodicy had the consequence of transforming religious criticism of the godless heathen into everwatchful concern over their own fidelity to the law' (SR p. 114). To explain why rationalism developed in this external legalistic direction rather than in an orientation towards inner-worldly asceticism requires that we take up the development of the Judaic worldview in the period of exile and post-exile.

The pre-exilic period in which Judaism takes on the characteristics of a universalistic religion was marked by the coincidence of interests between prophets and priests. The prophets' charismatic authority was grounded in the success of their re-interpretation of the covenant for explaining Israel's internal and external situation, while this re-interpretation similarly secured the interests of the priests in preserving their traditional authority over the plebeian masses. The routinisation of this new interpretation, its entrenchment within social life, during the period of exile and post-exile, however, sees the divergence of these interests; for whereas the prophets demanded a regime of inward reflection, the priests developed a regime of ritual obedience to the law. This divergence begins in the period of exile: 'It was a period in which the lack of external threats and the absence of propaganda against an unholy and unjust administration . . . resulted in an ethic that was more suited to everyday observance' (Schroeder 1992: 80). The consequence of this situation of relative peacefulness was the displacement of the rigorous ethic of the prophets by a rabbinical legalism. This process was also influenced by an increasing accommodation of the Judaic worldview to bourgeois interests (AJ p. 369). The implication of this accommodation, developed through the priestly elaboration of God's law, is as follows:

> Given that the priesthood maintained its control over believers by segregating them from non-believers through ritual means, the means to salvation also increasingly became narrowed to the formal observance of law and ritual. These more modest demands (because of their externality) went hand in hand with a change in the conceptions of Yahweh and of salvation. The tension between a severe wrathful ruler and an imperfect world, which had earlier been the basis for a radical devaluation of the world, was replaced by a more harmonious relation between a wise and beneficent governor of the world and a belief in a peaceful world.
>
> (Schroeder 1992: 81)

The central point here is, firstly, that the development of Judaism is governed by the ritual distinction between Jews and non-Jews, thus, securing the collective nature of the theodicy, and secondly, that this legalism pervades the elaboration of the Judaic worldview and mediates between Yahweh and the individual. Together these features prevent the development of a strict inner-worldly asceticism characterised both by an individualistic theodicy and an unmediated relation between the believer and the transcendent deity. Consequently, Weber can state with regard to Judaic rationalism in the economic sphere that

> Success in his occupation actually became the tangible proof of God's personal favor, for the Jew living in the ghetto. But the conception

of self-fulfillment (*Bewaehrung*) in a calling (*Beruf*) pleasing to god, in the sense of inner-worldly asceticism (*innerweltliche Askese*), is not applicable to the Jew. God's blessing was far less strongly anchored in a systematic, rational, methodical pattern of life (the only possible source of the *certitudo salutis*) for the Jew than the Puritan. Just as the Jewish sexual ethic remained naturalistic and anti-ascetic, so also did the economic ethic of ancient Judaism remain strongly traditionalistic in its basic tenets.

(SR p. 114)

The theme of collectivity and ritual segregation is expressed here in the fact that 'the traditionalistic precepts of the Jewish economic ethics naturally applied in their full scope only to one's fellow religionists, not to outsiders' (SR p. 115). However, while Judaism may not itself complete the development of Western rationalism, Weber certainly ascribes to Judaism the emergence of this rationalism. The construction in the Judaic worldview of the opposition between an omnipotent, universalistic god and an imperfect empirical world is constitutive of a will to knowledge, albeit one which takes the form of a historical (rather than scientific) reflection in the intellectual sphere and a self-reflection in terms of rabbinical law in the practical spheres. This transition from primitive to universal religion can be summed up in Nietzschean terms as the movement from a noble ethic predicated on the pathos of social distance to slave morality predicated on the pathos of metaphysical distance, this metaphysical distance being constructed upon the idea of a future 'messianic kingdom which would redeem the entire pariah community from its inferior position and in fact raise it to a position of mastery in the world' (SR p. 110) and articulated through the opposition of Jew and non-Jew. In other words, through the construction of a pathos of metaphysical distance, Judaism as the ground of Jewish culture enables the formation of goal-directed agency, while the other-worldly orientation of this agency implies that this culture does not possess the capacity to 'breed' autonomous individuals.[9]

Having delineated the significance of ancient Judaism for the emergence of Western rationalism in the transition from primitive to universal religion, we can move to the second transition in Western culture, that between Protestantism and modern secular culture, of which Weber states: 'The great historic process in the development of religion, the elimination of magic from the world, which had begun with the old Hebrew prophets and, in conjunction with Hellenistic scientific thought, had repudiated all magical means to salvation as superstition and sin, came here to its logical conclusion' (PE p. 105).[10]

107

THE PROTESTANT ETHIC 1: CHARISMA, CALLING AND LIFE-SPHERES

> One of the fundamental elements of the spirit of modern capitalism, and not only of that but of all modern culture: rational conduct on the basis of the idea of the calling, was born . . . from the spirit of Christian asceticism.
>
> (PE p. 180)

Weber's account of the Protestant ethic is conventionally read in terms of the impact of this ethic on the rationalisation of the economic sphere, and thereby as a contribution to the debate on the origins of capitalism.[11] However, as we have argued, Weber's primary concern is with the development of Western rationalism with respect to the possibility of individual autonomy in modern culture. In this context, it is the effect of the Protestant ethic on the rationalisation of the intellectual and political spheres which is of most direct import to our interests. Before taking up these topics, though, it is necessary to begin by specifying the Protestant worldview and the form of agency it facilitates. This issue can be addressed through an examination of the theodicy of predestination developed within Protestantism and the idea of a calling (*Beruf*) which attends it.

In our analysis of ancient Judaism, it was noted that religious charisma, exhibited by prophets, manifests itself in articulating the relationship between the deity, the individual and the world. In setting up the figure of the prophet as the bearer of religious charisma, Weber makes no real distinction between the 'founder of religion' and the 'renewer of religion'; in both cases the decisive features are the sense of personal calling and the claim of definite revelation (SR pp. 46–7). The various renewers of Christianity in its Protestant forms (most notably Luther and Calvin) may consequently be regarded as charismatic figures. However, we should note that religious charisma may exhibit itself in two distinct modes, namely, as *exemplary* prophecy or as *ethical* prophecy.[12] The former type is associated by Weber with a conception of the self as a *vessel* which exists in a personal relationship with an immanent divinity. The latter type is connected to a notion of the self as a *tool* expressing the will of a transcendent deity. While both are thus concerned with articulating the relationship between divinity, humanity and the world, the exemplary prophet achieves this by exhibiting the form of his life as a model, while the ethical prophet succeeds by way of a legislative teaching, that is, the construction of a moral law. The central point to note here is that the Protestant renewers of Christianity are of the second type, that is, they conceive of themselves as instruments of divine will and their charismatic authority expresses itself through the construction of a worldview around a moral legislation. What then are the features of this worldview and this legislation?

108

The central feature of the Protestant worldview is the idea of an absolutely transcendent god: 'everything of the flesh is separated from God by an unbridgeable gulf' (PE p. 103). In common with Judaism, Protestantism constructs an opposition between an omnipotent God and an imperfect world. Indeed, Protestantism is the 'logical conclusion' of the process initiated by Judaism simply because it rules out *any* mediation between God and the world. In contrast to Judaism, the Protestant God does not intervene in history on the basis of an ethical agreement; rather he has pre-ordained the totality of history in the moment of creation. Supplementing this vision of a transcendent God is the idea that only part of humanity, the elect, is saved and the rest are damned (PE p. 103). The reconciliation of these two features of the Protestant worldview finds its intellectual expression in the Calvinist idea of predestination. It is important to note that this theodicy is, for Weber, completely rational in a formal sense, that is, the combination of the idea of an absolutely transcendent god and the idea that humanity is divided into the saved and the damned can only be logically represented in the idea that ' "some men . . . are predestined unto everlasting life, and others foreordained to everlasting death" ' (PE p. 100). Moreover, the implication of this is that

> To assume that human merit or guilt play a part in determining this destiny would be to think of God's absolutely free decrees, which have been settled from eternity, as subject to change by human influence, an impossible contradiction.
>
> (PE p. 103)

In other words, the individual has either been granted God's grace or not, and not only is there no magical means of attaining this grace, there is no means whatsoever. As Weber notes:

> In its extreme inhumanity this doctrine must above all have had one consequence for the life of a generation which surrendered to its mag- nificent consistency. That was a feeling of unprecedented loneliness of the single individual.
>
> (PE p. 104)

Since this inner isolation is unredeemable by human action, Weber argues, it manifests itself in an antagonism 'to all the sensuous and emotional elements in culture and in religion, because they are of no use towards salvation' and, by contrast with Judaism, in a radical individualism (PE p. 105). Moreover, while the doctrine of predestination logically entails an ethos of fatalism, the emergence of the idea of proof of grace produces, as a psychological result, an entirely opposite ethos (PE p. 232 n. 66). To explore this psychological result requires that we attend to the idea of the calling.[13]

The heart of this idea, as formulated by Luther, is expressed in a rejection of the monastic flight from the world in favour of the claim that to live acceptably to God meant fulfilling the obligations of one's position within the world (PE p. 80). Individuals in adopting this calling constitute themselves as instruments of God's will, that is, the task of the individual is to transform the world in a moral (i.e. divine) direction. This labour in a calling is justified by Luther as 'the outward expression of brotherly love' on the grounds that 'the division of labour forces every individual to work for others' (PE p. 81). The rationale of brotherly love remains in the Calvinist transformation of Luther's idea; however, the anti-sensuous and individualistic impulses of Calvinism produce an alternative grounding of the expression of brotherly love:

> Brotherly love, since it may only be practised for the glory of God and not in the service of flesh, is expressed in the first place in the fulfilment of the daily tasks given by the *lex naturae*; and in the process this fulfilment assumes a peculiarly objective and impersonal character, that of service in the interest of the rational organisation of our social environment. For the wonderfully purposeful organisation and arrangement of this cosmos is, according to both the Bible and natural intuition, evidently designed by God to serve the utility of the human race. This makes labour in the service of impersonal social usefulness appear to promote the glory of God and hence to be willed by Him.
>
> (PE p. 109)

This idea of the calling of an individual to act as the instrument of God's will assumes its central significance for the development of Western rationalism with the emergence of the idea of proof of grace. Weber's argument is that the doctrine of predestination places the individual in an impossible psychological situation: on the one hand, the believer has an absolutely overriding ideal interest in knowing his state of grace; on the other hand, there is no possible means of attaining this knowledge, since God's eternal plan is inscrutable (PE pp. 109–11). However, with the entrenchment of this worldview, there emerges an accommodation to this ideal interest through two pastoral principles. Firstly, 'it is held to be an absolute duty to consider oneself chosen . . . since lack of self-confidence is the result of insufficient faith, hence of imperfect grace' (PE p. 111). Secondly, 'in order to attain that self-confidence intense worldly activity is recommended as the most suitable means' (PE p. 112).[14] In other words, what emerges here is 'the idea of the necessity of proving one's faith in worldly activity' (PE p. 121); the state of grace which marked out the elect could only be proved through 'a specific type of conduct unmistakably different from that of natural man' (PE p. 153). Moreover, this imperative towards worldly action is an ongoing injunction: 'only by a fundamental change in the whole meaning of life at every moment and in every action could the effects of grace transforming a man from the *status naturae* to the *status gratiae* be proved' (PE p. 118). In this context, worldly success becomes a sign of God's favour (PE p. 162). What follows from this, Weber argues, is that the individual has 'an incentive methodically to supervise his own state of grace in his own conduct, and thus to penetrate it with asceticism', where 'this ascetic conduct meant a rational planning of the whole of one's life in accordance with God's will' (PE p. 153). The form of this ascetic conduct, as we have noted, is rational action on the basis of a calling and Weber concludes this aspect of his argument by stressing this point: '[The] rationalisation of conduct within this world, but for the sake of the world beyond, was the consequence of the concept of calling of Protestant asceticism' (PE p. 154). The kernel of Weber's argument can thus be summarised as follows: Protestantism creates an imperative psychological need to master internal nature and the sign of this internal control is domination over external nature.[15]

Before going on to discuss the consequences of this inner-worldly asceticism for the differentiation of the life-spheres (and, thus, for the potential for change in a culture grounded in the Protestant worldview), however, the interests of our argument necessitate a specification of the type of man bred under the aegis of this worldview with respect to the constitution of goal-directed agency. Consider the following remark by Weber:

> The Puritan, like every rational type of ascetic, tried to enable a man to maintain and act upon his constant motives, especially those which it taught him itself, against the emotions. In this formal psychological sense of the term it tried to make him into a personality.
>
> (PE p. 119)

As with ancient Judaism, Protestantism provides a goal, that is, certain ultimate values which articulate the meaning of life. In this respect, Protestantism in common with all religions enables the constitution of goal-directed agency. The distinctiveness of the human type bred under Protestantism, however, lies in its *method* of achieving this and the *form* of agency it enables. While both these questions have been addressed in our discussion of the Protestant worldview and its effects on the individual, it is worthwhile to focus on them again at a more abstract level.

We can begin by recalling ancient Judaism in which goal-directed agency was constituted through a worldview predicated on the *chosen* status of the Jewish people which was articulated through the ritual distinction of Jew and non-Jew, and produced a form of agency reflexively oriented to Talmudic law. In Nietzschean terms, whereas the pathos of *inner* distance is tied to the pathos of *social* distance for the Jewish noble at the stage of Judaism as a primitive religion, the constitution of Judaism as a universal religion leads to the pathos of *inner* distance being predicated on the pathos of *metaphysical* distance. In other words, the constitution of goal-directed agency is no longer simply an unreflective internalisation of social distance; rather it involves a self-reflection mediated through the figure of the other, the non-Jew, as defined by Talmudic law. By contrast, the constitution of goal-directed agency under the aegis of Protestantism involves a self-reflection mediated only by the conscience of the individual. Thus, the distinctive feature of Protestant asceticism is that the pathos of *inner* distance – the individual's ability to command himself in relation to a goal – is reflexively constituted through adherence to a form of life defined in accordance with God's will as it is determined by the conscience of the individual.[16] In other words, through its construction of a regime of self-surveillance and self-suspicion, Protestant asceticism breeds a human type who becomes judge, victim and avenger of the moral law, that is, a human type with the capacity for reflexively constituting inner distance through adherence to a goal, that of rationally mastering the world for the glory of God.[17] At this stage, we may turn to the consequences of the development of this human type for the differentiation of the life-spheres.

As we have noted, the psychological effect of the Protestant ethic is to legislate an imperative towards the rationalisation of conduct, where this conduct is oriented to the rationalisation of all spheres of human activity as the expression of God's will. We can clarify this expression of Weber's position by noting that there is a distinction between the rationalisation of action and the rationalisation of spheres of activity. The first involves a rationality characterised by the calculation of the most efficient means to a given valuable end on the part of the individual. The second refers to institutional organisation of a given form of activity such that it facilitates this type of rational action to the maximum degree possible. The question which arises here concerns the determination of what count as valuable ends and the forms of organisation which facilitate the achievement of these ends. On one level, the response to this question is straightforward: the end to which ascetic action is geared is the fulfilment of God's will and this is most efficiently achieved through organisations which facilitate the impersonal pursuit of this duty. However, this answer – while trivially true – does not suffice to address the complexities of the issue. We can begin by recalling that God's will is defined as the maximisation of the utility of the resources he makes available (PE pp. 109, 162). Thus, in the economic sphere, this manifests itself as the pursuit of profit not for its own sake but 'as a performance of duty' (PE p. 163). It would be absurd, however, to suggest that the pursuit of profit is similarly the normative requirement in the spheres of science and politics, for example. On the contrary, the idea of fulfilling God's will in these spheres is expressed through normative commitments to knowledge and power respectively. Moreover, at an institutional level, this implies that the organisational structures within which these different activities are performed need to be oriented to be the requirements demanded for the pursuit of these distinct goals. Thus, while for Protestantism it was acceptable for the individual to combine callings on condition that justice was done to each or to change callings, the outcome of this rationalisation of actions and organisations was both to produce a growing differentiation between the spheres of life in so far as they were increasingly regarded as involving distinct normative commitments and to ground this differentiation in distinct types of institutional arrangement.

The purpose of this section has been to elaborate Weber's argument concerning the consequences of the Protestant ethic in terms of the human type to which it gives rise. We have focused on the method by which it produces this human type and the form of agency exhibited by this type. Finally, we have noted the implications of this type of goal-directed agency for the differentiation of the life-spheres. In terms of our discussion of Weber's methodology, this last point suggests that the routine form of life cultivated by Protestantism is a powerful force for cultural change. To address Weber's central concern with the possibility of individual autonomy in modernity, however, requires that we specify the directions of this cultural change in the spheres of science and politics.

THE PROTESTANT ETHIC 2: SCIENCE AND SECULARISATION

Three issues need to be addressed in this section. The first concerns the reason why the Protestant will to knowledge takes the form of scientific reflection. The second examines the inner logic of this will to knowledge. The third is the question of the institutional organisation of the pursuit of scientific knowledge. Together these issues inform Weber's account of the development of modern science and its consequences for modern culture.

In ancient Judaism, the will to knowledge takes the direction of historical reflection, the quest to uncover the ethical pattern of human history being the means by which knowledge of God is developed. In ancient Greece, the will to knowledge takes the form of scientific reflection, the path to uncovering the nature of true being.[18] The Protestant will to knowledge may be regarded as a synthetic rationalisation of these two developments.[19] On the one hand, it shares the Judaism conception of a transcendent deity and, consequently, is concerned to grasp knowledge of God or, more precisely, knowledge of God's divine plan. On the other hand, the absolutely transcendent character of the Protestant deity implies the fateful and impersonal character of the cosmos which leads not to reflection on history as the pattern of God's ethical interventions, but to the adoption and transformation of the Greek (i.e. Platonic) distinction between the realm of being and that of becoming. This is expressed in the idea that our empirical reality is the

113

epiphenomenal outcome generated by the mechanism of divine laws. Thus, this will to knowledge takes the form of scientific reflection on the laws of nature that God has ordained. Weber describes this Protestant will to knowledge as follows:

> If you recall Swammerdam's statement, 'Here I bring you the proof of God's providence in the anatomy of a louse,' you will see what the scientific worker, influenced (indirectly) by Protestantism and Puritanism, conceived to be his task: to show the path to God. People no longer found this path among the philosophers, with their concepts and deductions. All pietist theology of the time, above all Spener, knew that God was not found along the road by which the Middle Ages had sought him. God is hidden. His ways are not our ways, His thoughts are not our thoughts. In the exact sciences, however, where one could physically grasp His works, one hoped to come upon the traces of what He planned for the world.
>
> (SV p. 142)

The desire to read the Book of Nature as the correlate of the Bible governed the direction of this will to knowledge, whether it be physical or human nature that was the locus of attention, though Weber argues that Protestantism has a particular affinity with physics and the mathematical sciences (PE p. 249 n. 145).[20] In other words, the domination of nature in the intellectual sphere manifests itself as the rational construction of scientific accounts of nature. At this stage, we can turn to the second aspect of the Protestant ethic in the intellectual sphere, namely the question of how the will to knowledge constituted by it develops: what is its 'inner logic'?

For Weber, what must be recognised is that a tension arises within the intellectual sphere between scientific and religious forms of explanation. The attempt to read the Book of Nature, given the absolutely transcendent character of God, necessarily takes the form of *causal* explanation, which thereby implies a thesis of determinacy. The injunction to plan one's conduct rationally in accordance with God's revealed word, the Bible, however, generates explanation in terms of the *meaning* and value of one's life, which implies a thesis of free will. In other words, scientific activity presupposes a doctrine of free will, while scientific explanation presupposes a doctrine of necessity. The need to resolve this antinomy is, let us recall, the spur to the dualism of Kant's critical philosophy. Within the development of the 'inner logic' of this antinomy, however, Kant's peculiarly Protestant philosophy is merely a way-station. On Weber's account, the 'elective affinity' between the Calvinist doctrine of predestination and the thesis of causal determinacy implies that scientific explanation reveals itself in the progressive undermining of the meaning assigned to one's life by religious explanations. Science, for Weber, is a 'specifically irreligious power' which is 'apt to make the belief that there is such a thing as the "meaning" of the universe die out at its very roots' (SV p. 142). In these remarks Weber is echoing Nietzsche rather than Kant, and specifically Nietzsche's claim that it is the will to truth cultivated by Christianity which undermines Christian morality. The implication of the development of this 'inner logic' is that the Protestant will to knowledge increasingly undermines religious forms of explanation structured about *values* and ultimately, therefore, religion as such – which is itself the ground of meaning for scientific activity. The 'inner logic' of Protestantism is, paradoxically, a logic of secularisation in the face of which 'the ultimate and most sublime values have retreated from public life' (SV p. 155).[21] Thus, scientific explanation undermines moral values, only to discover that the ground of the meaning of moral values is also the ground of the meaning and value of scientific activity itself. Having traced this 'inner logic', we can turn to the final question to be addressed in this section, namely, that of the institutional arrangement through which this pursuit of knowledge manifests itself.

This is not a question which Weber directly addresses; however, by abstracting from his comments on both the institutional organisation of science in modernity and the character of the Protestant ethic, some tentative proposals may be suggested. Initially, it seems reasonable that the individualistic ethic of Protestantism manifests itself in the figure of the individual researcher. The imperative form of work in this sphere as a mode of glorifying not oneself but God, though, implies a rationalisation of scientific activity in a direction which maximises the utility of the resources, the gifts, provided by the Protestant deity. This rationalisation operates through the construction of the norms governing scientific activity, where these norms are simply those which maximise scientific productivity. At an individual level, the primary norm must be honesty in so far as fraud implies a quest for personal glory and, thus, a lack of grace. At an institutional level, the correlate of honesty is the open communication of ideas, discoveries, theories, etc. One might also suggest that specialisation in research (as the maximising of the resources of those engaged in scientific activity at a given time) and teaching (as the maximising of the resources of the next generation) also attend this normative rationalisation of scientific activity.[22] Needless to say, a condition of this organisational rationalisation is the construction of autonomous institutions (i.e. universities) in which this process is facilitated; this implies, for example, the separation of the administrative from the research and teaching functions![23] The Protestant ethic thus manifests itself with respect to scientific activity in terms of a rationalisation of both the institutional conditions of this activity and the mode of the activity itself. This rationalisation of the mode of scientific activity has, moreover, a further dimension in that, in so far as science undermines the Protestant worldview, it loses the ground of its legitimation, but this loss of worldview also has implications for the *direction* of scientific activity. Whereas science for the Protestant is legitimated as an expression of God's will and is given direction through an ideal interest in uncovering God's plan, the undermining of the Protestant worldview both renders scientific activity 'objectively' meaningless and undermines the ideal interest governing its direction. The implication of the latter point with respect to modernity is that the direction of rationalised science is increasingly determined purely and simply by material interests. The significance of this point emerges in conjunction with the fate of politics in modernity as we shall see shortly.

In concluding this section, we can note Weber's claim that the logic of secularisation inaugurated by Protestantism is completed in modernity; today, science cannot tell us how we should live nor can it ground the presupposition of its own value. Relating this to our comments on the structure of the life-sphere, we can say that while the norms governing scientific activity are embodied in the organisational structure of institutions of knowledge in modern culture, these norms no longer possess a purposive ground and, thus, assume an entirely instrumental character. In other words, on analogy with Weber's political sociology, the organisation of science in modernity has the form of legal-rational domination. Here we are confronted with the breeding ground of 'Specialists without spirit' (PE p. 182).

THE PROTESTANT ETHIC 3: POLITICS AND BUREAUCRATISATION

In taking up the effect of the Protestant ethic in and on the political sphere, we begin by focusing on the form of 'inner logic' assumed by the Protestant ethic in this sphere. This is followed by an elaboration of the organisational norms governing political institutions under the aegis of this ethic. Finally, we attend to the implications of these elements.

For Weber, the fundamental moral law of Christianity (and, indeed, of all salvation religions) is an ethic of brotherly love which comes into tension with the demands of political action (FMW pp. 333–40). The specificity of Protestantism lies in its development of a consistent 'inner-worldly' solution to this tension:

> Puritanism, with its particularism of grace and vocational asceticism, believes in the fixed and revealed commandments of a God who is otherwise incomprehensible. It interprets God's will to mean that these commandments should be imposed on the creatural world by the means of this world, namely, violence – for the world is subject to violence and ethical barbarism. And this means at least barriers which resist the obligation of brotherliness in the interests of God's cause.
>
> (FMW p. 336)

As will become apparent in our discussion of the 'inner logic' of Protestantism with respect to the political sphere, this last remark is slightly misleading. The important point to note here, however, is that just as there is an elective affinity between the Protestant will to knowledge and scientific activity, so too is there an affinity between the Protestant will to action (at least in its Puritan form) and political activity. At this stage, therefore, let us turn to the development of this 'inner logic'.[24]

We can begin by noting that, for Weber, politics has a peculiarly double character in that fulfilling God's will takes the form of facilitating rational action in all the life-spheres. To establish and clarify this, we can refer to the paradoxical form taken by the ethic of brotherly love under Protestantism:

> Brotherly love, since it may only be practised for the glory of God and not in the service of the flesh, is expressed in the first place in the fulfilment of the daily tasks given by the *lex naturae*; and in the process this fulfilment assumes a peculiarly objective and impersonal character, that of service in the interest of the rational organisation of our social environment. For the wonderfully purposeful organisation and arrangement of this cosmos is ... evidently designed by God to serve the utility of the human race. This makes labour in the service of impersonal social usefulness appear to promote the glory of God and hence to be willed by him.
>
> (PE p. 109)

Two themes emerge from this passage: firstly, the impersonal rationalisation of the social organisation provides an impetus towards the regulation of all public spheres of life on the basis of formal legal norms, and secondly, the maximisation of the utility of worldly resources requires the facilitation of rational activity in all the life-spheres which entails a conception of the state as providing the conditions of activity but not interfering in this activity. In other words, Weber's argument is that the 'inner logic' of Protestantism manifests an elective affinity with the emergence of legal rationalism on the basis of a contractarian conception of natural law and, concomitantly, with the development of liberalism (ES pp. 866–71). On the one hand, political activity under the aegis of Protestantism develops, on Weber's account, as the progressive destruction of traditional or affectual barriers to rational action. On the other hand, this activity is legitimated by natural law as the binding force of the public sphere, where natural law is viewed as the expression of God's will.[25] Together these developments imply that, for Weber, the Protestant ethic is connected to the emergence of the modern liberal-democratic state in which the pre-modern legitimation of political authority on the ground of tradition is displaced by an authority based on legal-rational grounds. With the development of the Protestant 'logic of secularisation', however, two problems emerge to confront the individual in modernity.

The implication of this process in the public spheres of life is that, while Protestantism has destroyed traditional or affectual grounds for action, the development of its 'inner logic' undermines the other-worldly ends to which rational action is oriented. Weber's conception of the outcome of this development has been succinctly expressed by Löwith:

> That which was originally a mere means (to an otherwise valuable end) becomes an end in itself. In this way, means as ends make themselves independent and thus lose their original 'meaning' or purpose, that is, they lose their original purposive rationality orientated to man and his needs. This reversal marks the whole of modern civilisation, whose arrangements, institutions and activities are so 'rationalised' that whereas humanity once established itself within them, now it is they which enclose and determine humanity like an 'iron cage'.
>
> (Löwith 1982: 47–8)

While political activity under Protestantism is oriented to providing formal norms which allow the expression of God's will in the life-spheres, the death of God signals the meaninglessness both of this political activity and of activity in the life-spheres as such. Moreover, the second dilemma merely serves to heighten the problem posed by the first in that the 'logic of secularisation' by undermining the very idea of natural law represents both the progressive destruction of the binding character of the public sphere and, ultimately, the impossibility of reconstituting this binding character on the basis of a criterion of legality.[26] The will to truth manifested by Protestantism, let us recall, not only undermines the moral values embodied in this worldview but is itself incapable of articulating a new set of values (including that of truth itself). The result of this development is that the political sphere is characterised by the perpetual clash of ungrounded worldviews. This dilemma which apparently denotes the fate of the modern individual can be given concrete exemplification by considering the organisation of the apparatus of the modern state.

What form is taken by the rationalisation of the structure of political institutions? We can begin by recalling that the Protestant ethic expresses itself in the fulfilment of God's will. In terms of politics, the facilitation of rational action entails the development of an administrative machine that enables both rational decision-making and the efficient translation of political will into practice. This is true, for Weber, at the level both of the party and of the state. In other words, rational political action requires a bureaucratic mode of administration. As Weber notes:

> The decisive reason for the advance of bureaucratic organisation has always been its purely technical superiority over any other form of organisation. The fully developed bureaucratic mechanism

compares with other organisations exactly as does the machine with non-mechanical modes of production.

(FMW p. 214)

Moreover, bureaucracy exhibits precisely those qualities of impersonality and resource maximisation to which the Protestant ethic is oriented:

Bureaucratisation offers above the optimum possibility of carrying through the principle of specialising administrative functions according to purely objective considerations. Individual performances are allocated to functionaries who have specialised training and who by constant practice learn more and more. The 'objective' discharge of business primarily means a discharge of business according to *calculable rules* and 'without regard for persons'.

(FMW p. 215)

Bureaucracy, in other words, is nothing other than an embodiment of *rational discipline*, that is, 'the consistently rationalised, methodically trained and exact execution of the received order, in which all personal criticism is unswervingly and exclusively set for carrying out the command' (FMW p. 253). With regard to the state, this rationalisation of the organisation of the administration apparatus recalls a comment of Kant's:

Now in many affairs conducted in the interests of the community, a certain mechanism is required by means of which some of its members must conduct themselves in an entirely passive manner so that through an artificial unanimity the government may guide them towards public ends, or at least prevent them from destroying such ends. Here one certainly must not argue, instead one must obey.

(Kant 1983: 42)

Kant's 'mechanism' is nothing other than bureaucracy and this 'passive manner' is ultimately legitimated by the idea of fulfilling God's will. Kant's argument in this instance may serve as an exemplification of Protestantism in that the 'special virtue' of bureaucracy is precisely its elimination from official business of 'love, hate, and all purely personal, irrational, and emotional elements which escape calculation' (FMW p. 216). For Weber, however, bureaucracy takes on a fateful character; there are two central grounds for this view. Firstly, because 'bureaucracy is amongst those social structures which are hardest to destroy . . . the idea of eliminating these organisations becomes more and more utopian' (FMW pp. 228–9). This characteristic of bureaucracy becomes problematic when linked to the second ground of Weber's pessimism which concerns the power position of the bureaucracy in the context of the disenchantment of the world. The first aspect of this is expressed as follows:

119

Under normal conditions, the power position of a fully developed bureaucracy is always overpowering. The 'political master' finds himself in the position of the 'dilettante' who stands opposite the 'expert,' facing the trained official who stands within the management of administration.

(FMW p. 232)

To the increasing dependence of the politician on the bureaucracy can be added the development of state bureaucrats as a distinct social stratum with a material interest in expanding the role of the state in social life. In so far as the Protestant worldview manifests itself politically through a form of liberalism predicated on natural law, this material interest is overridden by the ideal interest in fulfilling God's will. However, the disenchantment of the world signals both the demise of this ideal interest and the impossibility of constituting an alternative transcendent ideal interest to check the immanent expansionary tendencies of bureaucracy. To put it in Löwith's terms, bureaucracy as a means to the valuable end of fulfilling God's will becomes an end in itself. To summarise Weber's position with respect to the political sphere in modernity, we may say the 'polar night of icy darkness' (PV p. 128) that Weber sees before us is characterised by the increasing dependence of the political decision-making on bureaucracy, where this bureaucracy has a vested interest in increasing the role of the state, and yet where bureaucracy as a social structure is integral to the needs of modern society. This pessimism receives its expression in Weber's critique of socialism as the *telos* of this bureaucratic development in which the individual is reduced to being the instrument of an omnipotent state (Beetham 1974: 82–9), a view which echoes Nietzsche's comment that socialism 'expressly aspires to the annihilation of the individual, who appears to it as an unauthorised luxury of nature destined to be improved into a useful *organ of the community*' (HAH I. 473 p. 173).

To conclude this section, we can specify the problem which confronts modern politics. Firstly, the development of the 'logic of secularisation' represents the progressive destruction of the public sphere while ruling out the possibility of reconstituting this sphere on the basis of a principle of legality. Political activity is therefore rendered 'objectively' meaningless. Secondly, the development of legal norms to regulate social relationships facilitates the destruction of traditional and affectual forms of action and the promotion of rational action; however, with the disenchantment of the world, this action becomes substantively irrational. Thirdly, this rational action is facilitated through the construction of instrumentally rational forms of organisation which increasingly lessen the significance of individual action and 'enclose and determine humanity'. Finally, bureaucracy as the instrumentally rational form of administration within political organisations assumes an unfettered interest in expanding over the whole of social life, yet modern politics is necessarily dependent on this form of organisation.

THE FATE OF MODERNITY

Through his investigations, Weber constructs an account of both the loss of grounds which lend 'objective' meaning to science and politics and the transformation of the direction of scientific and political activity in so far as these activities are institutionalised in modernity. In both cases, the legitimation of these activities as distinct modes of expressing God's will is undermined by the logic of secularisation, but this also results in undermining the conceptions of fulfilling God's will which gave direction to these activities (in science, uncovering the divine design of the universe, and, in politics, transforming the world such that God's will may be expressed) such that science is increasingly transformed in the direction of technical knowledge concerning the achievement of material interests and politics is increasingly governed by technical decision-making on the basis of material interests. Both the loss of grounds of meaning and value of these activities and their transformation in the direction of material interests have profound implications for modern culture.

We have noted that, under the aegis of Protestantism, there is bred a human type with the capacity for the reflexive construction of inner distance and that, in so far as the logic of secularisation undermines the grounding of values in a transcendent deity, this entails the possibility of constructing inner distance through adherence to self-determined values for the modern individual, that is, the possibility of autonomous individuals being produced by modern culture.[27] However, as a result of this disenchantment of the world, modern culture lacks a ground of meaning and value capable of facilitating the realisation of this capacity which results in an ethos of flight from the meaninglessness of the world, either into mysticism or into an instrumentalisation of the self as, for example, a cog in the scientific or political machine.[28] At the same time, moreover, the transformation of the direction of science and politics into activities concerned simply with material interests creates a 'dialectic of domination'. On the one hand, the location of political decision-making as purely technical decision-making concerning the calculated pursuit of material ends increases the power of the bureaucracy. On the other hand, the location of scientific knowledge as purely technical knowledge on how to achieve material interests constructs a worldview in which the individual is conceived of simply as a means to material ends. Together these combine in that scientific knowledge increases the efficiency of the bureaucratic apparatus and, thereby, its power, while the growing power of the bureaucracy expresses itself in the increasing domination of rational discipline over social life and, thereby, transforms the world in a direction ever more subject to scientific prediction and control. The implication of this, for Weber, is that, while the modern individual possesses the capacity for autonomy, the possibility of realising this capacity is being progressively undermined by a process whose *telos* is the reduction of the individual to a position of absolute powerlessness and, ultimately, to a 'cheerful robot' (to borrow C. Wright Mill's phrase).[29] Weber's 'political' problem is, thus, not the possibility of utopia but how to resist this 'dialectic of domination'; for it is only in terms of this resistance that the possibility of enabling the emergence of the autonomous individual as the dominant human type of modern culture can be addressed.

7

THE POLITICS OF 'PERSONALITY'
Weber, maturity and modernity

Today the spirit of asceticism – whether finally, who knows? – has escaped from the cage. . . . The rosy blush of its laughing heir, the Enlightenment, seems also to be irretrievably fading, and the idea of duty in one's calling prowls about in our lives like the ghost of dead religious beliefs.

(PE pp. 181–2)

Certainly all historical experience confirms the truth – that man would not have attained the possible unless time and again he had reached out for the impossible. But to do that a man must be a leader, and not only a leader but a hero as well, in a very sober sense of the word.

(PV p. 128)

Weber's cultural science is structured around the concern to evaluate modernity with respect to the possibility of the autonomous individual becoming the dominant human type in modern culture. However, as we have noted, Weber's investigation of the genealogy of modern culture establishes its profoundly ambivalent character in regard to this possibility. On the one hand, the construction of a human type with the capacity for reflexively constituting inner distance and the logic of secularisation initiated by the Protestant ethic creates the possibility of individual autonomy. On the other hand, the chances of realising this possibility are increasingly undermined by the lack of a cultural ground of value and the 'dialectic of domination' which attends the reduction of science and politics to a concern with material interests. The concepts of disenchantment and rational discipline signal the fulfilment of the negative moment of this enterprise of evaluation. The positive moment of Weber's project requires the specification of an ideal capable of resisting the disenchantment of the age and the growth of the dominance of rational discipline. It will be argued that this ideal is embodied in Weber's idea of 'personality' in a calling.[1] Before focusing on this, however, we can specify further the extent of the crisis posed for the modern individual by disenchantment and rational discipline.

THE AMBIVALENCE OF MODERNITY

In the preceding chapter, we traced the impact of the Protestant ethic in the spheres of science and politics, while also noting the process of disenchantment to which it gives rise. In this section, our concern will be with specifying the fundamental ambivalence which attends modern culture with respect to the question of individual autonomy. This concern can be addressed by reference to two related topics, namely, the cultural conditions of possibility of individual autonomy and the institutional conditions of possibility of individual autonomy.

The first of these concerns relates to the capacity for autonomy of the human type produced under the aegis of the Protestant ethic. The central feature here is Protestantism's breeding of a type of man capable of the reflexive constitution of 'inner distance' through adherence to a form of life prescribed by Puritan morality. Weber's account of this development is structured about Protestant asceticism's construction of a regime of self-reflection in which the moral conscience of the individual becomes its own judge.[2] The crucial idea here is that of a calling characterised by 'the valuation of the fulfilment of duty in worldly affairs as the highest form which the moral activity of the individual could assume' (PE p. 80), where this fulfilment of duty expresses the consciousness of grace which marks out the individual as one of the elect. It follows from this, Weber argues, that the individual has an incentive methodically to 'supervise his state of grace in his own conduct, and thus to penetrate it with asceticism' where 'this ascetic conduct meant a rational planning of one's whole life in accordance with God's will' (PE p. 153). Moreover, whereas the Puritan type is characterised simply by goal-directed agency, the disenchantment of the world (the death of God) entails the possibility of the self-determination of goals on the part of the individual. However, the death of God also entails that work within a calling is 'objectively' meaningless and this lack of meaning produces self-narcoticism expressed either as an ethos of flight from the world into mysticism or as an ethos of adaptation to the world through mechanical activity.[3] The implication of this, for Weber, is that while the modern individual possesses the capacity for autonomy, modern culture is characterised by the lack of a ground of meaning and value for human existence which might mobilise this capacity.

However, as we have noted, the lack of structures of recognition which enable the formation of autonomous individuals does not describe the full extent of the ambivalence of modern culture. On the contrary, this culture is characterised by the decreasing possibility of constructing such value-structures; this is expressed in the increasing spread of *rational discipline* over all areas of social life. Consider the following passage:

> An inanimate machine is mind objectified. Only this provides it with the power to force men into its service and to dominate their

everyday working life as completely as is the case in the factory. Objectified intelligence is also the animate machine, that bureaucratic organisation, with its specialisation of trained skills, its division of jurisdiction, its rules and hierarchical relations of authority. Together with the inanimate machine it is busy fabricating the shell of bondage which men will perhaps be forced to inhabit some day, as powerless as the fellahs of ancient Egypt. . . . Who would want to deny that such a potentiality lies in the womb of the future?

(ES p. 1402)

Here the question which arises is how it is possible to preserve the possibility of individual autonomy, that is, to 'save *any remnants* of "individualistic" freedom in any sense?' (ES p. 1403). Moreover, in so far as modern culture does not provide a ground on the basis of which this development may be resisted, it paves 'the way for the eventual rise of a new human species' described by Mommsen as

the fully adjusted men of a bureaucratic age who no longer strive for goals which lie beyond their intellectual horizon, which is in any case likely to be exclusively defined by their most immediate material needs.

(Mommsen 1974: 20)[4]

In the face of this vision, Weber's question concerning the conditions of possibility of individual autonomy in modern culture attends to the possibility of facilitating resistance to the domination of *rational discipline*, that is, the instrumentalisation of the individual.[5]

In this context, it is apparent that, for Weber, while modern culture raises the possibility of individual autonomy, it also undermines this possibility through facilitating a human type defined entirely in terms of material interests. The question which arises for the positive moment of Weber's cultural science is how to establish resistance to the development of a human species fully adjusted to a bureaucratic age both at the level of the ground of culture and at the level of institutions. We shall examine Weber's position at each of these levels.

THE IDEA OF 'PERSONALITY': WEBER'S CULTURAL IDEAL

The fruit of the tree of knowledge, which is distasteful to the complacent but which is, nonetheless, inescapable, consists in the insight that in every single important activity and ultimately life as a whole, if it is not to be permitted to run on as an event in nature but is instead to be consciously guided, is a series of ultimate decisions through which the soul – as in Plato – chooses its own fate, i.e., the meaning of its activity and existence.

(MSS p. 18)

This passage presents Weber's conception of the transcendental presupposition of cultural science, namely, 'that we are *cultural beings*, endowed with the capacity and the will to take a deliberative attitude towards the world and lend it *significance*' (MSS p. 81). It is precisely this, however, which is threatened by the dominance of rational discipline in so far as the *telos* of this dominance is reduction of the individual to an instrument which is subject to scientific prediction and control.[6] This dominance expresses not just the powerlessness of the individual but the 'breeding' of a new 'human' type who exists as 'an event in nature'. The 'transcendental presupposition' of Weber's cultural science, thus, stands as the ground of his concern to resist this development.[7] We can note here also though that this passage, despite its reference to Plato, echoes Nietzsche's injunction to become what you are. It will be recalled that Nietzsche argues that one is always 'becoming what one is', simply because the narrative constitutive of 'what one is' (the self) is always already ongoing, but that *what is needful* is to be reflexively active in this process and this exhibits itself in giving style to one's character through adherence to a single taste. Weber's position too stresses the need for this becoming what one is to be 'consciously guided' even claiming that it is this reflexivity which separates human action from natural events. Moreover, although Weber does not adopt Nietzsche's aesthetic vocabulary, [8] his conception of giving 'personality' to one's character through the constraint of 'a constant and intrinsic relation to certain ultimate "values" and "meanings" of life' (RK p. 192) clearly recalls Nietzsche's idea of giving style to one's character.[9]

How then does the idea of 'personality' express itself, for Weber, in modernity? It is a consequence of the disenchantment of the world, for Weber, that 'the ultimate and most sublime values have retreated from public life' (SV p. 155), the collapse of grounds for values expressing itself in the emergence of moral relativism. The implication of this for the idea of 'personality' is that individuals must 'choose' their own 'ultimate "values" and "meanings" of life'. As Weber puts it:

> so long as life remains immanent and is interpreted in its own terms, it knows only an unceasing struggle of these gods [ultimate values] with one another. Or speaking directly, the ultimately possible attitudes towards life are irreconcilable, and hence their struggle can never be brought to a final conclusion. Thus it is necessary to make a decisive choice.

> (SV p. 152)

Or again: 'ultimate *Weltanschauungen* clash, world views among which in the end one has to make a choice' (PV p. 117). 'Personality' is thus constituted at this level through the choice of, and adherence to, a particular worldview and 'the dignity of the "personality" lies in the fact that for it there exist values about which it organises its life' (MSS p. 55).

126

In other words, as for Nietzsche, the labour of self-overcoming through which one constitutes oneself as an autonomous individual is articulated by adherence to self-determined values which enable the reflexive construction of inner distance.

It should also be noted that, for Weber, choosing a worldview entails that 'you serve this god and you offend the other god when you adhere to this position' (SV p. 151). The implication of this claim is that the ruling value is probity (*Redlichkeit*) in that the degree to which one constitutes oneself as a 'personality' depends on the probity one manifests in relation to adherence to one's 'ultimate "values" and "meanings" of life'. It must be stated though that, as with Nietzsche, probity is the value which is constitutive of the structure of self-legislation; it is the value which attends the reflexive *becoming* of what one is as opposed to the *what one is* that one becomes in that it articulates not the values to be posited and adhered to, but the process of positing and adhering to these values.[10] At this stage, however, we confront the moment at which Nietzsche's and Weber's positions depart from each other. This emerges when we take up the question of the structure of probity. For Nietzsche, as we have argued, the constraint of probity is embodied in the doctrine of eternal recurrence. Weber, however, quite explicitly rejects this doctrine:

> Fatalism is, of course, the only logical consequence of predestination. But on account of the idea of proof the psychological result was precisely the opposite. For essentially similar reasons the followers of Nietzsche claim a positive ethical significance for the idea of eternal recurrence. This case, however, is concerned with responsibility for a future life which is connected with the active individual by no conscious thread of continuity, while for the Puritan it was *tua res agitur*.
>
> (PE p. 232 n. 66)

It is apparent from this passage that Weber reads eternal recurrence as a *cosmological* doctrine, whereas we have already shown that, for Nietzsche, eternal recurrence represents a *psychological* doctrine. Indeed, Nietzsche recognises that a cosmological interpretation of eternal necessarily leads to the ethos of fatalism embodied in the Spirit of Gravity.[11] On this point, at least, Weber's critique of Nietzsche, which appears to draw on the reading presented in Simmel's *Schopenhauer and Nietzsche*,[12] is hardly marked by his characteristic perspicacity. However, the distinction between Nietzsche's and Weber's positions can be rendered clearer by focusing on the following passage:

> In the field of science only he who is devoted *solely* to the work at hand has 'personality'. And this holds not only for the field of science; we know of no great artist who has ever done anything but serve his

work and only his work. As far as his art was concerned, even with a personality of Goethe's rank, it has been detrimental to take the liberty of trying to make his 'life' into a work of art. And even if one doubts this, one has to be a Goethe in order to dare to permit oneself such a liberty. Everyone will admit at least this much: that even with a man like Goethe, who appears once in a thousand years, this liberty did not go unpaid for. In politics matters are not different, but we shall not discuss that today.

(SV p. 137)

Despite the qualifications Weber introduces into this passage, it is manifestly apparent that he is concerned to distance himself from the Nietzschean ideal of making one's life a work of art. It appears, in Yeat's words, as if 'The intellect of man is forced to choose/Perfection of the life or of the work' (Yeats 1974: 153), and whereas Nietzsche's ideal is the former, Weber's is the latter.[13] The reasons for this transformation of the concept of probity lie in Weber's recognition that the individual is inscribed not simply within the struggle of competing worldviews but also within the struggle of competing life-spheres constituted by their own immanent norms and obligations: 'The Puritan wanted to work in a calling; we are forced to do so' (PE p. 181). 'Personality' thus entails not merely a choice of, and adherence to, 'certain ultimate "values" and "meanings" of life' but also the choice of, and adherence to, a particular life-sphere. Weber's point here is that this-worldly rational-teleological action in modernity can only express itself through labour in a given life-sphere, where this labour involves commitment to norms and obligations which are irreconcilable with those of the other life-spheres: 'We are placed into different life-spheres, each of which is governed by different laws' (PV p. 123). What, then, are the consequences of this transformation for the concept of probity? What is entailed by this idea of serving the needs of one's vocation?

THE IDEA OF A 'CALLING': WEBER'S VOCATIONAL ETHIC

A route into this discussion is provided by the suggestion that while 'personality' requires commitment to 'certain ultimate "values" and "meanings" of life', the nature of this commitment is distinct in the different life-spheres. In other words, the structure of probity is dependent on the life-sphere in which this commitment expresses itself, that is, each life-sphere embodies its own criteria of probity. This suggestion can be grounded by specifying the distinct criteria of probity in the spheres of science and politics.[14]

To begin we may note that the passage we cited by Weber with respect

128

to Goethe suggests that probity in all life-spheres is characterised by exclusive devotion to the work at hand (SV p. 137); this 'devotion' taking the form of setting out 'to work and meet the "demands of the day" ' (SV p. 156). On Weber's account, this devotion to meeting the demands of the day in one's calling leads to a conception of probity as the threefold relation of 'passion, a feeling of responsibility, and a sense of proportion' (PV p. 115). More precisely, this threefold relation consists of a passionate devotion to one's ultimate values, a recognition of the demands of the day in one's vocation, and the sense of distance required to mediate between one's ultimate values and these demands. Although Weber specifies these constituents of probity in relation to the figure of the politician, they are *formal* requirements of the idea of probity as such. This emerges when we consider how these elements of probity exhibit themselves in the spheres of science and politics; we shall treat each of these spheres in turn.

In the sphere of politics, passionate devotion to one's ultimate values is expressed through 'devotion to a "cause, " to the god or demon who is its overlord' (PV p. 115). This alone, however, is not constitutive of probity, 'unless passion as devotion to a "cause" also makes responsibility to this cause the guiding star of action' (PV p. 115) and for this 'a sense of proportion is needed' (PV p. 115). Weber continues:

> This is the decisive psychological quality of the politician: his ability to let realities work upon him with inner concentration and calmness. Hence his *distance* to things and men. 'Lack of distance' *per se* is one of the deadly sins of every politician. For the problem is simply how can warm passion and a cool sense of proportion be forged together in one and the same soul?
>
> (PV p. 115)

Weber's answer is that while passion is necessary as the root of political commitment, this passion can be made responsible 'only through habitation to detachment in every sense of the word' (PV p. 116). Consequently, he concludes that the ' "strength" of a political "personality" means, in the first place, the possession of these qualities of passion, responsibility, and proportion' (PV p. 116).

In the sphere of science, passionate devotion to one's ultimate values expresses itself both in one's conception of science and in the 'evaluative ideas' through which the scientist selects and ranks phenomena in terms of their cultural significance. Again, however, this passion is not enough in itself to constitute probity: 'it is a fact that no amount of enthusiasm, however sincere and profound it may be, can compel a problem to yield scientific results' (SV p. 135). On the contrary, there is needed a feeling of responsibility which manifests itself as a concern with the 'demands of the day', which in the sphere of science means a concern with the great cultural problems of the age. To realise this feeling of responsibility as

129

scientific practice requires the capacity to distance oneself both from the activity of science as a cultural product through methodological reflection and from one's values through the construction of ideal-types in which one's 'evaluative ideas' are given 'objective' form in relation to the cultural problems of the age.

The central point to this discussion though is that the choice of life-sphere determines the structure of probity; the necessity of choosing a life-sphere lies both in the fact that work in a calling is the condition of possibility of exhibiting probity in the conditions of modern culture and in the fact that the criteria of probity – what it is to exhibit probity – in the different life-spheres are irreconcilable. To summarise Weber's ideal, let us recall once more his formal definition of 'personality' as a 'constant and intrinsic relation to certain ultimate "values" and "meanings" of life' (RK p. 152). In the context of our discussion, we can now state that 'personality' in modernity consists in choosing and adhering to 'certain ultimate "values"' *and* choosing and adhering to the form of 'constant and intrinsic relation' one exhibits with respect to these values.[15] At this stage, let us turn to the question of what is required, on Weber's account, to resist the spread of rational discipline.

THE POLITICS OF RESISTANCE

The confrontation here is between rational discipline as that force which changes people 'from without' and charisma which changes people 'from within' (ES p. 1116). In the context of this confrontation, it is useful to recall the following passage:

> Without exception every order of social relations (however constituted) is, if one wishes to *evaluate* it, ultimately to be examined in terms of the human type (*menschlichen Typus*) to which it, by way of external or internal (motivational) selection, provides the optimal chances of becoming the dominant type.
>
> (GAW p. 517, cited in Hennis 1988: 59)

Weber's profoundly pessimistic prognosis for modernity is based on the fact that modern culture is characterised by the increasing dominance of *rational discipline* and this external process of selection provides the 'optimal chances' for the dominant human type of modernity being the fully adjusted men of a bureaucratic age. In contrast, though, Weber's ideal of 'personality' in a calling constructs an internal process of selection which provides the 'optimal chances' for the autonomous individual becoming the dominant type of modernity. In making this claim, we are, of course, positing a relation between the idea of 'personality' in a calling and charisma.[16] This claim seems justified both by the 'heroic' character of 'personality' in a calling (ES p. 1116) and by Weber's comment that charisma 'is the root of the idea of a *calling* in its highest expression' (PV p. 79); however, it may be as well to specify this relation further. This can be done by referring back to Nietzsche's politics.

Nietzsche's politics is constructed about two types of judgement: a judgement of style (probity) which entitles the individual to enter the *agon* of competing values, and a judgement of taste (value) which determines the authority of individuals in terms of their capacity to create a community of judgement which recognises their authority. A similar 'politics' may be said to inform Weber's account with the crucial difference that the criteria of these judgements are distinct in the different life-spheres. In science, one might say that commitment to the norms and obligation immanent to this sphere determines the entitlement of the individual to enter the *agon* of worldviews in this sphere, whereas the judgement of the adequacy of the ideal-typical explanations constructed through their 'evaluative ideas' determines the authority of these 'evaluative ideas', this authority being dependent on the community of judgement they constitute. Again, in politics, it may be stated that commitment to the form assumed by probity in this sphere is the condition of entitlement, whereas the authority of politicians is dependent on the community of judgement they can constitute by virtue of their personal qualities and ideas. To put this in relation to the concept of charisma, the claim being developed here is that 'personality' in a calling is the condition of charismatic authority, but that whether or not charisma is held depends on its ability to create a community of judgement which recognises its authority.[17] In the sphere of science, this charismatic authority is embodied in the 'evaluative ideas' of the scientific genius, while in the sphere of politics, charismatic authority inheres in the personal qualities of the political leader. In so far as Weber's 'political vision' is concerned with preventing the dominance of this external process over the internal process of selection, this can be articulated by attending to Weber's account of the role of the charismatic politician and the charismatic scientist. In both cases, it will become apparent that the role of charisma is to give *direction* to activity within the life-sphere; we shall address each in turn.

The distinctive feature of the charismatic politician is his capacity to ground 'certain ultimate "values" and "meanings" of life' in his person. In contrast to bureaucratic politics in which decision-making is predicated on a utilitarian weighing of material interests, the politician with a calling bases decision-making on a *responsible* commitment to ultimate values. What is involved in this idea of 'value-responsibility' becomes clear with a contrast between the bureaucratic ethic and the 'ethic of ultimate ends'. On the one hand, bureaucratic politics, for Weber, does not involve values; it exhibits itself purely as instrumental rationality (*Zweckrationalität*), that is, as political action totally oriented to means, and this is 'dangerous because it is incompatible with genuine autonomy' (Brubaker 1984: 106).

131

On the other hand, dogmatic conviction politics expresses itself purely as value-rationality (*Wertrationalität*), that is, as political action totally oriented to ultimate ends, and this is dangerous because it does not consider the consequences of action as ethically significant. Weber's rejection of the ethic of instrumentality exemplified by the bureaucrat is predicated on the ground that it is fundamentally antagonistic to the possibility of individual autonomy. His rejection of the ethic of ultimate ends is based on the recognition that it legislates obedience to ultimate values without respect for the conditions under which political activity occurs. The ironic implication of the latter ethic is that, as occurred with Protestantism, unconditioned commitment to ultimate ends may result not in the realisation of these values in the world but, on the contrary, in creating conditions which undermine the possibility of realising these ends. As such, Weber's argument is that *genuine* commitment to ultimate values in modernity entails the attempt to calculate the consequences of one's action for realising these values. In other words, 'the ethic of responsibility can best be understood as an attempt by Weber to integrate *Wertrationalität* and *Zweckrationalität*, the passionate commitment to ultimate values with the dispassionate analysis of alternative means of pursuing them' (Brubaker 1984: 108),[18] this ethic of responsibility, of course, being nothing other than the structure of probity in the political sphere. Now the implication of this point with respect to charismatic politicians is that grounding the authority of certain ultimate values in their person enables them to place the bureaucratic apparatus in the service of ultimate values. In fact, the relation between bureaucracy (instrumental administration) and politics (the struggle of values) in modernity mirrors the ethic of responsibility embodied by the charismatic leader. By placing bureaucracy in the service of ultimate values, the charismatic politician restricts it to the consideration of means, that is, the calculation of the consequences of various courses of action, and thereby enables resistance to the spread of rational discipline over social life.[19] There is *pathos* to this position that Weber takes up in his recognition that, while rational discipline is inherently durable, charisma is inherently unstable. Charismatic political leaders are holders of charisma only in so far as they can continually constitute and reconstitute a community of judgement which recognises their authority:

> Charisma knows only inner determination and inner constraint. The holder of charisma seizes the task that is adequate for him and demands obedience and a following by virtue of his mission. His success determines whether he finds them. His charismatic claim breaks down if his mission is not recognised by those to whom he feels he has been sent. If they recognise him, he is their master – so long as he knows how to maintain recognition through 'proving' himself.
>
> (FMW p. 246)

Again: 'The charismatic leader gains and maintains authority solely by proving his strength in life' (FMW p. 249). Given that Weber's central question in its most pronounced political mode is how to preserve the possibility of individual autonomy, the opposition of discipline as a persistent social force and charisma as an unstable social force requires an account of how Weber's ethic of responsibility as the condition of political charisma in modernity is to be entrenched. For the moment, however, let us turn to the other side of resistance to rational discipline, that is, the charismatic scientist.

At first sight, the very idea of connecting science and charisma might seem a contradiction in terms in that science is a specifically disenchanting power and charisma, if nothing else, is power grounded on enchantment. It must, after all, be emphasised that science, on Weber's account, 'cannot tell anyone what he *should* do', that is, the question as to whether a person should adhere to certain ultimate values rather than others 'involves will and conscience, not empirical knowledge' (MSS p. 54). The role of science is to tell the individual 'what he *can* do – and under certain circumstances – what he wishes to do' (MSS p. 54). To address this question, let us begin by distinguishing the scientist with a calling from the 'technician'.[20] The characteristic of the technician is to provide knowledge based on the means-end schema of science of how to achieve interests, that is to say that the perspective from which the technician interrogates reality is one constructed purely in relation to creating instrumental knowledge through the determination of causal laws. We can approach the distinction between this technical ethos and the ethos of the scientist with a calling by asking why Weber insists that cultural science must operate both in terms of causal explanation and in terms of interpretive understanding. The crucial point here is that, in so far as human behaviour is governed by material and ideal interests, it is susceptible to causal explanation, while in so far as this behaviour is constitutive of material and ideal interests, it requires interpretive understanding. Technical science, however, in so far as it is purely concerned with generating knowledge concerning the means by which interests may be achieved is also implicitly characterised by a conception of the individual as purely a 'thing' whose being is *essentially* determined. In this respect, the technician is the correlate of, and partner of, the bureaucrat. Whereas bureaucratic politics reduces the individual to an instrument at the level of practice, technical science reduces the individual to an instrument at the level of theory. As such, this science manifests an 'elective affinity' with rational discipline in that, ironically, it is only with the total dominance of rational discipline that this science can achieve its immanent interest in explanatory totality.[21] The correlate of the bureaucratic *ethic* of instrumentality is thus a scientific *thesis* of determinacy. We should note here that there is also a correlate to the political ethic of ultimate ends in a scientific thesis of freedom. This emerges if we consider that this type of ethic implicitly (or, indeed, perhaps explicitly) is concerned with human behaviour purely as constitutive of material and ideal interests and, at least implicitly, defines the individual purely as an 'end' whose being is *essentially* free. This leads to a science which is purely concerned with the interpretive understanding of human action, that is, with clarifying the meaning of a person's action, and whose knowledge, like the acts performed under the ethic of ultimate ends, consequently 'can and shall have only exemplary value' (PV p. 121), in other words, a science whose impotence from the standpoint of generating knowledge about how to achieve ends directly correlates to a politics unconcerned with consequences. In contrast to both these types of science stands the scientist with a calling, the political ethic of responsibility finding its correlate in the scientific thesis that human behaviour is both governed by, and constitutive of, ideal and material interests. The central feature of this science is that it can force, or at least help, the individual 'to give himself an *account of the ultimate meaning of his own conduct*' (SV p. 152), where this consists in specifying the *means* by which a goal in a given life-sphere may be achieved and the *meaning* of using such and such a means for the individual given his commitment to both a particular life-sphere and certain ultimate values. In relation to politics, this means that science can tell the politician the means by which a given practical end may be realised and the meaning that this conduct will have for him in the respect of the form and substance of his political commitment. To put this in slightly clearer terms, science may be said to specify the conditions of meaningful action in a life-sphere at both institutional and individual levels. This, however, is nothing other than the meaning of probity in the scientific sphere. How does this relate to charisma?

It was argued earlier that having a calling is the condition of charisma, although whether a scientific account based on certain 'evaluative' ideas is charismatic or not depends on its capacity to constitute a community of judgement which acknowledges its authority. In the light of this, consider the following remark:

> the values to which the scientific genius relates the object of his inquiry may determine, i.e., decide the 'conception' of a whole epoch, not only concerning what is 'valuable' but also concerning what is significant or insignificant, 'important' or 'unimportant' in the phenomena.
>
> (MSS p. 82)

The suggestion to be developed here is that the scientific genius is the correlate of the charismatic politician – but in what sense? Let us re-emphasise that science, for Weber, cannot tell the individual what he should do; rather science tells the individual what he can do by specifying the conditions of meaningful action. The important point at this juncture is to note that this specification of the conditions of meaningful action is grounded in the determination of what aspect of a phenomenon (e.g. science or politics) is significant, 'valuable' or 'important' and this is dependent on the 'the values to which the scientific genius relates the object of his inquiry', that is, the scientist's ultimate values. This is manifestly so with regard to Weber's own cultural science at the level both of methodological reflection and of concrete analysis, as Löwith has astutely noted, in that

> the ultimate assumption inherent in Weber's 'individualistic' definition of so-called social 'structures' is this: that today only the 'individual', the self-sufficient single person, is true and real and entitled to existence, because objectivities of all kinds have been demystified (through rationalisation) and no longer have any independent meaning.
>
> (Löwith 1982: 39)

It is precisely this inherent assumption which emerges in Weber's conception of 'personality' and which generates his concern with specifying the conditions of 'personality' in relation to the disenchantment of modern culture. Let us be clear what is at stake here: whereas the charismatic politician *legislates* values, the charismatic scientist *legislates* the conditions of meaningful action. In both cases, the force of this legislation depends on creating and maintaining a community of judgement which accepts this legislation. Again, moreover, there is a *pathos* in Weber's position in that again this charismatic authority is unstable in that science is chained to the course of 'progress', the light of the great cultural problems moves on, and the capacity of particular 'evaluative ideas' to generate accounts of the conditions of meaningful conduct which sustain its authority is necessarily surpassed. In this context, given that scientific charisma is dependent on what we may call the scientific ethic of probity (in that this science specifies the criteria of probity in the different life-spheres), Weber's question must be how to ground this in modern culture.

In this section, we have noted Weber's concern with resisting the 'dialectic of domination' formed by the elective affinity of bureaucratic politics and technical science, and expressed as rational discipline. This concern finds voice in the 'dialectic of resistance' constituted by the elective affinity of *responsible* science and politics in their charismatic forms, although the ambivalences inherent in this responsibility entail that it can only be resistance to, and not abolition of, rational discipline. Weber's problem given the instability of charismatic authority is how to entrench the ethic of responsibility in the sphere of politics and the ethic of probity in the sphere of science in so far as these describe the conditions of emergence of charisma.

AMBIVALENT ETHICS: SCIENCE AND POLITICS
AS VOCATIONS

There is, perhaps, a certain 'Machiavellianism' to Weber's strategy in the essays on science and politics as vocations. On the one hand, there is a certain similarity between Weber's essays and Machiavelli's *The Prince* in that both authors can be seen as specifying what is involved in following a particular calling, that is, what the conditions of meaningful action within these callings are.[22] Moreover, Weber's acerbic comments on the ethic of ultimate ends subverts Kantian ethics in a way reminiscent of Machiavelli's deliberate reversals of Renaissance conceptions of virtue. However, the significant point for our concern lies in Machiavelli's duplicitous strategy of writing. In *The Prince*, Machiavelli's strategy consists in providing cogent reasons (honour and glory) for the prince to adopt a particular form of behaviour, yet the goal to which the text is directed is not the honour and glory of the prince but the effects of this mode of behaviour. Given that the effects which Machiavelli is attempting to produce are the creation of political stability and the unification of Italy as the conditions in which civic *virtù* and, thereby, a republic may develop, his 'guide to princes' is profoundly ironic. Weber's essays on science and politics may be read as deploying a variation of this strategy in that they provide cogent reasons ('personality') for adopting particular types of behaviour within these life-spheres, yet the goals to which the essays are directed are as much the effects of this type of behaviour as the scientist and politician as exemplars of the ideal of 'personality'. To explore this approach to the vocations essays, we can take each up in turn.

In 'Science as a Vocation', Weber begins by delineating the external conditions of scientific activity, notably, specialisation; it soon becomes clear though that his major concern is the internal meaning of science as a vocation. This topic takes on a tragic dimension in two respects: firstly, science, unlike art, is chained to the course of progress, it asks to be 'surpassed and outdated' (SV p. 138), and, secondly, science can give us no answer to the question of how we should live, it is 'objectively' meaningless (SV p. 143). However, science 'can force the individual, or at least we can help him, to give himself an *account of the ultimate meaning of his own conduct*' (SV p. 152). Weber summarises this conception of the vocation of science in all its tragic *pathos* in the following comments:

> Science today is a 'vocation' organised in special disciplines in the service of self-clarification and knowledge of interrelated facts. It is not the gift of grace of seers and prophets dispensing sacred values and revelations, nor does it partake of the contemplation of sages and philosophers about the meaning of the universe. This, to be sure, is the inescapable condition of our historical situation. We cannot evade so long as we remain true to ourselves.
> (SV p. 152)

We can describe this as presenting an ethic of probity in that it appears that the calling of science is to specify the structures of probity (including its own) which govern meaningful activity within the life-spheres (Weber's vocation essays themselves exemplify this calling); it is this formal specification of the structure of probity in a given life-sphere which enables science, in its charismatic mode, to force or help the individual committed to this life-sphere and certain ultimate values to clarify '*the ultimate meaning of his own conduct*' (SV p. 152). In other words, the scientist as a teacher exhibits 'intellectual integrity' (*intellektuelle Redlichkeit*) in specifying the formal conditions of meaningful action in the different life-spheres, which is nothing other than a *legislation* of the distinct structures of probity entailed within these different life-spheres. Moreover, in so far as this necessarily requires both causal explanation (knowledge of interrelated facts) and interpretive understanding (self-clarification), this calling exhibits a tragic *pathos* of which Weber was only too cognisant, namely, that while science as interpretive understanding posits the individual as an end, science as causal explanation posits the individual as a means. In other words, while science forces, or helps, the individual to gain clarity about the meaning of his life, it is also a specifically disenchanting power.

The fundamental ambivalence of this ethic of probity, however, emerges in relation to the duty of clarifying the meaning of individuals' conduct to them: 'we can force the individual, or at least we can help him, . . .' (SV p. 152). In other words, this task has the form of an imperative for the scientist; to constitute himself as an autonomous individual, as a 'personality', the scientist must 'force, or at least help, [the individual] to give himself an *account of the ultimate meaning of his own conduct*' (SV p. 152). This is precisely reminiscent of the task of Nietzsche's world-historical *Übermensch* with all the ambivalence that figure entailed; however, there is a crucial difference. The legislation of the *Übermensch* is grounded in an unlimited economy of violence, whereas the legislation of the scientist is grounded in *charisma*, that is, the capacity of the scientist to constitute a community of judgement which accepts the authority of this legislation, and this is constituted by the capacity of a scientist's 'legislation' to enable individuals to constitute themselves as autonomous individuals, a capacity which manifests itself in the figure of the scientist as an exemplar. Weber does not resolve the ambivalences endemic to Nietzsche's politics here; rather, the legislative and exemplary moments of Nietzsche's position are fused. The scientist as redeeming legislator is inextricably tied to the scientist as exemplar of 'personality'.

What then of 'Politics as a Vocation'? Again Weber begins by delineating the external conditions of politics before moving to the question of the internal conditions of meaningful activity in the sphere of politics, these conditions (i.e. the structure of political probity) being nothing other than the ethic of responsibility; it is by acting in accordance with this ethic that the politician constitutes himself as a 'personality'. How does this form of conduct manifest itself? Through the value-rational selection of political ends and the instrumentally rational selection of means. The tragic *pathos* of this ethic is that while it is oriented to realising values, that is, preserving the possibility of individual autonomy, to realise this requires treating individuals as means towards political ends. This pathos emerges at another level in Weber's recognition that while politics is concerned with resisting the spread of rational discipline, bureaucracy is indispensable to modern mass democracy; this is the fate of modernity. The fundamental ambivalence of this ethic, however, emerges in relation to the preservation of human freedom being articulated through the legislation of certain ultimate values. This is apparent if we consider that a condition of 'personality' is choosing one's own ultimate values, yet the political leader can only preserve the possibility of individual autonomy by imposing her ultimate values on cultural life. Again, however, it must be noted that the capacity of the politician to legislate these values is grounded in charisma, where this charisma is dependent on the capacity of the politician to constitute a community of judgement which accepts her authority and this capacity is ultimately grounded in the probity of the politician. In other words, we find again that the figure of the politician as redeeming legislator is tied to the politician as exemplar of 'personality'.

These ambivalences inherent in these ethics, however, do not exhaust the ambivalence of Weber's position. Indeed, the constitutive ambivalence of this position only emerges when we read these essays together with respect to the question of entrenchment.[23] We can begin by noting that, for Weber, the effect of the charismatic politician is to create the *external* conditions of possibility of individual autonomy, while the effect of the charismatic scientist is to create the *internal* conditions of possibility of individual autonomy. The implication of this is that the charismatic scientist is the means by which the political ethic of responsibility is entrenched, while the charismatic politician is the means by which the scientific ethic of probity is rendered possible. In other words, the figures of the scientist and the politician are bound to each other as the condition of constituting the autonomous individual as the dominant type in modern culture. Yet the political 'personality' from the perspective of the scientist is both a means and an end: on the one hand, legislating the ethic of responsibility in the political sphere is one of the means by which the scientist constitutes his own 'personality', and, on the other hand, the charismatic politician is an end in so far as this politician constitutes the external conditions of possibility of 'personality' as such. Similarly, the scientific 'personality' is both a means and an end from the perspective of the politician: on the one hand, preserving the possibility of scientific 'personality' is one of the means by which the politician constitutes his own 'personality', and, on the other hand, the charismatic scientist is an end in so far as this science constitutes the internal conditions of possibility of 'personality' as such. In other words, the possibility of individual autonomy in the sphere of science is dependent on the possibility of individual autonomy in the sphere of politics and *vice versa*, yet while these types of 'personality' are necessary to each other, they conceive of each other not purely as ends but as both means and ends. This ambivalence inhabits the heart of Weber's cultural science and is ultimately its fate.

CONCLUSION: THE AUTHORITY OF WEBER

We can conclude our examination of Weber by noting that his transformation of Nietzsche's project abandons the utopian moment within the enterprise of critique but reproduces in heightened form the ambivalences which plagued Nietzsche's politics. Given these ambivalences, with what authority does Weber's critique of modernity speak?

As with Nietzsche, this question is necessarily preceded by the question of relevance. This is, of course, explicitly recognised by Weber in that the condition of his authority is that *his* questions remain *our* questions, that the light of the great cultural problems has not moved on. Weber's authority itself is based on the *charisma* of his tortured reflections on the fate of the individual in modern culture, that is, the capacity of these reflections to bring into being a community of judgement which recognises their authority. Weber, in other words, is prepared to enter the scientific *agon*. The dilemma which attends the legitimation of this thought is that its ambivalence manifests itself in a politics in which exemplification and legislation are inextricably entwined. Weber's legacy is thus marked by his attempt to enable individuals to heroically confront the disenchantment of the modern world, where the tragic fate of this thought is that it cannot create the conditions of its own realisation. In other words, the fulfilment of Weber's concern with making the autonomous individual the dominant type of modern culture requires both a science and a politics, yet Weber in taking up the role of the scientist can do no other than exclude himself from the political arena.[24]

8

GENEALOGY AS HISTORICAL ONTOLOGY
Foucault, methodology and critique

> Let us imagine that the *Berlinische Monatschrift* still exists and that it
> is asking its readers the question: What is modern philosophy?
> Perhaps one could respond with an echo: modern philosophy is the
> philosophy that is attempting to answer the question raised so
> imprudently two centuries ago: *Was ist Aufklärung?*
>
> (FR p. 32)

Michel Foucault's location of his theoretical trajectory within a form of
reflection which runs from 'Hegel through Nietzsche or Max Weber to
Horkheimer or Habermas' (FR p. 32)[1] as a thinking of the question 'What
is Enlightenment?' provides a site of entry into his work in so far as it raises
a series of questions: What is the character of this form of reflection? How
does Foucault's elaboration of this mode of thinking differ from that of
the philosophers he refers to in making this claim? How is this form of
reflection to be methodologically articulated? In what sense is this mode
of thinking critical? It is these questions which define the tasks of this
chapter as an attempt to identify and situate the philosophical *ethos* and
methodological apparatus which exhibits itself in Foucault's work. To
begin then, let us reflect on Foucault's general characterisation of this
form of reflection within which he locates his own enterprise.

ENLIGHTENMENT, HUMANISM, MODERNITY

We may initiate discussion of this topic by referring to Foucault's reading
of Kant's essay 'Answering the Question: What is Enlightenment?' as 'a
reflection by Kant on the contemporary status of his own enterprise' (FR
p. 38).[2] The significance of this text for Foucault is that it introduces a
mode of thinking the present as 'neither a world era to which one belongs,
nor an event whose signs are perceived, nor the dawning of an
accomplishment' (FR p. 34) but, rather, as a 'reflection on "today" as
difference in history and as a motive for a particular philosphical task' (FR
p. 38).[3] The philosophical task which is motivated by this reflection, on

140

Foucault's reading, is a 'critical ontology of ourselves', that is, an investigation of how we have become what we are today which both discloses the limits of what we are and raises the possibility of being otherwise than we are.

At this juncture, before elaborating on Foucault's conception of this form of reflection, let us pause to reflect on the figures in relation to whom Foucault situates himself with respect to this mode of thinking, namely, Hegel, Nietzsche, Weber and the Frankfurt School.[4] Recalling the reading of Kant's essay on enlightenment which opened this text, we may briefly highlight two points: firstly, Kant's emphasis on our *construction* of ourselves as autonomous agents and, secondly, Kant's identification of autonomy and morality. With this in mind, we may suggest, no doubt as an oversimplification, that there is a certain bifurcation to be located here with respect to reflection on the question 'What is Enlightenment?' which exhibits itself as the opposition between *dialectical* and *agonistic* styles of reasoning. On the one hand, we may note that in re-interpreting Kant's position concerning maturity as our construction of ourselves as autonomous agents through critical reason, the Hegelian trajectory elaborates the theme of morality in seeking to give positive content to the formalism which manifests itself in Kant's thought.[5] On the other hand, the Nietzschean trajectory articulates the relationship between critical reason and autonomy through a focus on the theme of self-construction.[6] The critical movement from *Moralität* to *Sittlichkeit* in Hegel and from autonomy as moral to autonomy as extra-moral in Nietzsche denotes the initial divergence of these trajectories in their relation to Kant's thought. Expanding on this suggestion, we may note that the Hegelian project becomes that of clarifying grounds for identifying and promoting the ethical basis of human community through the elaboration of normative criteria of judgement with respect to action, while the Nietzschean project recognises 'the possibility that action cannot be grounded in universal, ahistorical theories of the individual subject . . . or in the conditions of community and speaking, and that in fact such attempts promote what all parties agree is most troubling in our current situation' (Dreyfus and Rabinow 1986: 118). The *raison d'être* of these tentative reflections is not simply to legitimate the reading of Foucault in relation to Nietzsche and Weber in which this text engages, but to provide a context within which both Foucault's articulation of the project of a critical ontology of the present and the critical reactions to the form of this articulation (specifically those of Habermas) become intelligible.[7] With these comments in mind, then, let us return to Foucault's essay on enlightenment.

The significance of Kant's inauguration of thinking of the present as difference in history, for Foucault, lies in its status as the locus of emergence of an *ethos* which Foucault locates as constitutive of our modernity. Modernity, in other words, is not an epochal concept in this instance but rather a specific 'mode of relating to contemporary reality' (FR p. 39). To flesh out this *ethos*, Foucault refers to the 'almost indispensable' figure of Baudelaire.[8] There are two aspects of Baudelaire's consciousness of modernity which Foucault highlights in delineating the *ethos* which emerges with the question of enlightenment. Firstly, there is a will to 'heroize' the present. For Baudelaire, on Foucault's reading, being modern does not merely consist in recognising our consciousness of modernity as ' "the ephemeral, the fleeting, the contingent" ' but 'in adopting a certain attitude with respect to this movement' which 'consists in recapturing something eternal that is not beyond the present instant, nor behind it, but within it' (FR p. 39). Modernity is that *ethos* which grasps the 'heroic' aspect of the present. There is, however, a second element of this *ethos* which is that of irony:

> The attitude of modernity does not treat the passing moment as sacred in order to try to maintain or perpetuate it. . . . For the attitude of modernity, the high value of the present is indissociable from a desperate eagerness to imagine it, to imagine it otherwise than it is, and to transform it not by destroying it but by grasping it in what it is.
>
> (FR pp. 40–1)

Within the *ethos* of modernity, the will to 'heroize' is ironic in its recognition of the contingency of the present which it 'heroizes' and in its desire to transfigure this present through 'the practice of a liberty which simultaneously respects this reality and violates it' (FR p. 40). However, in so far as our modernity is constituted by this ironic heroization of the present, this entails a certain *rapport à soi* – it is here that Foucault's relationship to the Nietzschean perspective clearly emerges – in which one does not simply 'accept oneself as in the flux of the passing moments' but takes oneself 'as [the] object of a complex and difficult elaboration' (FR p. 41):

> Modern man, for Baudelaire, is not the man who goes off to discover himself, his secrets and his hidden truth; he is the man who tries to invent himself. This modernity does not 'liberate man in his own being'; it compels him to face the task of producing himself.
>
> (FR p. 42)

In further echoes of Nietzsche, one's modernity consists in making oneself a work of art.[9]

In this essay, then, Foucault connects Kant's thinking of the question of enlightenment with the emergence of an *ethos* which finds its elaboration in Baudelaire. What though does this signify? For Foucault's own reflections on the question '*Was ist Aufklärung?*', the significance of this connection appears to be the idea that the thread which connects us to the enlightenment 'is not faithfulness to its doctrinal elements, but rather the permanent reactivation of an attitude – that is, of a philo-sophical ethos that could be described as a permanent critique of our historical era' (FR p. 42).[10] The implications of this claim are twofold, attending to the topic of humanism and that of critique. Firstly, to think of enlightenment in terms of a mode of reflective relation to the present establishes a certain disjunction between enlightenment and humanism in so far as the latter 'serves to color and to justify the conceptions of man to which it is, after all, obliged to take recourse', while the former denotes 'the principle of a critique and a permanent creation of ourselves in our autonomy' (FR p. 44).[11] From this perspective, as Foucault notes, the relationship between enlightenment and humanism is one of 'tension rather than identity' (FR p. 44). Secondly, the principle of critique which discloses itself within this philosophical ethos is that of a *limit-attitude*, an analysis and reflection on limits. The liminal thinking[12] which operates, however, marks a departure from that exhibited in Kant's critical philosophy:

> if the Kantian question was that of knowing the limits knowledge has to renounce transgressing, it seems to me that the critical question today has to be turned back into a positive one: in what is given to us as universal, necessary, obligatory, what place is occupied by whatever is singular, contingent, and the product of arbitrary constraints? The point, in brief, is to transform the critique conducted in the form of a necessary limitation into a practical critique that takes the form of a possible transgression.
>
> (FR p. 45)

From the twofold nature of the claim that enlightenment may be located as a philosophical *ethos*, there consequently arises the twofold task of elaborating an anti-humanist methodology which is capable both of accounting for how we have become what we are and of operating as a form of practical critique. To explore the form of Foucault's thought in relation to these tasks without imposing an artifical unity on his texts requires that we begin by tracing the development of his reflections on method attending to the question of whether these reflections exemplify the philosophical *ethos* he elaborates as a coherent and cogent project of critical reason.

IRONIC HEROIZATION AS ARCHAEOLOGICAL DETACHMENT

The initial methodology developed by Foucault is presented under the name of 'archaeology' and articulated through the concept of the *episteme*. To delineate the dimensions and limitations of this project, we can begin by specifying the task of archaeology as the attempt to disclose 'a *positive unconscious* of knowledge: a level which eludes the consciousness of the scientist and yet is part of scientific discourse' (OT p. xi).[13] Foucault's concern is with isolating 'rules of formation, which were never articulated in their own right, but are to be found only in widely different theories, concepts, and objects of study' (OT p. xi). This task is clarified further by Foucault's outlining of the concept of the *episteme*:

> what I am trying to bring to light is the epistemological field, the *episteme*, in which knowledge, envisaged apart from all criteria having reference to its rational value or to its objective forms, grounds its positivity and thereby manifest a history which is not that of its growing perfection, but rather that of its conditions of possibility; in this account, what should appear are those configurations of knowledge which have given rise to the diverse forms of empirical science.
>
> (OT p. xxii)

As an archaeologist, Foucault's concern is to uncover the 'rules of formation' which govern particular configurations of knowledge and to highlight the epistemological breaks which mark the movement from one *episteme* to another.[14] It is this second archaeological concern which led to the simplistic description of Foucault as 'a philosopher who founds his theory of history on discontinuity' (FR pp. 53–4).[15] What is clear, however, is that the archaeological gaze is one of detachment; in focusing on discourses at the level of rules of formation, Foucault not only dispenses with the transcendental subject but, further, engages in a bracketing of questions of truth and meaning. An *episteme* thus denotes a regime governing the realm of what may be intelligibly spoken; it is not here a question of the truth or falsity of a statement but of whether a statement enters the realm of being 'up for grabs' as true or false.[16] In the Kantian terms deployed by Foucault, an *episteme* is the 'historical *a priori*' (OT p. xxii) on the basis of which certain forms of knowledge become possible.

In reflecting on this archaeological project, however, we may note that while Foucault deploys the language on a non-transcendental Kantianism, it may be more appropriate to explore a parallel with Nietzsche's thought. In this context, consider the following quotation:

> That individual philosophical concepts are not something arbitrary, something growing up autonomously, but on the contrary grow up connected and related to one another; that, however suddenly and arbitrarily they appear to emerge in the history of thought, they nonetheless belong just as much together as do the members of the fauna of a continent: that fact is in the end also shown in the fact that the most diverse philosophies unfailing fill out again and again a certain basic scheme of possible philosophies.
>
> (BGE 20 p. 32)

144

To explain (and justify) this claim, Nietzsche refers to consciousness as governed by 'the unconscious domination' of grammatical functions as opening up certain possibilities of knowledge while 'the road seems barred to certain other possibilities of world interpretation' (BGE 20 p. 32). Reading Foucault's archaeological project through this parallel, we may suggest that an *episteme* denotes the 'grammatical rules' governing the formation of 'scientific' statements. The felicitude of this analogy is that it raises a series of questions with respect to the adequacy of archaeology as methodology and critique: What is the status of this epistemological grammar? How are transformations of this grammar to be accounted for? In what sense is archaeology critical?

This topic can be explored by returning to the concept of the *episteme* in relation to the question of how the archaeologist uncovers the rules of epistemological grammar. Foucault provides an outline of this aspect of his methodology in defining the concept of the *episteme* as

> the total set of relations that unite, at a given period, the discursive practices that give rise to epistemological figures, sciences, and possibly formalised systems. . . . The episteme is not a form of knowledge or type of rationality, which, crossing the boundaries of the most varied sciences, manifests the sovereign unity of a subject, a spirit or a period; *it is the totality of relations that can be discovered, for a given period, between the sciences when one analyses them at the level of discursive regularities*.
>
> (AK p. 191, my emphasis)

The concept of the *episteme* disclosed in this passage, when read with the earlier outlines of this concept as 'historical *a priori*' and 'rules of epistemological grammar', reveals an ambivalence within Foucault's archaeological method concerning the status of the *episteme*, namely, whether this concept is descriptive or prescriptive. We can specify this ambivalence further by noting that the central issue is whether the grammar of epistemological discourses is *constituted* by these discourses or is *constitutive* of these discourses. On the one hand, it is clear that Foucault locates an *episteme* as grounding configurations of positive knowledge in the sense of *governing* the formation of epistemological statements. On the other hand, in so far as Foucault (unlike Nietzsche) treats discourse as *autonomous*, he cannot locate the formation of rules of epistemological grammar in non-discursive practices but, rather, must attempt to show how these rules are simultaneously constituted by, and constitutive of, discourse. As Dreyfus and Rabinow have acutely indicated, this attempt 'to pass from an *analysis* of positivities into elements to an *analytic* providing the ground of the possibility of its own method and its objects' reproduces the ambivalent relationship between the empirical and the transcendental which characterises humanist discourse (Dreyfus and Rabinow 1983: 92). At this juncture, however, let us merely note that the dilemma which attends Foucault's archaeological method is that, in treating discourses as autonomous, it is incapable of accounting for its own conditions of possibility. In other words, while archaeology eludes the 'anthropological sleep' of humanism by dispensing with the transcendental subject, it reproduces an ambivalence which is isomorphic with that endemic to humanist discourse.

The question remains, however, of the critical character of archaeology in the sense that if we were to treat the concept of *episteme* as purely descriptive (and thereby bracket the problems attendant to Foucault's treatment of discourse as autonomous), wherein would its critical force lie? The point that this query raises for us is to suggest that, while a descriptive analysis may indicate aporias and ambivalences, this analysis can only endow itself with critical force relative to discourses in a given period if it can constitute itself as an analytic, that is, if it can show that these aporias and ambivalences are *necessarily* endemic to these discourses. As a purely descriptive concept, however, the methodological construct of *episteme* is incapable of fulfilling this critical function.[17]

We can conclude this section by turning to a final topic, namely that of the *politics* of archaeology. This issue becomes significant because there is an important sense in which archaeology does embody the ethos of ironic heroization which Foucault locates as constitutive of our modernity. The archaeological gaze, through the concept of *episteme*, constructs ironic monuments, monuments whose totality is only visible at a distance and whose irony lies in this distance in the sense that it is only when we are beyond a given *episteme* that it becomes possible for us to analyse it. In other words, we are always already within an *episteme* whose rules we cannot know and whose boundaries we cannot escape. As such the ironic heroization exhibited by archaeology is not that of Baudelaire which impels us to transfigure our present but, rather, that which paralyses as the heroic always already retreats into the distance and irony becomes impotence. As Habermas appropriately comments:

> Under the *stoic* gaze of the archaeologist, history hardens into an iceberg covered with the crystalline forms of arbitrary formations of discourses.
>
> (Habermas 1987: 253)[18]

IRONIC HEROIZATION AS GENEALOGICAL ENGAGEMENT

Foucault's movement from an archaeological method to a genealogical mode of accounting may be read as addressing the ambivalence which the concept of *episteme* exemplified through an abandoning of the methodological commitment to the autonomy of discourse. This shift is signalled by Foucault's deployment of the concept of *dispositif* whose relationship to that of *episteme* is characterised as follows:

> what I call an apparatus [*dispositif*] is a much more general case of the *episteme*; or rather, that the *episteme* is a specifically discursive apparatus, whereas the apparatus in general form is both discursive and non-discursive, its elements being more heterogeneous.
>
> (P/K p. 197)

To clarify the project of genealogy and the philosophical character of the concept of *dispositif*, we can turn initially to Foucault's reflections on a genealogical approach to history in the essay 'Nietzsche, Genealogy, History' before addressing the issue of the methodological and critical adequacy of Foucault's formulations. In approaching this essay, it is not my concern to examine its fidelity to Nietzsche's texts[19] nor to treat it as a masked self-reflection on the part of Foucault; rather, I want simply to highlight those points which Foucault recognises as characterising genealogy and to take these as signposts guiding the analysis of Foucault's own position.

In examining Nietzsche's notion of genealogy, Foucault attempts to specify the difference of genealogy as a method through a double opposition – to metaphysics and to traditional history – which reveals the philosophical and methodological character of genealogy. In distinguishing genealogy from metaphysics, Foucault stresses a conception of metaphysics based on a commitment to the pursuit of the origin,[20] the features of the idea of the origin outlined being those of an atemporal essence, a unitary perfection, and a site of truth as the correspondence of words and things. Concomitantly, genealogy as a challenge to the metaphysics of the origin defines itself in terms of a historical anti-essentialism which exhibits itself as an ironic dispersal and as a scepticism towards (the authority of) truth (FR pp. 78–9).[21] To put this in terms we have used in discussing Nietzsche and Weber, it appears that genealogy denotes the calling into question of the will to truth. Consequently, a central task of genealogy in accounting for its own conditions of possibility is to generate an account of how it is that the will to truth becomes conscious of itself as a problem. Before returning to this issue, however, let us examine the other dimension of genealogy's oppositional identification of itself.

The opposition of genealogy as 'effective history' (*wirkliche Historie*) to 'traditional history' is predicated on an identification of traditional history as infused with metaphysical assumptions, namely, the idea of the transcendental subject and the correspondence theory of truth, which exhibit themselves as the claim to a suprahistorical perspective. By contrast to this traditional history, the anti-foundational stance of genealogy entails dispensing with the idea of the transcendental subject and the correspondence theory of truth (at least in its metaphysical form),[22] and, concomitantly, eschews the very idea of a suprahistorical perspective. This eschewal has both methodological and critical consequences. Firstly, it entails a reformulation of the relationship between proximity and distance:

> It reverses the surreptious practice of historians, their pretension to examine things furthest from themselves, the groveling manner in which they approach this promising distance (like the meta-physicians who proclaim the existence of an afterlife, situated at a distance from this world, as a promise of their reward). Effective history studies what is closest, but in an abrupt dispossession, so as to seize it at a distance (an approach similar to that of the doctor who looks closely, who plunges to make a diagnosis and to state its difference).
>
> (FR pp. 89–90)

Genealogy is thus 'reflection on "today" as difference in history' (FR p. 38). The second consequence of the eschewal of the claim to a suprahistorical perspective is that genealogy 'refuses the certainty of absolutes' and, thereby, deprives us of the forces of reassurance offered by 'an apocalyptic objectivity' (FR p. 87); it acknowledges the contingency of what we are and 'confirms our existence among countless lost events' (FR p. 89). In this dimension of its self-definition, genealogy situates itself as a product of the historical process it is engaged in investigating; its perspectives are immanent to the historical process and acknowledge their interested character.

Summarising the issues highlighted by Foucault, we can identify genealogy as a mode of intellectual inquiry which exhibits the following features: a dispensing with the idea of the transcendental subject, a scepticism towards (the authority of) truth, a commitment to investigating the constitution of the present as difference in history, an ironic eschewal of absolutes, and an acknowledgement of interestedness of knowledge. Concomitant wth this outline of genealogy is the construction of two tasks immanent to genealogy: firstly, a methodological bracketing of 'truth' and a historical account of how the will to truth is constituted as a problem, and, secondly, a methodological bracketing of the 'transcendental subject' and a historical account of how this idea is constituted. Taking this outline and these tasks, let us return to Foucault's conception of genealogy as historical ontology and his concept of *dispositif*.

We may note initially that the concept of *dispositif*, like that of *episteme*, dispenses with the transcendental subject and concerns itself with the discursive and non-discursive practices constitutive of subjectivity, that is, with what we have referred to as *structures of recognition*. Foucault's recognition of this dimension of his own conception of genealogy is quite explicit:

One has to dispense with the constituent subject, to get rid of the subject itself, that's to say, to arrive an analysis which can account for the constitution of the subject within a historical framework.

(FR p. 59)

Again like the *episteme*, the *dispositif* also brackets the question of 'truth', yet the form of this bracketing is distinct in so far as archaeology's focus of discourse entailed a methodological avoidance of both the non-discursive practices which inform the constitution of an epistemological grammar and the practices which such a grammar makes possible. It is with this inclusion of the non-discursive that Foucault raises, initially, the question of power and, latterly, the question of ethics as these relate to the politics of truth (by which Foucault is referring to the ways in which a 'regime of truth' operates in the constitution of subjectivity). We will return to the adequacy of this methodology in a later section; for the moment, however, it is useful to note the shift in the philosophical character of Foucault's central methodological constructions.

The point to be indicated in this shift from *episteme* to *dispositif*, which is marked by Foucault's movement from a quasi-Kantian to Nietzschean vocabulary, is the commitment to a perspectival conception of knowledge in which a given *dispositif* acknowledges its own interested character, its 'system of injustice' (FR p. 90). As such, the *dispositif* – which Dreyfus and Rabinow have noted may be usefully translated as 'grid of intelligibility' (Dreyfus and Rabinow 1983: 121) – displays the philosophical character which Karl Löwith ascribed to Weber's idea of the ideal-type, namely, that 'it lays open reality while at the same time constructing it' (Löwith 1982: 62 fn. 36). Like the ideal-type, the concept of *dispositif* seeks to render intelligible a heterogeneous complex of practices through isolating and abstracting the *significant* relationships within this complex, where the assignation of significance is governed by the interest of the genealogical account.[23] We shall see the operation of such a construct in Foucault's notion of 'biopolitics'; at this juncture though we may simply note that the concept of *dispositif* denotes a twofold departure from Foucault's archaeological method: firstly, the inclusion of the non-discursive and, secondly, the movement to perspectivism. What are the implications of this for Foucault's method as an exemplification of the ethos of ironic heroization which marks the attitude of modernity?

Contrasting genealogy to archaeology, we can note the transformation attendant on this ethos in that whereas the concept of *episteme* entailed that one could not formulate the epistemic grammar of one's present, the concept of *dispositif* locates the formulation of the significant relationships of the discursive and non-discursive practices constitutive of the present as articulated through interests which are precisely those of the present (namely, what Weber would refer to as the great cultural problems of the

149

age).[24] To put this slightly differently, we may say that genealogy displaces the ironic monumental history of archaeology with an ironic critical history. This point becomes clear if we recall that the ironic force of archaeology's heroization was dependent on its distance, whereas we have seen that genealogy transforms the relationship between proximity and distance such that it is in grasping our being in its proximity that genealogy heroizes the present, while the gesture of 'abrupt dispossession' constitutes the distance which ironizes this heroization. More specifically, genealogy's moment of heroization lies in its disclosure of what we are – the difference of our modern subjectivity – while the moment of irony lies in its showing how we *become* what we are – the sheer contingency of our being what we are. This double moment of ironic heroization is critical precisely because, in revealing the contingency of what we are, genealogy opens a space in which we can envisage ourselves as other than we are. Thus the impotent irony of archaeology is displaced by the engaged irony of genealogy. It is in this way that genealogy functions as 'an exercise in which extreme attention to what is real is confronted by the practice of a liberty that simultaneously respects this reality and violates it' (FR p. 41) and, thus, exemplifies the *ethos* of modernity.

It must be recalled, however, that we have left suspended the question of the adequacy of the methodological apparatus Foucault develops around the topics of truth, power and ethics in relation to the immanent tasks of genealogy. We will consider this issue in detail shortly; however, we can conclude our general reflections on Foucault's method by briefly examining the reformulation of the relationship between archaeology and genealogy which attends his final thoughts.

THE DOUBLE GAZE: PROBLEMATICS AND PRACTICES

An initial point of entry into these reflections[25] on the reflection between archaeology and genealogy is offered in the introduction to *The Use of Pleasure* where Foucault – retrospectively – characterises the form of his thought as follows:

> It was a matter of analyzing, not behaviours or ideas, nor societies and their 'ideologies,' but the *problematizations* through which being offers itself to be, necessarily, thought – and the *practices* on the basis of which these problematizations are formed.
>
> (UP p. 11)

By the use of the term 'problematization', Foucault is conceptualising the focus of his analyses as a concern with the ways in which specific issues come to be recognised as problematic:

> There was a problematization of madness and illness arising out of

social and medical practices, and defining a certain pattern of 'normalization'; a problematization of life, language, and labor in discursive practices that conformed to certain 'epistemic' rules; and a problematization of crime and criminal behaviour emerging from certain punitive practices conforming to a 'disciplinary' model.

(UP p. 12)

To put this into terms used throughout this study, we may state that Foucault's concern with problematisations and practices is a concern with the ways in which the cultural *a priori* judgements that constitute our *structures of recognition* become visible, become questioned and are transformed. How does Foucault place archaeology and genealogy in relation to this concern? As follows:

The archaeological dimension of the analysis made it possible to examine the forms [of problematisations] themselves; its genealogical dimension enabled me to analyze their formation out of practices and the modifications undergone by the latter.

(UP pp. 11–2)

In other words, archaeology provides a series of snapshots or synchronic analyses which specify the forms of the problematisation of an issue, while genealogy operates diachronically in seeking to illustrate the emergence and descent of these nodal points, that is, the practices through which they arise and those that they make possible.

It is clear, no doubt, that the idea of archaeology deployed here is distinct from that examined earlier in that, while it attends to discourse and seeks to illuminate the 'grammar' of our thinking of our being, this grammar is situated as constituted through non-discursive practices. At the same time, the location of the *episteme* as a restricted form of *dispositif* entails that archaeology, like genealogy, recognises its own interested character. Foucault's introduction of the idea of problematisation, though, serves to clarify the function that an archaeological analysis can perform in so far as the identification of the breaks in, and transformations of, our *structures of recognition* provides genealogy with signposts indicating the path it has to map in order to account for our being as we are. In this respect, it is notable that Foucault does not talk of archaeology and genealogy as distinct but as complementary dimensions of an adequate analysis. The form of this complementarity is revealed further in relation to the critical function of Foucault's mode of analysis when he suggests that criticism is 'genealogical in its design and archaeological in its method' (FR p. 46). To clarify this enigmatic utterance, Foucault continues as follows:

Archaeological – and not transcendental – in the sense that it will not seek to identify the universal structures of all knowledge or all possible moral action, but will seek to treat the instances of discourse that articulate what we think, say, and do as so many historical events. And this critique will be genealogical in the sense that it will not deduce from the form of what we are what it is impossible for us to do and to know; but it will separate out, from the contingency that has made us what we are, the possibility of no longer being, doing, or thinking what we are, do, or think.

(FR p. 46)

The complementarity exhibited in this passage is that of a double gaze in which the archaeological concern with specific structures of consciousness and will within the site of a problematisation and the genealogical concern with the formation and implications of structures of consciousness and will denote the moments of detachment and engagement as the theoretical and practical dimensions of critique.

At this juncture, particularly having abruptly introduced the notions of 'consciousness' and 'will' in the previous paragraph, it is necessary to turn to the much suspended topic of the form and adequacy of the methodological apparatus which Foucault develops and deploys in confronting the tasks of genealogy.

EXPLANATION AND HISTORICAL ONTOLOGY

We have noted that the methodological task immanent to a genealogical mode of explanation attends the bracketing of 'truth' and the 'constituent subject' in that this bracketing requires the formulation of a methodological apparatus which can account for the production of regimes of truth and modes of subjectivity. Foucault's recognition of this task emerges when he asks himself the question 'How can one analyze the connection between ways of distinguishing true and false and ways of governing oneself and others?' (QM p. 82). To unpack this question, we may begin by asking what Foucault means by 'ways of distinguishing true and false' and 'ways of governing oneself and others'; only when this has been clarified will it be possible to pose the question of the connection between these methodological themes.

We can initiate this discussion by noting that Foucault locates genealogy as a mode of analysis operating around three axes:

First, a historical ontology of ourselves in relation to truth through which we constitute ourselves as subjects of knowledge; second, a historical ontology of ourselves in relation to a field of power through which we constitute ourselves as subjects acting on others; third, a historical ontology of ourselves in relation to ethics through which we constitute ourselves as moral agents.

(FR p. 351)

The first of these dimensions attends to 'ways of distinguishing true and false' as an analysis of relations of knowledge, the second dimension corresponds to 'ways of governing others' as an analysis of relations of power, and the final dimension relates to 'ways of governing oneself' as an analysis of relations of ethics. To place this sketch in a more conventional vocabulary and in the context of Foucault's anti-humanism, it may be stated that the first dimension of genealogy attends to the constitution of *consciousness*, while the latter dimensions relate to the constitution of the *will* in its other-directed and self-directed moments. In so far as Foucault is concerned with analysing the form of modern subjectivity, it is clear why it is necessary for him to analyse the connection between, on the one hand, relations of knowledge and, on the other hand, relations of power and of ethics. At this stage, our task becomes that of examining Foucault's mode of conceptualising these elements.

What does Foucault mean when he refers to relations of knowledge, of power or of ethics? Consider the following comments on power:

> In effect, what defines a relationship of power is that it is a mode of action which does not act directly and immediately on others. Instead it acts upon their actions: an action upon an action, on existing actions or on those which may arise in the present or the future.
>
> (SP p. 220)

To attempt to clarify this further, Foucault continues as follows:

> Perhaps the equivocal nature of the term *conduct* is one of the best aids for coming to terms with the specificity of power relations. For to 'conduct' is at the same time to 'lead' others . . . and a way of behaving within a more or less open field of possibilities.
>
> (SP pp. 220–1)

A power relationship is thus a mode of action which 'leads' others through structuring their possible field of action; it is a conducting of the conduct of others.[26] On this basis, we may reasonably suggest that by relations of ethics Foucault is referring to a conducting of the conduct of the self. What though of relations of knowledge? Continuing the analogy, we may argue that the specificity of a relationship of knowledge is a mode of thought which structures a possible field of thought (one might refer here to the way in which Kant's thinking on enlightenment structures the possible field of thought by opening up the way to Hegelian and Nietzschean modes of thought).

This manner of conceiving of relations of knowledge, of power and of ethics has significant philosophical implications which can again be clarified by an initial reference to Foucault's comments on relations of power:

When one defines the exercise of power as a mode of action upon the actions of others, when one characterises these actions by the government of men by other men – in the broadest sense of the term – one includes an important element: freedom. Power is only exercised over free subjects, and only in so far as they are free.

(SP p. 221)

Foucault's point is straightforward: the concept of power, if it is to be intelligible, requires the thesis that the actions of an individual are capable of being affected by the actions of another individual. This leads to the following formulation:

At the heart of the power relationship, and constantly provoking it, are the recalcitrance of the will and the intransigence of freedom. Rather than speaking of an essential freedom, it would be better to speak of an 'agonism' – of a relationship which is at the same time reciprocal incitation and struggle; less of a face to face confrontation which paralyses both sides than a permanent provocation.

(SP pp. 221–2)

To unpack this position, we should begin by noting that the concept of ethics as the conducting of one's own conduct similarly presupposes that one's conduct is capable of being conducted (i.e. is not exclusively determined) and that this conducting of conduct also involves 'the recalcitrance of the will and the intransigence of freedom'. This becomes clear if we consider that, for Foucault, it is through relations of power and of ethics that the *will* – at any given time – is constituted, that is, that we are constituted as agents with certain capacities; consequently, any further conducting of our conduct by others or by ourselves can only be exercised in relation to those capacities for action we have and, in so far as this exercise of power or ethics presupposes our capacity for acting in a given way, it also presupposes that we may not exercise this capacity.[27] We can clarify this further through an example in relation to power:

The characteristic feature of power is that some men can more or less entirely determine other men's conduct – but never exhaustively or coercively. A man who is chained up and beaten is subject to force being exerted over him. Not power. But if he can be induced to speak, when his ultimate recourse could have been to hold his tongue, preferring death, then he has been caused to behave in a certain way. His freedom has been subjected to power. If an individual can remain free, however little his freedom may be, power can subject him to government. There is no power with potential refusal or revolt.

(PPC pp. 83–4)

In this example, torture as a mode of conducting the conduct of an

154

individual presupposes the capacity of the individual to speak and provide certain information; however, in so far as the individual has the capacity to perform this act he also has the possibility of not exercising this capacity. In this context, we may suggest that the *will* at any given time is constituted as a configuration of relations of power and recalcitrance, and of ethics and recalcitrance, where relations of power and of ethics denote the potential reconstitution of the *will* and where recalcitrance to power relations and to relations of ethics signifies the resistance of the *will* as it is constituted to this process of reconstitution. We will return to this issue to clarify it further in considering the relationship between relations of power and relations of ethics; however, at this juncture, we should consider the implications of Foucault's mode of analysis with respect to relations of knowledge and the constitution of *consciousness*. If we continue the mode of argument by analogy which has been developed, it is apparent that relations of knowledge as a mode of thinking which structures a possible field of thought also presuppose freedom in the sense that they pre-suppose that consciousness is not exclusively determined and is capable of reflecting on itself. An exercise of knowledge, in this respect, can structure the form of consciousness only in so far as consciousness has the capacity for a given mode of reflection and, thereby, also the possibility of not exercising this capacity. Consequently, we might say that the consti-tution of consciousness is the *agonistic* product of relations of knowledge which seek to develop a particular mode of reflection and a recalcitrance predicated on the existing relation of consciousness to itself.[28]

At this stage, further clarification of Foucault's conceptual apparatus requires that we pose the question of the connection between 'ways of distinguishing true and false' and 'ways of governing oneself and others'. This should not surprise since outlining the concepts of power, ethics and knowledge has entailed treating the question of the will and that of consciousness separately and, as the last paragraph may unwittingly illustrate, this strategy of clarification rapidly reaches the limits beyond which it threatens to conceal more than it reveals. How then may we approach the question of how Foucault analyses the connection at stake here? Let us note initially that the site of the question Foucault poses to himself involves three dimensions: the relationship between ethics and knowledge, that between power and knowledge, and that between ethics and power. We can begin by examining Foucault's thought in relation to these dimensions before attending to the methodological apparatus he deploys.

Let us note initially that the questions of how to analyse the connection between power and knowledge and between ethics and knowledge are structurally isomorphic in that both involve asking how we can analyse the relationship between structures constitutive of consciousness and structures constitutive of the will (in its other-directed and self-directed moments).[29] In other words, in so far as ethics refers to that 'power' one exercises in relation to one's self, a mode of analysing the connection between power and knowledge will also function as a way of analysing the connection between ethics and knowledge. With this in mind, consider the following hypothesis advanced by Foucault:

> Perhaps we should abandon the belief that power makes mad and that, by the same token, the renunciation of power is one of the conditions of knowledge. We should admit rather that power produces knowledge . . . ; that power and knowledge directly imply one another; that there is no power relation without the correlative constitution of a field of knowledge, nor any knowledge that does not presuppose and constitute at the same time power relations.
>
> (DP p. 27)

We should note that Foucault is not asserting the dialectical identity of power and knowledge;[30] on the contrary, his claim is simply that relations of knowledge as the structures constitutive of consciousness are immanently related to relations of power (and ethics) as the structures constitutive of the will. The phrase 'power-knowledge' denotes this claim of a relationship between the modes of rationality constitutive of the form of consciousness and the kinds of practices constitutive of the modality of the will. We can express this claim as the idea that forms of rationality open up fields of possible practices, while modes of practice open up fields of possible rationalities. More precisely, we may say that the *actual* ways in which we constitute ourselves as subjects of knowledge govern the ways in which we can reflect on others and ourselves and, thereby, define a field of *possible* ways of acting on others and ourselves; while, at the same time, the *actual* ways in which we act on others and ourselves govern the *possible* ways in which we can constitute ourselves as subjects of knowledge.[31] Viewed in this way, Foucault's project of historical ontology may be situated as a mode of accounting for the emergence and development of the *structures of recognition* constitutive of our subjectivity through a tracing of the movement from fields of possibility to patterns of actuality in the interplay of structures of consciousness and structures of the will.

The Nietzschean radicalism of this project lies in Foucault's emphasis on the contingent (but not arbitrary) character of the relationship between possibilities and actuality. This emphasis manifests itself within his methodological reflections as the conception of power-knowledge relations as 'intentional and nonsubjective' (HS p. 94). By this phrase, Foucault is presenting the hypothesis that while specific power-knowledge relations 'are imbued, through and through, with calculation: there is no power without a series of aim and objectives' (HS p. 95), there is no subject which co-ordinates these power-knowledge relations.[32] In this sense, Foucault may be read as presenting an analysis of power-knowledge relations which operates analogously to a vectoral analysis in which the direction and force of the vectoral totality is the product of the interaction of directional forces, yet the resultant vector can in no way be said to be a co-ordinated product; rather, it is radically contingent. In the same way, the intentionality of the totality of power-knowledge relations is a product of the interaction of these power-knowledge relations, yet this product is not the result of a co-ordinating agency.[33] Foucault's position on this issue has far-reaching implications; most notably, that it entails the rejection of the Hegelian idea of the Subject of history and, concomitantly, the claim that history manifests an immanent *telos*. In other words, the direction of our history is contingent and cannot be subject to control. We may note in passing here that Foucault thus eliminates the remnants of the idea of the world-historical individual which still attended Nietzsche's notion of the world-historical *Übermensch* and, to a lesser extent, Weber's notions of the scientific genius and the charismatic politician.[34] In both Nietzsche's and Weber's case, the possibility of consciously controlling the formation of *structures of recognition* persisted in the legislative moments of their thought; with Foucault, this echo of utopianism is finally silenced.[35]

Having examined how Foucault conceptualises the relationship between power and knowledge (and, thereby, also ethics and knowledge), we are in a position to approach the question of how he analyses the *structures of recognition* constitutive of our subjectivity. Foucault sets out this mode of analysis most clearly in *The Use of Pleasure* with respect to relations of ethics-knowledge; however, I will suggest that the same methodological apparatus serves to analyse relations of power-knowledge. We can begin by noting that to analyse the *structures of recognition* constitutive of consciousness and the will in their self-directed aspects entails, on Foucault's account, attending to four dimensions: a determination of the ethical substance (*substance éthique*), an identification of the mode of subjection (*mode d'assujettissement*), a location of the ethical work (*travail éthique*) or form of asceticism (*practique de soi*), and an elaboration of the *telos* (*téléologie*), these four dimensions denoting, respectively, the ontological, deontological, ascetic and teleological axes of our experience of ourselves as ethical subjects.[36]

Elaborating on this initial outline, we may clarify each of these axes of analysis. Firstly, the determination of ethical substance refers to 'the way in which the individual has to constitute this or that part of himself as the prime material of his moral conduct' (UP p. 26). In other words, Foucault is concerned here with identifying the object of ethical reflection (e.g. bodily desire or conscious intentions). Secondly, the mode of subjection signifies 'the way in which an individual establishes his relation to a rule and recognises himself as obligated to put it into practice' (UP p. 27). Thus, for example, one may recognise the rule of faithfulness to a conjugal partner on a variety of grounds:

157

because one acknowledges oneself to be a member of a group that accepts it . . . [or] because one regards oneself as an heir to a spiritual tradition that one has the responsibility of maintaining and reviving; one can also practice fidelity in response to an appeal, by offering oneself as an example, or by seeking to give one's personal life a form that answers to criteria of brilliance, beauty, nobility, or perfection.

(UP p. 27)

With this axis, Foucault is attempting to locate the possible modalities of reflection which operate within a given ethico-epistemological grammar. In ancient Greece, for example, he suggests that the modalities of reflection are governed by a politico-aesthetic grammar which manifests itself in a conscious decisionism, whereas, in mediaeval Christianity, the modalities of reflection are governed by juridico-theological grammar which manifests itself as an ongoing self-deciphering (FR pp. 357–8). Thirdly, ethical work refers to the type of self-forming activity one operates on oneself – '*asceticism* in a very broad sense' (FR p. 355) – 'not only in order to bring one's conduct into compliance with a given rule, but to attempt to transform oneself into the ethical subject of one's behaviour' (UP p. 27). Thus, for example, the practice of sexual austerity may be articulated through 'a long effort of learning, memorization, and assimilation of a systematic ensemble of precepts, and through a regular checking of conduct aimed at measuring the exactness with which one is applying these rules' or 'a sudden, all-embracing, and definitive renunciation of pleasures' or 'a relentless combat whose vicissitudes . . . can have meaning and value in themselves' or 'a decipherment . . . of the movement of desire in all its hidden forms' (UP p. 27). In this dimension, Foucault is concerned with the possible forms of practice opened up by modalities of reflection and the actual *techne* developed within this field of possibility. Finally, the *telos* refers to 'the kind of being to which we aspire when we behave in a moral way' (FR p. 355). As Foucault puts this point:

A moral action tends towards its own accomplishment; but it also aims beyond the latter, to the establishing of a moral conduct that commits an individual, not only to other actions always in conformity with values and rules, but to a certain mode of being, a mode of being characteristic of the ethical subject.

(UP p. 28)

The *telos* might be, for example, self-mastery, tranquility, impersonality or salvation (UP p. 28). Expressing Foucault's point in Nietzschean terms, we might say that the *telos* defines the stylistic parameters of the self as ethical subject within which the labour of self-overcoming occurs.[37]

Reflecting on these four dimensions in relation to the constitution of consciousness and the will, we may note that broadly speaking the determination of ethical substance and the mode of subjection are constitutive of the structure of consciousness, while the ethical work and the *telos* are constitutive of the structure of the will. At this juncture, we should indicate that, although Foucault never explicitly theorises the issue as such, this mode of analysing the *structures of recognition* constitutive of consciousness and the will in their self-directed aspect, perhaps unsurprisingly, also enables an analysis of these *structures of recognition* in their other-directed aspect. This can be briefly illustrated in principle by translating the operations Foucault sets out into the vocabulary of power-knowledge relations.

First, there is the *substance of subjugation* by which is meant the way in which an aspect of the other is constituted as the prime material of their conduct. Second, the *mode of subjection* signifies the relation of the other to a rule and its obligated practical exercise which the conducting of conduct requires. Third, there are the *ascetics of domination*, that is, the *techne* which are deployed not only to bring the other's conduct into compliance with a certain rule, but to attempt to transform the other into the subjugated subject of their behaviour. Fourth, there is the *telos of domination* which refers to the kind of being which power-knowledge relations attempt to produce. To adapt Foucault, we might say that a subjugated action aims towards its own accomplishment; but also aims beyond the latter to the establishing of a subjugated conduct that commits the other to a certain mode of being, a mode of being characteristic of the subjugated subject.[38]

This way of setting up Foucault's concern enables us to locate the final dimension of his mode of analysis, that is, the question of how to analyse the relationship between ethics and power. The conceptualisation of this connection is one of agency as constituted through the articulation of power and ethics. More precisely, Foucault's mode of analysis may be read as locating subjectivity as constituted through the articulation of power-knowledge and ethics-knowledge. We can, perhaps, clarify this position as follows: in so far as we are subject to the exercise of power as the other-conducting of our conduct and, thus, the formation of a specific mode of subjectivity, this exercise of power is subject to potential resistance predicated on ethical relations, that is, the self-conducting of our conduct. Thus, in accounting for how we have become what we are, Foucault's genealogy operates through a tracing of the *structures of recognition* constitutive of our subjectivity, where this subjectivity is located as a configuration of relations of knowledge, of power and of ethics, and where the emergence, development and transformation of *structures of recognition* may be accounted for in terms of the interplay of power-knowledge and ethics-knowledge.[39]

To conclude this section, it may be useful to refer back to the question with which we began: how is it possible to analyse the connection between ways of distinguishing true and false and ways of governing oneself and others? We can now suggest that the question being asked here concerns the analysis of the relationship between the structures constitutive of the grammar of consciousness and those constitutive of the grammar of the will. Recalling Foucault's 'double gaze', we may note that the archaeological dimension is simply concerned with the grammar of consciousness, whereas genealogy necessarily addresses the question of the connection between consciousness and the will. Genealogy as historical ontology engages in this analysis through, firstly, a reconstruction of *structures of other-recognition* and *structures of self-recognition* – where these structures are seen as complex ensembles constitutive of objects of reflection, modalities of reflection, forms of agency and objectives of agency – and, secondly, a tracing of the relationships between these complex ensembles. We should also reiterate here that the methodological apparatus Foucault deploys allows him to account for the direction of history as radically contingent. The question which arises, at this juncture, with respect to this mode of analysis is that concerning the sense in which genealogy as historical ontology may be said to be critical.

HISTORICAL ONTOLOGY AS CRITIQUE

In our earlier discussion of Foucault's 'double gaze', we cited a passage in which Foucault describes genealogy as critical in the sense of showing us the possibility of being otherwise than we are. It is through this showing that genealogy seeks 'to give new impetus, as far and as wide as possible, to the undefined work of freedom' (FR p. 46).[40] However, critics such as Habermas have suggested that Foucault's genealogical method is incapable of answering the question 'why fight?'.[41] After all, to illustrate the possibility of being otherwise is distinctly different from providing reasons why we should want to be otherwise. Habermas's point – and in this he is quite correct – is that Foucault cannot provide *moral* reasons why we should resist power relations, why we should trangress constraints exercised on us. This should not, perhaps, surprise us in that Foucault's methodology, like those of Nietzsche and Weber, involves a commitment to value-freedom as the ethical stance of refusing to legislate values.[42] It is not simply that Foucault's methodological position is incapable of providing grounds on which he might engage in such legislation (although this is the case), but further that Foucault quite explicitly rejects any such role as appropriate to the intellectual:

> The role of the intellectual is not to tell others what they have to do. By what right would he do so? And remember all the prophecies, promises, injunctions, and programs that intellectuals have managed to formulate over the last two centuries and whose effects we can now see.

> (PPC p. 265)

The 'failure' of Foucault's methodology to be able to provide *moral* reasons for resistance is thus not an unfortunate unconscious lacunae within his thinking but a quite deliberate ethical stance.[43] At this stage, it may perhaps be clear why it was necessary in the discussion of the theoretical trajectory within which Foucault locates himself to distinguish between Nietzschean and Hegelian traditions. The latter, it will be recalled, articulate the relationship between autonomy and critique through a thinking of autonomy in terms of *Sittlichkeit* which locates critique as the elaboration of normative criteria of judgement. By contrast, the Nietzschean trajectory of thought articulates the relationship between autonomy and critique in terms of a thinking of autonomy as the activity of self-construction which locates critique as the specification of the form of this activity. In this context, we may attempt to grasp Foucault's conception of 'the principle of a critique and a permanent creation of ourselves in our autonomy' (FR p. 44) in terms of the question Habermas does *not* ask, namely, whether genealogy as historical ontology provides *extra-moral* reasons for resistance.

We can begin by noting that a condition of possibility of genealogy as an investigation of the historical contingency of how we have become what we are is that our time has a historical structure.[44] In this context, consider the following passage:

> It is through revolt that subjectivity (not that of great men but that of whomever) introduces itself into history and gives it the breath of life. A delinquent puts his life into balance against absurd punishments; a madman can no longer accept confinement and the forfeiture of his rights; a people refuses the regime which oppresses it. This does not make the rebel in the first case innocent, nor does it cure in the second, and it does not assure the third rebel of the promised tomorrow. One does not have to be in solidarity with them. One does not have to maintain that these confused voices sound better than the others and express the ultimate truth. For there to be a sense in listening to them and in searching for what they have to say, it is sufficient that they exist and they have against them so much which is set up to silence them. . . . All the disenchantments of history amount to nothing: it is due to such voices that the time of men does not have the form of an evolution, but precisely that of a history.
>
> (UR p. 8)

It was noted earlier that the *possibility* of resistance is the condition of possibility of the exercise of power; however, it is the *exercise* of resistance to power which is the form of freedom. In other words, in so far as the emergence, development and transformation of our *structures of recognition* is the product of the 'agonism' of power and ethics, it is only through resistance to power that the non-identity of power and ethics is maintained and historical time is constituted. The significance of this point is that it implies that resistance is the condition of possibility of genealogy. As such there is an immanent relationship between genealogy and resistance which expresses itself both in the *idea* of genealogy in so far as a concern with showing how we have become what we are is predicated on the possibility of being otherwise than we are and in the *practice* of genealogy as an investigation of how we can be otherwise than we are.

Referring back to Foucault's notion of 'the principle of a critique and a permanent creation of ourselves in our autonomy', we can now specify these elements. The former is expressed in the following passage:

> the important question here, it seems to me, is not whether a culture without constraints is possible or even desirable but whether the system of constraints in which a society functions leaves individuals the liberty to transform the system . . . a system of constraint becomes truly intolerable when the individuals who are affected by it don't have the means of modifying it.
>
> (PPC p. 294)

By examining relationships between ethics and power, genealogy enables us to locate those sites where relations of power and relations of ethics approach a condition of identity. In other words, genealogy enables us to identify the degrees of entrenchment of particular forms of constraint within our culture and the possibilities for resistance available. The important point to note here, however, is that the immanent relation of genealogy to resistance entails a principle of critique in terms of which forms of constraint may be evaluated. The relationship of this principle of critique to the theme of autonomy is identical with the relationship of genealogy and resistance in that it is the ongoing exercise of resistance which constitutes our permanent creation of ourselves in our autonomy.

To conclude, we may note that Foucault's project of genealogy operates as a Nietzschean mode of critique in which the concern for autonomy, no less than in Hegelian forms of critique, animates his mode of analysis. To grasp the urgency with which Foucault endows this project and to examine why the politics of truth is the dominant concern in the construction of his history of the present requires that we reconstruct his genealogical investigations.

9

THE GENEALOGY OF MODERNITY
Foucault, humanism and biopolitics

For Foucault, as for Nietzsche and Weber, the task of genealogy is to construct an account of how we have become what we are. However, as Foucault notes in his essay on Nietzsche's genealogy, this task requires the deployment of a 'system of injustice' or, in Weber's terms, an 'evaluative idea' which governs the perspective from which the cultural significance of phenomena is determined and ranked. To take up Foucault's genealogical studies, consequently, entails that we begin by specifying the 'central question' that operates within Foucault's investigations. Reflecting on this issue, we may recall that it has already been indicated in the previous chapter that an integral task of genealogy in accounting for its own conditions of possibility is to specify how it is that the will to truth becomes constituted as a problem. On this basis, we may suggest that the animating interest of Foucault's genealogies is in specifying the form of the will to truth in contemporary culture, tracing the emergence and descent of this will to truth, and indicating its implications for humanity.[1]

A starting point for our analysis of Foucault's position is provided by his location of two distinct modes of philosophical reflection as emerging in the writings of Kant. On the one hand, there is a line of interrogation which revolves about the question 'What is Man?' and takes the form of a philosophical anthropology seeking to establish foundations upon which the questions of thought – what can I know? what should I do? what can I hope for? – which are constitutive of the question 'What is Man?' may be definitively answered.[2] On the other hand, there is that trajectory of thought which engages the question 'What is enlightenment?' and takes the form of a critical ontology of ourselves. In so far as Foucault argues that there is a tension between these modes of reflection which manifests itself as a tension between humanism as a form of will to truth and genealogy as a problematisation of the will to truth, it follows that the concern of his investigations must be with accounting for humanism and indicating the problematic form of this modality of the will to truth.[3]

In approaching this issue, we will follow Foucault's procedure by initially sketching his archaeology of humanism as it is presented in his

163

reflections on modern thought. This archaeological gaze will then be supplemented by Foucault's genealogical studies of specific rationalities and practices through which humanism emerges; in particular, we will address the topics of punishment, sexuality and politics. We will conclude by delineating the implications of these analyses for the constitution of modern subjectivity and the 'agonism' of power and freedom.

AN ARCHAEOLOGY OF HUMANISM

For Foucault, modern philosophical humanism is characterised by an 'analytic of finitude', this phrase describing the curious idea of 'a being who is sovereign precisely by virtue of being enslaved, a being whose very finitude allows him to take the place of God' (Dreyfus and Rabinow 1983: 30):

> At the foundation of all the empirical positivities, and of everything that can indicate itself as a concrete limitation of man's existence, we discover a finitude – which is in a sense the same: . . . and yet it is radically other: in this sense, the limitation is expressed not as a determination imposed on man from outside (because he has a nature or history), but as a fundamental finitude which rests on nothing but its own existence as fact, and opens upon the positivity of all concrete limitation.
>
> (OT p. 315)

This finite being whose very finitude presents itself as both determination and ground is 'Man' and, Foucault argues, modern philosophy from Kant onwards is conceived as a reflection on this figure. The question 'What is Man?' is constituted as the site of reflection, where the task of this philosophical reflection is a paradoxical demonstration of the identity and difference of man's determinate limitations (finitude as the positivities) with the conditions of determinateness (finitude as the fundamental): 'From one end of experience to the other, finitude answers itself; it is the identity and the difference of the positivities, and of their foundation, within the figure of the *Same*' (OT p. 315). In other words, modern thought faces the task of generating a coherent account of man as an object produced by the world as identical to, and different from, man as the subject that constitutes the world. Foucault's argument is that this reflection has taken, more or less successively, three forms in which we see 'the transcendental repeat the empirical, the cogito repeat the unthought, the return of the origin repeat its retreat' (OT p. 316).[4]

The empirical–transcendental doublet denotes the initial form of the analytic of finitude which emerges with Kant's conception of the limitations on human knowledge as the ground of the possibility of knowledge. Man is conceived of both as a transcendental subject who constitutes the objects of his experience and, simultaneously, as an empirical object of that experience. Kant's philosophy attempts to ground finitude in itself by divorcing the *form* of experience (finitude as the fundamental) from the *contents* of experience (finitude as the positivities). However, although this radical dualism entails that Kant can account for the difference between man as subject and man as object, it also entails that he cannot account for the identity of man as subject and as object. On Foucault's account, the attempt to overcome this dilemma in post-Kantian philosophy takes the form of a reduction of the transcendental to the empirical, where the empirical is conceived of as either *nature* or *history*. The former of these locates the form of experience as governed by 'anatomo-physiological conditions' and attempts to ground finitude in itself by showing 'that there is a *nature* of human knowledge that determines its forms and that can at the same time be made manifest to it in its own empirical contents' (OT p. 319).[5] The latter locates the form of experience as governed by 'historical, social, or economic conditions' and attempts to ground finitude in itself by showing that 'there was a *history* of human knowledge which could be both given to empirical knowledge and prescribe its forms' (OT p. 319). However, both of these forms of reduction are caught within a dilemma, namely, that of truth itself:

> there must, in fact, exist a truth that is of the same order as the object – the truth that is gradually outlined, formed, stabilised, and expressed through the body and the rudiments of perception; the truth that appears as illusions are dissipated, and as history establishes a disalienated status for itself; but there must also exist a truth that is of the order of discourse – a truth that makes it possible to employ, when dealing with the nature or history of knowledge, a language that will be true. It is the status of this true discourse that remains ambiguous.
>
> (OT p. 320)

This 'true discourse', Foucault argues, may take either of two forms: firstly, a 'positivist' discourse – 'the truth of the object determines the truth of the discourse that describes its formation', or, secondly, an 'eschatological' discourse – 'the truth of the philosophical discourse constitutes the truth in formation' (OT p. 320). In fact, Foucault argues, 'a discourse attempting to be both empirical and critical cannot but be both positivist and eschatological; man appears in it as a truth both reduced and promised' (OT p. 320).[6] The central claim of this argument is that the attempt to reduce the transcendental to the empirical simply ends up by repeating the transcendental in the requirement of 'a truth that is of the order of discourse'.

If man is 'the locus of an empirico-transcendental doublet', the attempt to think finitude as its own foundation in terms of a reduction of the transcendental to the empirical necessarily reproduces that which it attempts to exclude. In this context, there emerges a second strategy for thinking finitude in its own foundation which avoids this ambivalence by changing the focus of reflection to man as 'a mode of being which accommodates that dimension – always open, never finally delimited, yet constantly traversed – which extends from a part of himself not reflected in a *cogito* to the act of thought by which he apprehends that part' (OT p. 322). Modern thought renounces the pure transparency of the Cartesian *cogito* in the recognition that the *cogito* is intrinsically tied to an unthought which escapes the reflection of the *cogito* even as it makes this reflection possible. In Kant, this unthought was the noumenal realm of the thing-in-itself; however, for post-Kantian thought, 'the unthought is a dimension of our own reality, an otherness we must find in ourselves' (Gutting 1989: 203).[7] The question of man's being, thus, takes the form of a reflection on the unthought which, as the horizon of being, constitutes it. To ground finitude in itself, the task of thought under the aegis of the *cogito*/unthought double becomes that of thinking the unthought, of constituting the Other as the Same:

> the whole of modern thought is imbued with the necessity of thinking the unthought – of reflecting the contents of the *In-itself* in the form of the *For-itself*, of ending man's alienation by reconciling him with his own essence, of making explicit the horizon that provides experience with its background of immediate and disarmed proof, of lifting the veil of the Unconscious, of becoming absorbed in its silence, or of straining to catch its endless murmur.
>
> (OT p. 327)

With this necessity, this imperative, reflection constitutes itself as that *action* in which reflection on the unthought which defines man's being transforms this being. If modern thought is notable for its inability to formulate a morality, Foucault argues, it is because the imperative lodged within this mode of reflection itself constitutes 'the form and content of the ethical' (OT p. 328). Thinking under the *cogito*/unthought double, however, is marked by its own ambivalence in that to ground finitude in itself requires the identity and difference of the *cogito* and the unthought. This ambivalence emerges in that the unthought as the ground of action in so far as it is thought loses its capacity to ground action. Foucault's argument here parallels those offered by Nietzsche and Weber in their accounts of the will to truth as constitutive of, respectively, nihilism and disenchantment. Thinking the unthought as will to truth aims at a *cogito* transparent to itself, yet whose very transparency renders its being groundless. When Foucault states that this mode of reflection 'cannot help but liberate and enslave' and that 'knowledge of man . . . is always linked, even in its vaguest form, to ethics or politics' (OT p. 328), his argument is that thinking the unthought produces a liberation from the authority of the Other (e.g. tradition, ideology, the unconscious) in so far as it is constitutive of a *cogito* transparent to itself, that is, a self sovereign over its own actions, yet, to the same degree as it constitutes this sovereign self, it enslaves by destroying the (unthought) grounds on which action has meaning. Again, it appears as if an instability is engendered at the heart of thought.

The final double under which modern thought attempts to present finitude as its own foundation is that of the retreat and return of the origin. The recognition of the irreducibility of man as an empirico-transcendent doublet, and of his mode of being as inextricably entwined in the mutuality of the *cogito* and the unthought, manifests itself as a reflection on his relation to the origin. The relation between the positive and the fundamental being expressed here conceives of man as an object which always already exists within a history which is not his own and man as a subject as the condition of possibility of time, of history, as such. The task for thought is 'that of contesting the origin of things, but of contesting it in order to give it a foundation, by rediscovering the mode upon which the possibility of time is constituted' (OT p. 332).[8] To ground finitude in itself means thinking man's history as identical to, and different from, the condition of possibility of history, that is to say it means thinking 'the origin without origin or beginning, on the basis of which everything is able to come into being' (OT p. 332). In other words, to present finitude as its own foundation requires the thinking of that which makes thinking possible, that is, the thinking of the original. The form of this reflection is paradoxical, for in so far as thinking is constitutive of time, the attempt to think the original is necessarily constitutive of that temporality which separates man from his non-temporal origin: 'in setting itself the task of restoring the domain of the original, modern thought immediately encounters the recession of the origin' (OT p. 333). The solution proposed by modern thought is, paradoxically, that 'of advancing in the direction of this ever-deepening recession; it tries to make it appear on the far side of experience, as that which sustains it by its very retreat, as that which is nearest to its most visible possibility, as that which is, within thought, imminent' (OT pp. 333–4). In other words, the origin of temporality is posited as that which is nothing other than structure of man's being-in-the-world; the origin is that which returns to man's being in the thought of its being as Being. Foucault locates two types of thought of this return. On the one hand, there is the idea of a thought which thinks itself as totality:

a thought which, by the movement in which it is accomplished . . . curves over upon itself, illuminates its own plenitude, brings its circle to completion, recognises itself in all the strange figures of its odyssey, and accepts its own disappearance into the ocean from which it sprang.

(OT p. 334)

This is, for example, the Hegelian thought of the Absolute, a thought which in its overcoming of all diremption is 'enveloped in "the night of self-consciousness," the night in which everything is lost, in which reason which has coursed through all reality is cast again upon an unknown sea' (Gillespie 1984: 114). On the other hand, there is a thought which 'is neither a completion nor curve, but rather that ceaseless rendering open which frees the origin in exactly that degree to which it recedes' (OT p. 334). This is a thought which does not reflect in its movement its own plenitude, but which, rather, traces in its movement a lack, a void, that consumes it. In contrast to the fullness of meaning which denotes the thought of return as totality, the thought of return as opening represents the collapse of meaning. In both cases, however, this thought of return is the return to authentic Being 'in that plenitude or in that nothing which he is himself' (OT p. 334); finitude 'is the insurmountable relation of man's being with time' (OT p. 335). This mode of reflection, for all its profundity, however, does not escape the ambivalence of modern thought; rather it constitutes this ambivalence as its essence: 'Time – the time that he himself is – cuts him off not only from the dawn from which he sprung but also from that other dawn promised him as still to come' (OT p. 335). Being as time cannot return to its non-temporal origin precisely because the non-temporality of this origin stands inevitably as the site of non-Being. To put it slightly differently, we may say the historicity of being cannot *be* outside of history; the thought of return (in either of its modes) cannot return to itself.

In respect of the analytic of finitude, it is notable that reflection is instituted by the question *'Was ist das Mensch?'*, that is, the project of philosophical anthropology. In this sense, the ambivalence which Foucault traces through his examination of the figure of Man and his doubles is the ambivalence of humanism as a specific modality of the will to truth. In *The Order of Things*, Foucault locates the possibility of beginning to think beyond this anthropological mode with Nietzsche: 'Perhaps we should see the first attempt at uprooting this Anthropology – to which, no doubt, contemporary thought is dedicated – in the Nietzschean experience' (OT p. 342). The form of this experience is a thinking of the integral connection between the idea of man as a transcendental subject and the idea of God: 'Nietzsche rediscovered the point at which man and God belong to each other, at which the death of the second is synonymous with the disappearance of the first, and at which the promise of the superman signifies first and foremost the imminence of the death of man' (OT p. 342). Foucault's point here is that Nietzsche's genealogical critique of the transcendental subject under the principle of will to power, a critique which exposes the contingency of the idea of 'man', creates the space for a thinking which is not tied to a philosophical anthropology: 'In this, Nietzsche, offering this future to us as both promise and task, marks the threshold beyond which contemporary philosophy can begin thinking again; and he will no doubt continue for a long time to dominate its advance' (OT p. 342). Later, in the essay 'What is Enlightenment?', Foucault seems to be implicitly suggesting that Kant's reflections on 'today' as difference in history prefigures the development of genealogy which emerges with Nietzsche. We will return to the genealogical mode of thinking within which Foucault locates his own thinking in the next chapter.

To conclude this section, the significant issue to note for our investigation is the ambivalence which, in the form of the three doubles, runs through this modern will to truth and whose effect is to structure this will to truth in terms of an ongoing dynamic; thus, for example, the *cogito*/unthought double constitutes the task of thinking the unthought as an endless imperative. At this same juncture, we should also note that the emergence of 'Man', that is, the formation of the subject of knowledge as simultaneously an object of knowledge, makes possible that modality of the will to knowledge which Foucault refers to as the human sciences. As we shall see, the structuring of this will to knowledge through the form of modern humanism's will to truth has profound implications for the modalities of ethics and power constitutive of modern subjectivity. To examine this topic, however, requires that we begin by reconstructing Foucault's genealogical studies of the emergence and development of the will to truth constitutive of modern humanism.

ON PUNITIVE REASON: OBJECTIFYING INDIVIDUALS

In *Discipline and Punish*, Foucault defines his task as presenting a 'history of the modern soul and of a new power to judge' (DP p. 23) through an analysis of 'the metamorphosis of punitive methods on the basis of a political technology of the body in which might be read a common history of power relations and object relations' (DP p. 24). In other words, Foucault's question concerns the transformations of the 'modalities according to which the power to punish is exercised' and the implications of these transformations for the constitution of the modern individual as an object of knowledge, that is, the government of the other as object.[9] This genealogy of punitive reason may be schematically identified as involving two analytically distinct transformations: firstly, a movement from a technology of power constructed about the figure of 'the tortured body' to one predicated on the figure of 'the soul and its manipulated representations' and, secondly, a movement from the technology structured as soul/representation to a modality of power constructed around the figure of 'the body subjected to training' (DP p. 131). Our analysis will briefly sketch these transformations before focusing on the modern modality of punishment.

169

The technology of 'the tortured body' is characterised by two moments: the secret investigation and the public execution. The model of penal truth which characterised the investigation took the form of 'an arithmetic modulated by casuistry, whose function is to define how a legal proof is to be constructed', where the specialised form of knowledge involved both 'reinforces the principle of secrecy' and acts as a constraint on the magistrate (DP p. 37). What emerges here is the penal investigation as a machine for producing the truth in the absence of the accused. However, the lack of need for the presence of the accused in the procedure of establishing truth leads to the confession both as a form of proof which 'almost discharged the prosecution of the obligation to provide further evidence' and as 'the complement to the written, secret preliminary investigation' (DP p. 38). The confession assumes a doubly ambiguous role in this penal apparatus. Firstly, although it was only one type of proof and did not itself strictly guarantee guilt, it also transcended other types of evidence in that as 'an element in the calculation of the truth, it was also the act by which the accused accepted the charge and recognised its truth; it transformed an investigation carried out without him into a voluntary affirmation' (DP p. 38). Secondly, as a type of proof which in its strength minimised the work of the investigation, it was highly valued and 'every possible coercion would be used to obtain it'; however, its coerced production had to be ritually reaffirmed as a 'spontaneous' confession to the court by which the accused 'signed the truth of the preliminary investigation' (DP p. 39).[10] The principle reflected in this procedural secrecy is the absolute right of the sovereign and his judicial agents to determine truth: 'Before the justice of the sovereign, all voices must be still' (DP p. 36). The economy of this judicial apparatus is one in which 'the ritual that produced the truth went side by side with the ritual that imposed punishment' where these rituals are interlocked through the body of the accused as 'the point of application of the punishment and the locus of extortion of the truth' (DP p. 42). This interlocking continues, moreover, in the public execution of the penalty in which 'the body of the condemned man was once again an essential element in the ceremonial of public punishment' (DP p. 43). Whereas the secret nature of judicial investigation attests to the absolute right of the sovereign to determine the truth, the public execution proclaims the absolute power of the sovereign to punish. This political economy of the public execution can be grasped by noting that crime functions within classical political discourse both as an injury to the prince's kingdom and as an affront to his person, and as such punishment demands both redress for the injury and revenge for the affront. The body of the condemned man through the public liturgy of punishment functions as the symbolic site of a relationship between the sovereign and the people defined by a policy of terror in which sovereignty manifested and re-charged itself 'in the ritual display of its reality as "super-power" ' (DP p. 57).

170

How is it then that this technology of power structured around the figure of the tortured body is displaced by a technology of 'humane' punishment? Foucault begins with a reason which 'is internal to the public execution itself: at once an element of its functioning and the principle of its perpetual disorder' (DP p. 57). This reason attends to the necessary presence of the public at the execution in so far as the *raison d'être* of the execution is not only to make an example but also to burn the omnipotence of the sovereign into the minds of the spectators through the symbol of the tortured body. However, as Foucault points out, the role of the people is ambiguous. On the one hand, they are spectators, witnesses and participants within the dramatic unfolding of the ritual of execution. In the latter role, the crowd is called upon to manifest a circumscribed violence such as the execution in effigy of the condemned man. On the other hand, this point of participation could function as the site of a rejection of this punitive power through popular protests which prevented execution, turned on the executioner, abused judges and denounced sentences. Not only was it the case that 'the great spectacle of punishment ran the risk of being rejected by the very people to whom it was addressed' but further 'the terror of the public execution created centres of illegality' in that the crowd became a scene of both violence and theft (DP p. 63). Above all though, 'the people never felt closer to those who paid the penalty than in those rituals intended to show the horror of the crime and the invincibility of power' (DP p. 63). The very excess of this power, its logic of atrocity, could serve to constitute a relation of solidarity between the condemned and the mass which manifested itself, at the extreme, in a reversal of the order of violence in which the condemned man is freed and the executioner killed. The ambiguity of private judicial torture as an ordeal between accused and magistrate is reproduced in the public execution as an ordeal between the power of the sovereign and the power of the crowd. One of the criticisms offered by the eighteenth and nineteenth century reformers of the public execution was, in effect, that this modality of the power to punish 'provided a support for a confrontation between the violence of the king and the violence of the people. . . . in this violence . . . tyranny confronts rebellion; each calls forth the other' (DP pp. 73–4). The target of this critique is the element of personal revenge manifest in the public execution; its watchword is that punishment should address injury rather than affront. This critique is facilitated at the level of judicial-political discourse through the idea of 'humanity', predicated on the notion of the social contract, as that which must be respected in all individuals and, thus, constitutes 'the legitimate frontier of the power to punish' (DP p. 74). What emerges here is the idea that 'punishment must have "humanity" as its "measure", without any definitive meaning being given to this principle, which nevertheless is regarded as insuperable' (DP p. 75). Throughout the eighteenth century,

Foucault argues, a new apparatus of punishment emerges whose rationale is 'not to punish less, but to punish better; to punish with an attenuated severity perhaps, but in order to punish with more universality and necessity; to insert the power to punish more deeply into the social body' (DP p. 82).

The judicial rationality of this new modality of punishment is expressed in the theory of the social contract. Within this framework, the criminal is constituted as a 'juridically paradoxical being' in that, as a member of the society, he has accepted the law by which he is punished, while in divorcing himself from membership in the act of crime, he threatens the foundation of the law itself.[11] The right to punish is constructed here as the absolute defence of the social body; it is the defence by law of its own foundation. This right is itself a return to a form of 'super-power' in which the criminal is opposed by the whole of society; however, at the same time, this 'super-power' is modulated by a principle of moderation in that the 'humanity' of the criminal which renders him subject to the law also serves as a limit of punishment. The criminal as that 'monster' who in transgressing law denies his own humanity must nonetheless be treated in accordance with that humanity. But, as we have noted, the principle of 'humanity' raised here as a cry from the heart of the reformers remains theoretically indeterminate, whereby this very indeterminacy leads to the location of this limit in 'the sensibility of the reasonable man' (DP p. 91). This situating of the rationality of punishment in the idea of 'sensibility' transforms both the objective and modality of punishment towards a principle of non-repetition and a calculation of effects, that is, an economy of power which functions to prevent the repetition of the crime by either the criminal in question or imitators through a punishment which addresses the crime in terms of its effects.[12]

Foucault delineates this technology as a 'semio-technique' constructed around a series of theoretical rules: (i) a linking to the idea of the crime of a punishment whose harm exceeds the benefit derivable from the crime; (ii) a location of the idea of pain, its representation rather than actuality, as the instrument of this technique; (iii) a formulating of representation in terms of its effects on potential offenders: 'if one could be sure the criminal could not repeat the crime, it would be enough to make others believe he had been punished' (DP p. 95); (iv) a doubling of publicity and surveillance: on the one hand, the laws and the procedures of their deployment (the system of justice) must be known and, on the other hand, the gaze of the law to be effective must be eternally vigilant (the system of policing); (v) a determination of the truth of the crime through common reason rather than casuistry; and (vi) an optimal specification of punishment along the axes of crime/punishment and sentence/criminal through which there emerges a code-individualisation link expressed in the idea of a 'table' of crimes and penalties 'so that each particular offence and each punishable individual might come . . . within the provisions of a general law' (DP p. 99). The formation of these rules, Foucault argues, denotes the emergence of two lines of objectification of the crime and the criminal: on the one hand, the location of the criminal 'designated as the enemy of all, whom it is in the interest of all to track down, falls outside the pact, disqualifies himself as a citizen and emerges, bearing within him as it were, a wild fragment of nature'[13] and, on the other hand, 'the need to measure, from within, the effects of the punitive power prescribes tactics of intervention over all criminals, actual or potential' (DP p. 101).[14] However, while the former of these lines of objectification remains only a potentiality, the latter directly constitutes a series of effects which emerge in the construction and organisation of penal practices as 'theatres of punishment'.

This technology of penal semiotics, which combines the idea of the social contract with a theory of representation and a principle of utility, counterposes to the technology of the tortured body, an operation on the mind of the convict and the public in which punishment links the two in a theatre of morals. Yet this semiotic system of penal practices was barely put into practice before being rapidly displaced by the universalising of the practice of detention which had been merely one of its modes; the 'punitive city' in which punishment exhibits itself as a moral street-theatre is displaced by the 'reformatory' as an enclosed laboratory of discipline.

Foucault's argument is that the emergence of the prison as the site of punitive reason is a specific instance of the emergence of a certain technology of domination characterised by disciplinary techniques. He suggests that the emergence of these techniques represents the discovery of 'the body as object and target of power':

> The great book of Man-the-Machine was written simultaneously on two registers: the anatomo-metaphysical register, of which Descartes wrote the first pages and which the physicians and philosophers continued, and the technico-political register, which was constituted by a whole set of regulations and by empirical and calculated methods relating to the army, the school, and the hospital, for controlling or correcting the operations of the body. These two registers are quite distinct, since it was a question, on the one hand, of submission and use and, on the other hand, of functioning and explanation: there was a useful body and an intelligible body.
>
> (DP p. 136)

Foucault's claim here is not that disciplinary techniques suddenly emerge *ex nihilo*; on the contrary, he recognises that such techniques had long existed in the monastery,[15] the army and the workshop; rather, his claim is that, in the seventeenth and eighteenth centuries, these techniques 'became general formulas of domination' aimed at the production of 'subjected and practised bodies', that is, economically useful and political obedient bodies. We can begin to analyse the operation of this technology of domination by outlining the general features of discipline. Firstly, Foucault identifies discipline as proceeding through the distribution of individuals in space. This is facilitated through techniques of enclosure and partitioning which organise an analytical space, a space which is not simply architectural but also functional (it denotes a 'place' in a series) and hierarchical (it denotes a 'rank' in a series). This analytical space of distribution is thus also the supervisable space of intelligibility; distribution and observation are tied to each other in the figure of the table as 'both a technique of power and a procedure of knowledge' (DP p. 148); however, although 'the procedures of disciplinary distribution had their place amongst contemporary techniques of classification and tabulation . . . they also introduced into them the specific problem of individuals and multiplicity' (DP p. 156). Secondly, Foucault notes the control of activity in these 'cellular' spaces through a series of techniques: the time-table through which precision and application are articulated; the temporal elaboration of the act in which the act is broken down into its constituent elements; the correlation of the body and the gesture which imposes the optimal relation for efficiency 'between a gesture and the overall position of the body' (DP p. 152), the body–object articulation which breaks down the 'total gesture into two parallel series: that of the parts of the body to be used . . . and that of the parts of the object manipulated' (DP p. 153) and integrates these series into a fixed sequence of elements; and the technique of exhaustive use which seeks the maximisation of both efficiency and speed. Through these techniques, Foucault argues, a new object emerges which is not that of the mechanical body, but rather that of the natural body, 'a body of exercise, rather than of speculative physics; a body manipulated by authority, rather than imbued with animal spirits; a body of useful training and not of rational mechanics, but one in which, by virtue of that very fact, a number of natural requirements and functional constraints are beginning to emerge' (DP p. 155). Consequently, these two dimensions of discipline – distribution and control – entail that disciplinary power 'has as its correlative an individuality which is not only analytical and "cellular", but also natural and "organic" ' (DP p. 156).[16] Thirdly, moreover, Foucault argues that disciplinary power is dynamic rather than static; tied to a principle of progression it manifests an 'evolutive' form of time which 'tends towards a subjection which has never reached its limit' (DP p. 162). Finally, Foucault suggests, this form of power further seeks to constitute the body as an element of a machine which transcends its component parts through a spatial and temporal insertion of the body into an ensemble over which it is articulated through precise commands (e.g. a military unit). These four dimensions of disciplinary power can be summarised thus:

it might be said that discipline creates out of the bodies it controls four types of individuality, or rather an individuality that is endowed with four characteristics: it is cellular (by the play of spatial distribution), it is organic (by the coding of activities), it is genetic (by the accumulation of time), it is combinatory (by the composition of forces) . . . in doing so, it operates four great techniques: it draws up tables; it prescribes movements; it imposes exercises; . . . it arranges 'tactics'.

(DP p. 167)

Discipline, in other words, 'makes' individuals; 'it is the specific technique of a power that regards individuals both as objects and as instruments of its exercise' (DP p. 170).[17] At this juncture, then, let us turn from the techniques of disciplinary power to the instruments through which the operations of these techniques were deployed and regulated, namely, 'hierarchical observation, normalizing judgement and their combination in a procedure that is specific to it, the examination' (DP p. 170).

To begin with the exercise of discipline presupposes surveillance of the space within which individuals are linked and divided, the initial model for this 'observatory' being the military camp in which the disciplinary gaze operates by means of general visibility. The expansion of this principle of internal visibility to schools, factories, prisons and housing estates, for example, denotes its gradual refinement as an instrument of individualisation which not only analytically separates individuals but also allows for altering them. However, for the analytical individualisation of the gaze to function as the ground of discipline requires a standard of judgement in terms of which the deployment of penalties may be articulated. This role is taken up by normalising judgement which addresses the deviation from an order which is set out as formal regulations where these are defined by substantive norms; punishment here is articulated on a ground of formal equality linked to substantive normality. This normalising judgement 'refers individual actions to a whole that is at once a field of comparison, a space of differentiation and the principle of a rule to be followed' (DP p. 182). By contrast with a judicial penalty, normalising judgement refers not to laws which are transgressed but to non-conformity to norms. The combination of hierarchical observation and normalising judgement emerges in the examination in which a certain type of power and a certain form of knowledge become linked. Firstly, the examination subjects those upon whom it is directed to a 'compulsory visibility', it 'holds them in a mechanism of objectification' (DP p. 187). Secondly, the examination introduces individuality into the field of documentation through procedures which correlate individual data within cumulative systems 'making it possible to classify, to form categories, to determine averages, to fix norms' (DP p. 190). In this respect, the examination makes possible both 'the constitution of the individual as a describable, analysable object' and 'the constitution of a comparative system that made possible the measurement of overall phenomena, the description of groups, the characterisation of collective facts, the calculation of gaps between individuals, their distribution in a given "population" ' (DP p. 190). Thirdly, the examination makes each individual 'a case which at one and the same time constitutes an object for a branch of knowledge and a hold for a branch of power' (DP p. 191). The examination as instrument of discipline marks here 'the reversal of the political axis of individualization' in that it is no longer the case that individualisation is greatest in the upper echelons of power but, rather, individualisation increases as power grows more anonymous in its descent: 'In a system of discipline, the child is more individualised than the adult, the patient more than the healthy man, the madman and delinquent more than the normal and non-delinquent' (DP p. 193). It is, Foucault argues, in the epistemological space opened up by this reversal, by this production of the modern individual as object and instrument of power that the 'objectifying' human sciences emerge. The procedures of individualisation and objectification which manifest their combination in the examination denote the conditions of emergence of a 'science of individuals'. To illustrate this claim, we can turn, firstly, to the development of 'panopticism' and, secondly, to the emergence of the penitentiary technique and the figure of the 'delinquent'.

The formation of panopticism marks the entwinement of two pre-existing projects of power: on the one hand, the rituals of exclusion characteristic of the treatment of lepers and, on the other hand, the segmentation and surveillance characteristic of plague control. Embodied in these two projects are distinct modes of exercising power:

> The leper was caught up in a practice of rejection, of exile-enclosure; he was left to his doom in a mass amongst which it was useless to differentiate; those sick of the plague were caught up in a meticulous tactical partitioning in which individual differentiations were the constricting effects of a power that multiplied, articulated and subdivided itself; the great confinement on the one hand; the correct training on the other.

(DP p. 198)

Moreover, these two modes of power exhibit distinct political dreams: the tactic of exclusion is tied to the idea of the pure community, the tactic of training is tied to the idea of a disciplined society. However, despite these differences, these projects become linked in the nineteenth century which applies to 'the space of exclusion of which the leper was the symbolic inhabitant . . . the technique of power proper to disciplinary partitioning':

> On the one hand, the lepers are treated as plague victims; the tactics

176

of individualizing disciplines are imposed on the excluded; and, on the other hand, the universality of disciplinary controls makes it possible to brand the 'leper' and to bring into play against him the dualistic mechanisms of exclusion. The constant division between the normal and abnormal, to which every individual is subjected, brings us back to our own time, by applying the binary branding and exile of the leper to quite different objects; the existence of a whole set of techniques and institutions for measuring, supervising and correcting the abnormal brings into play disciplinary mechanisms to which the fear of the plague gave rise.

(DP p. 199)

The entwinement of the projects of exclusion and discipline is given architectural form in the figure of Bentham's Panopticon in which a central tower allows the permanent surveillance of prisoners who are confined to single cells in a building around this tower. Moreover, the tower as the source of light guarantees both the visibility of the prisoner and the invisibility of the supervisor, while the partitioning of the cells implies the invisibility of other prisoners: 'The Panopticon is a machine for dissociating the see/being seen dyad: in the peripheric ring, one is totally seen, without ever seeing; in the central tower, one sees everything without ever being seen' (DP pp. 201–2). This optical relation makes the exercise of power automatic in that the prisoner, because he cannot be sure as to whether he is being observed, becomes his own supervisor, 'he becomes the principle of his own subjection' (DP p. 203). This disciplinary machine, however, is not marked simply by the self-supervision of the inmate; on the contrary, its architectural arrangement also qualifies the Panopticon as a individualising machine:

It makes it possible to draw up differences: among patients, to observe the symptoms of each individual, without the proximity of beds, the circulation of miasmas, the effects of contagion confusing the clinical tables; among schoolchildren, it makes it possible to observe performances (without there being any imitation or copying), to map aptitudes, to assess characters, to draw up rigorous classifications and, in relation to normal development, to distinguish 'laziness and stubbornness' from 'incurable imbecility'; among workers, it makes it possible to note the aptitudes of each worker, compare the time he takes to perform a task, and if they are paid by the day, to calculate their wages.

(DP p. 203)

As these examples illustrate, the Panopticon is polyvalent in its applications as a site of knowledge production. Yet this does not exhaust the operation of this machine in that it also functions as a laboratory of power: 'it could be used as a machine to carry out experiments, to alter behaviour, to train or correct individuals' (DP p. 203). The Panopticon represents 'a privileged place for experiments on men, and for analysing with complete certainty the transformations that may be obtained from them' (DP p. 204). Foucault's argument in analysing the emergence of the idea of the Panopticon is not to suggest the institutional realisation of this figure in its ideal but, rather, to suggest that this imaginary utopia 'is the diagram of a mechanism of power reduced to its ideal form' and the fact that it has given rise to so many projected or realised programmes indicates 'the imaginary intensity it has possessed for almost two hundred years' (DP p. 205). Foucault's claim is that this panoptic schema becomes a generalised functional mechanism for discipline which denotes the formation of the disciplinary society, that is, the spread of mechanisms of discipline through the social body during the seventeenth and eighteenth centuries. It is in this context that penal justice takes as its point of application the disciplined individual rather than the tortured body or juridical subject; the prison as the universal site of penal punishment is a specific instance of the development of disciplinary power.

What then of this universalisation of detention as the form of punishment? How is it that the prison becomes the 'self-evident' site of punishment? Foucault notes initially that this 'self-evident' character is based on the idea of 'deprivation of liberty':

> How could the prison not be the penalty *par excellence* in a society in which liberty is a good that belongs to all in the same way and to which each individual is attached, as Duport put it, by a 'universal and constant' feeling? Its loss has therefore the same value for all: unlike the fine, it is an 'egalitarian' punishment. The prison is the clearest, simplest, most equitable of penalties. Moreover, it makes it possible to quantify the penalty exactly according to the variable of time.
>
> (DP p. 232)

The prisoner pays his debt to society, makes reparation for his crime, through the work he performs in the prison over a given time. However, the self-evidence of the prison is not simply based on this juridico-economic logic; rather, it is also based on its role in transforming individuals: 'How could the prison not be immediately accepted when, by locking up, retraining and rendering docile, it merely reproduces, with a little more emphasis, all the mechanisms that are found in the social body?' (DP p. 233). From the beginning of the nineteenth century, Foucault argues, the foundation of the prison is both juridico-economic and technico-disciplinary. The prison in this respect always already exceeds the simple deprivation of liberty and it does so through three schemata which define the penitentiary technique: 'the politico-moral schema of individual isolation and hierarchy; the economic model of force applied

178

to compulsory work; the technico-medical model of cure and normal-isation' (DP p. 248). The prison as the site not only of punishment but also of observation and experiment is the privileged site of realisation of the panoptic programme; it is not simply a case of surveillance but also of objectification, of knowing the individual as a point of application of punitive mechanisms. In other words, the penitentiary apparatus receives an 'offender' and substitutes for this figure of juridical knowledge, the 'delinquent', that is, a figure of 'criminological' knowledge:

> The delinquent is to be distinguished from the offender by the fact that it is not so much his act as his life that is relevant in characterising him. . . . The delinquent is also to be distinguished from the offender in that he is not only the author of his acts (the author responsible in terms of certain criteria of free, conscious will), but is linked to his offence by a whole bundle of complex threads (instincts, drives, tendencies, character). The penitentiary technique bears not on the relation between author and crime, but on the criminal's affinity with his crime.
>
> (DP p. 253)

It is in the space defined by the figure of the delinquent that there emerges the constitution of 'a new objectivity in which the criminal belongs to a typo-logy that is both natural and deviant' (DP p. 253). In taking up the initial form of this typology in the classification of Ferrus, we can also illustrate the operation of the penitentiary technique as a technology of domination.

This criminological discourse constructs three major types of delinquent:

1 those who are endowed 'with intellectual resources above the average of intelligence that we have established', but who have been perverted either by the 'tendencies of their organization' and a 'native pre-disposition', or by 'pernicious logic', an 'iniquitous morality', a 'dangerous attitude to social duties' (DP p. 253);
2 those who are 'vicious, stupid or passive convicts, who have been led into evil by indifference to either shame or honour, through coward-ice, that is to say, laziness, and because of a lack of resistance to bad incitements' (DP pp. 253–4);
3 those who are 'inept or incapable convicts', who are 'rendered incapable, by an incomplete organization, of any occupation re-quiring considered effort and consistent will, . . . and who . . . are led to evil by their very incapacity' (DP p. 254).

This identification of the criminal's *nature* denotes the identification of the *substance* which is the target of the technology, that is, the determination of that part of the individual which is constituted as the prime material of their criminal conduct. The mode of subjection denotes the relation to, and form of recognition of, normal behaviour to be aimed at in relation to each type. This is expressed in the ascetics of domination developed to attend each type of delinquent:

1   The intelligent convict having the cognitive and conceptual resources to recognise their own deviancy will be placed in the position of having to reflect on this. They require 'isolation day and night, solitary exercise' (DP p. 253).

2   The passive delinquents will be provided with the conceptual resources they lack: 'the regime suitable to them is not so much that of punishment as of education: isolation at night, work in common during the day, conversations permitted provided they are conducted aloud, reading in common, followed by mutual questioning, for which rewards may be given' (DP p. 254).

3   The incapable convicts must 'live in common, but in such a way as to form small groups, constantly stimulated by collective operations, and subjected to rigid surveillance' (DP p. 254).

While these disciplinary practices attempt to produce docile bodies, that is, to maximise the conductability of inmates, they also, it may be argued, aim beyond themselves to the *telos* of this technology of domination: the production of 'normal' individuals. Foucault's concern is not immediately with the success or failure of this technology, but rather with noting that the penitentiary technique and the figure of the delinquent are co-productive, and that this technico-disciplinary economy of punishment increasingly invests the juridical apparatus, that is, the delinquent increasingly displaces the offender: 'Delinquency is the vengeance of the prison on justice. It is a revenge formidable enough to leave the judge speechless. It is at this point that the criminologists raise their voices' (DP p. 255). We can refer back at this juncture to the two potential but divergent lines of objectification which emerged with the discourse of penal reform: 'the first was the series of "monsters", moral or political, who had fallen outside the social pact; the second was that of the judicial subject rehabilitated by punishment' (DP p. 256). In the figure of the delinquent, these two lines of objectification are integrated as 'an individual in whom the offender of the law and the object of a scientific technique are superimposed – or almost – upon one another' (DP p. 256). In this context, Foucault suggests that one of the reasons for the enduring acceptance of the prison is that 'in fabricating delinquency, it gave criminal justice a unitary field of objects, authenticated by the "sciences", and thus enabled it to function on a general horizon of "truth" ' (DP p. 256); '[k]nowable man (soul, individuality, consciousness, conduct, whatever it is called) is the object-effect of this analytical investment, of this domination-observation' (DP p. 305). This production of truth, however, must be taken up in relation to a final feature of prisons, namely, their failure to perform as sites of rehabilitation.

The failure of prisons to achieve their stated aims and the various projects of reform wrought on prisons are not, on Foucault's account, divorced from the persistence of the prison as the privileged site of punishment. Rather, he argues, these elements should be situated as part of a system comprising

> the additional, disciplinary element of the prison – the element of 'super-power'; the production of an objectivity, a technique, a penitentiary 'rationality' – the element of auxiliary knowledge; the *de facto* reintroduction, if not actual increase, of a criminality that the prison sought to destroy – the element of inverted efficiency; lastly, the repetition of a 'reform' that is isomorphic, despite its 'idealism', with the disciplinary functioning of the prison – the element of utopian duplication.
>
> (DP p. 271)

In taking this stance, Foucault's argument is that 'failure' of the prison needs to be addressed in terms of the ends achieved by this failure. Taking up this question, Foucault suggests that 'the prison, and no doubt punishment in general, is not intended to eliminate offences, but to distinguish them, to distribute them, to use them; ... they tend to assimilate the trangression of the laws in a general tactics of subjection' (DP p. 272). Not the least aspect of this 'failure' of the prison as an element of the carceral system is that it serves to legitimate the extension of disciplinary power. Resistance to the technologies of domination deployed in the prison becomes the ground for a refinement and elaboration of these techniques both within and beyond the prison. Thus Foucault notes that the normalising judgement has become one of the central elements of our society:

> The judges of normality are everywhere. We are in the society of the teacher-judge, the doctor-judge, the educator-judge, the 'social worker'-judge; it is on them that the universal reign of the normative is based; and each individual, wherever he may find himself, subjects to it his body, his gestures, his behaviour, his aptitudes, his achievements. The carceral network, in its compact or disseminated forms, with its systems of insertion, distribution, surveillance, observation, has been the greatest support, in modern society, of the normalizing power.
>
> (DP p. 304)

The 'failure' of prisons itself seems to provide a ground for the expansion of normalising power in the government of the individual considered as an object of the disciplinary gaze. The pernicious character of this modality of power/knowledge – in which disciplinary practices create the epistemological space for the scientific treatment of man as an object and the 'structural' human sciences create the 'truth'-space of normalising judgement – lies in its capacity to locate failure as a need for intensifying and extending its gaze. If we are increasingly today caught with structures of objectification, Foucault argues, it is not least because resistance to disciplinary power, resistance to the government of 'man' as an objectified other, serves to incite the reproduction and intensification of its normalising gaze.

ON SEXUAL REASON: SUBJECTIFYING INDIVIDUALS

In considering the punitive rationality developed around the site of the prison, we were concerned with power relations and object relations, that is, the panoptic technologies through which the other is constituted as an object. In addressing the emergence of sexual rationality, our concern is with power relations, ethical relations, and subject relations, that is, the confessional technologies through which we both constitute ourselves as subjects and are produced as objects. To analyse Foucault's account, we can begin by constructing the apparatus he deploys to analyse sexual reason before examining his account of the emergence of sex as the site on which an ascetics of truth-telling is linked to the subjectification of individuals.

Foucault's approach to the domain of sexual rationality can be clarified by his distinction between a *deployment of alliance* and a *deployment of sexuality*, where the former of these refers to 'a system of marriage, of fixation and development of kinship ties, of transmission of names and possessions' (HS p. 106) and the latter refers to secret desires, bodily pleasures, and private fantasies. Moreover, while the deployment of alliance is articulated through a juridical discourse which attends to 'the legitimate or illegitimate character of the act of sexual congress' (HS p. 108), the deployment of sexuality is articulated through a normative discourse which concerns the truth of sex as 'the very essence of the individual human being and the core of personal identity' (Dreyfus and Rabinow 1983: 171). In this respect, Foucault's concern, as in his study of punitive rationality, is with how a normative discourse is grafted onto, and penetrates, a juridical discourse, that is, his genealogical task is to trace the emergence and development of the deployment of sexuality in relation to the deployment of alliance and to indicate the implications of the process for the constitution of the modern individual. To reconstruct this genealogy, we can direct our initial focus to the emergence of the deployment of sexuality by reference to 'a gradual progression away from the problematic of relations to the problematic of the "flesh" ' (HS p. 108) in the Christian pastoral and the transformation of the problematic of the flesh into a problematic of sexuality within a secularisation of pastoral care.

We can begin with Foucault's identification of a generalisation and intensification of the confession of the flesh within the Christian pastoral in the seventeenth century. Although the confession as a mode of transforming sex into discourse had functioned for centuries in a monastic setting, it now becomes both universalised in the form of a general imperative and deepens its gaze by both assigning a priority to sins of the flesh in relation to various other modes of sinning and requiring the verbalisation not only of sexual acts but also of desire in all its forms. This activity of rendering desire into discourse was not merely the prologue to the performance of penance, on Foucault's account; rather this ascetics of truth-telling was immanently linked to a *telos* of self-renunciation in that the very activity itself was located as producing specific (desirable) effects on desire such as mastery and detachment but also spiritual reconversion and renewal.[18] Indeed, we arrive here at a central element of Foucault's argument:

> This is the essential thing: that Western man has been drawn for three centuries to the task of telling everything concerning his sex; that since the classical age there has been a constant optimization and an increasing valourization of sex; and that this carefully analytical discourse was meant to yield multiple effects of displacement, intensification, reorientation, and modification of desire itself.
>
> (HS p. 23)

This claim, of course, remains to be demonstrated; what is significant at this stage is the emphasis which the Christian pastoral places on sexual desire within the practice of confession and the idea that the activity of telling the truth about oneself in the form of one's desires is itself constitutive of freedom from desire, that there is an immanent relationship between truth and freedom. However, we should note that confession 'is also a ritual that unfolds within a power relationship, for one does not confess without the presence (or virtual presence) of a partner' (HS p. 61). This partner, on Foucault's account, is both the interlocutor whose questions are integral to the teasing out of a truth whose resistance to disclosure is its corroboration and the authority who requires, interprets and judges this truth. Thus, to the ethical relationship of truth and freedom embodied in this pastoral rationality, there must be added a further dimension, namely, that the production of truth requires the figure of the interlocutor/authority. The development and refinement of this technology within Christianity, Foucault argues, 'went through a long series of theoretical elaborations until, at the end of the eighteenth century, it became fixed in expressions capable of symbolising the mitigated strictness of Alfonso de' Liguori in the one case and Wesleyan pedagogy in the other' (HS p. 116).

While Christianity continued to elaborate its confessional technologies throughout the eighteenth century, this period also saw the constitution of sex as a matter which required the attention of secular institutions of government: 'sex became a "police" matter' (HS p. 24). It is within this gradual displacement of the Christian pastoral by a secular state pastoral that the problematic of flesh becomes that of sexuality and that this deployment of sexuality is grafted onto the deployment of alliance. This articulation of sex as something requiring management is signalled by the emergence of the political problematic of 'population'. This problematic denotes a crucial shift for Foucault in so far as it marks, on the one hand, the severing of the art of government from the model of the family and, on the other hand, the emergence into prominence of the family 'considered as an element internal to population and as a fundamental instrument in its government' (G p. 99).[19] With specific regard to sex, this political problematic of population as the target of government expresses itself through, on the one hand, the emergence of statistical analyses of phenomena such as birth rates, the age of marriage, the frequency of sexual relations, fertility rates, etc. and, on the other hand, a series of interventions which sought to conduct the sexual conduct of subjects. Foucault suggests that this government of sexuality developed along three axes:

> that of pedagogy, having as its objective the specific sexuality of children; that of medicine, whose objective was the sexual physiology peculiar to women; and last, that of demography, whose objective was the spontaneous or concerted regulation of births.
>
> (HS p. 116)

In this respect, the secular government of sexuality marked a continuity with Christianity in which these three axes had emerged in terms of spiritual pedagogy, the phenomena of possession, and the regulation of conjugal relations (HS p. 117). However, this continuity is also the site of a transformation in so far as the form of sexual reason which emerges 'was ordered in relation to the medical institution, the exigency of normality, and . . . the problem of life and illness' (HS p. 117). Thus, Foucault suggests that by the end of the eighteenth century the family is 'the interchange of sexuality and alliance' in that the medical discourse of sexuality, which at this juncture becomes separate from the medicine of the body, interpenetrates the juridical discourse of alliance along the three axes of development of the deployment of sexuality. This inter-penetration, on Foucault's account, operates through 'four great strategic unities which, beginning in the eighteenth century, formed specific mechanisms of knowledge and power centering on sex' (HS p. 103): firstly, a hysterisation of women's bodies as a threefold process whereby woman's body is constituted as 'saturated with sexuality', integrated into medical discourses and practices 'by reason of a pathology intrinsic to it', and situated as 'in organic communication with the social body . . ., the

184

family space . . ., and the life of children' (HS p. 104); secondly, a pedagogisation of children's sex whereby the child's capacity for indulging in sexual activity (e.g. masturbation) is located as both natural and dangerous, such that it requires the continual supervision of parents and experts to care for 'this precious and perilous, dangerous and endangered sexual potential' (HS p. 104); thirdly, a socialisation of procreative behaviour which operates economically through fiscal measures attending the fertility of couples, politically by designating couples as responsible to the social body, and medically by 'attributing a pathogenic value – for the individual and the species – to birth-control practices' (HS p. 105). Finally, a psychiatrisation of perverse pleasure wherey the sexual instinct is isolated, analysed in terms of possible anomalies, assigned a normal or pathological role relative to behaviour, and submitted to corrective technologies. Thus, through the figures of the hysterical women, the masturbating child, the Malthusian couple and the perverse adult, medical theories of sex operate a normative gaze over individuals.

In this reconstruction of Foucault's account, it was noted – almost as an aside – that the medicine of sex is set apart from the medicine of the body or, to put this another way, that from the beginning of the nineteenth century 'sex seems to have been incorporated into two very distinct orders of knowledge: a biology of reproduction, which developed continuously according to a general scientific normativity, and a medicine of sex conforming to quite different rules of formation' (HS p. 54). While we have noted the context within which this science of sex emerged and the normative figures which facilitate its primary lines of articulation, it does remain necessary to specify its rules of formation in terms of how it takes up and transforms the confessional technologies developed within the Christian pastoral.

Foucault's comments on this issue may be taken as starting with the observations that the confession has operated in a number of contexts as 'one of the West's most highly valued techniques for producing truth' (HS p. 59) and that from the Christian penance onwards sex has been a privileged theme of confession. The crucial development, on Foucault's account, is that 'with the rise of Protestantism, the Counter Reformation, eighteenth century pedagogy, and nineteenth century medicine, [confession] gradually lost its ritualistic and exclusive localization' (HS p. 63), that is, confessional technologies, like panoptic technologies in the same period, become generalised through the social body as techniques of truth production; while the form of the truth-telling enacted within the confessional becomes 'a discourse which had to model itself after that which spoke, not of sin and salvation, but of bodies and life-processes – the discourse of science' (HS p. 64). In other words, throughout the eighteenth century with its political problematic of policing populations, we can see both a generalising of confessional techniques for the production of truth and a shift in the modality of truth-statements from a theological to scientific register, where these two dimensions of the regime of truth interact as the need to reconcile procedures of confession with a scientific discursivity. The articulation of this interest, however, is by no means a smooth or automatic process. As Foucault notes:

> The scientific discourse was scandalised, or in any case repelled, when it had to take charge of this whole discourse from below. It was also faced with a theoretical and methodological paradox: the long discussions concerning the possibility of constituting a science of the subject, the validity of introspection, lived experience as evidence, or the presence of consciousness to itself were responses to this problem that is inherent in the functioning of truth in our society: can one articulate the production of truth according to the old juridico-religious model of confession, and the extortion of confidential evidence according to the rules of scientific discourse?
>
> (HS p. 64)

It is in the context of the formation of this epistemological problematic that the separation of the medicine of sex from that of the body at the beginning of the nineteenth century emerges as a central element. This becomes clear if we detail the five procedures Foucault identifies governing the constitution of sexual confession within a scientific discursivity.

1 *Through a clinical codification of the inducement to speak* – this procedure denotes the combining of confession with the examination (inter-rogation, questionnaire, hypnosis) as a way of 'reinscribing the procedure of confession in the field of scientifically acceptable observations' (HS p. 65).

2 *Through the postulate of a general and diffuse causality* – the legitimation of the confession–examination through an isolation of the sexual instinct as the primary principle of agency: 'the principle of sex as a "cause of any and everything" was the theoretical underside of a con-fession that had to be thorough, meticulous, and constant, and at the same time operate within a scientific type of practice' (HS pp. 65–6).

3 *Through the principle of a latency intrinsic to sexuality* – the shift in the focus of confession from that which the subject hides to that which is hidden from the subject and which, thereby, links confession to scientific practice as the process of forcing a secretive truth to reveal itself.

4 *Through the method of interpretation* – the identification of the labour of confession as integral to the scientific validation of the truth produced in so far as this truth 'was constituted in two stages: present but incomplete, blind to itself, in the one who spoke, it could only reach

completion in the one who assimilated and recorded it' (HS p. 66), this interlocutive other operating as the authority who constitutes and verifies the truth of confession as a sign through deciphering its hidden meaning.

5   *Through the medicalisation of the effects of confession* – the reconfiguring of the activity of confession and its effects as therapeutic operations within a regime governed by the rule of the normal and the pathological. This implies both that sex is constituted as 'an extremely unstable pathological field' which requires medical supervision and intervention, and that the activity of confessing to the appropriate medical authority is itself a therapeutic operation.

We can recognise in these procedures several elements drawn from the confession of the flesh within the Christian pastoral but recodified within a scientific discourse. At this juncture though the issue to stress is that Foucault's account illustrates how, through the scientisation of confessional technologies, there emerges that linkage between power relations, ethical relations and subject relations whereby the conduct of the other is conducted through practices of normalisation predicated on discourses of the truth of the other's subjectivity. Foucault's point is not merely that this confessional science of sex marks the formation of that epistemological space within which the interpretive or hermeneutic human sciences become possible, but also that the constitution of an immanent relationship between truth and freedom within this epistemological space functions such that resistance to this modality of power incites the expansion and refinement of its normalising gaze.

We can clarify the latter claim by noting that, within this dimension of humanist structures of recognition, the linkage between ethical relations and subject relations is structured in terms of the truth of one's subjectivity, that is, the *telos* of one's ethical practices is *authenticity*, where this denotes a conception of autonomy as the self-legislation of the law of one's true or essential being. As such resistance to power relations operates through opposing an alternative interpretation of one's authentic personal identity to that legislated by the 'scientific expert'; however, within the logic of the confession as sign, this alternative interpretation is situated as a supplementary signification requiring an extension and deepening of the interpretative activity of science. In other words, as with panoptic technologies, confessional technologies operate to link the expansion of capacities to the intensification of power relations.

To conclude this section, let us note that in his study of sexual reason Foucault has provided an account which complements that offered in the study of punitive reason by addressing itself to subject relations rather than object relations. The penetration and subsumption of the deployment of alliance by that of sexuality, like the envelopment of the deployment of crime by that of delinquency, expresses the displacement of a juridical modality of power by a normative modality of power. Moreover, although *The History of Sexuality* lacks the historical detail of *Discipline and Punish* (it was after all only intended as an introduction to future volumes), it does point beyond the account of punitive reason in so far as the epistemological problematic which marked the interface of confessional techniques and scientific discursivity is located in terms of a political problematic, namely, the secularisation of a pastoral modality of power. In taking up the relationship of these accounts of punitive and sexual reason to the ambivalent structure of the modern humanist will to truth, we need to address this political dimension of humanism.

ON POLITICAL REASON: BEING AND BIOPOLITICS

In our consideration of sexual reason, it was noted that the development of the four great strategic unities identified by Foucault emerges with the intertwinement of a concern with the individual and a concern with the population.[20] Foucault's suggestion is that this double concern denotes the formation of a political rationality in which the state and its agencies function simultaneously as sites of individualisation and totalisation. More precisely, Foucault notes two forms of political rationality exhibited in the Western tradition: on the one hand, there is the shepherd–flock game characterised by a focus on individuals, a concern for the truth of their being, and a theme of other-worldly salvation; and on the other hand, there is the city–citizens game characterised by a focus on the collective, a concern for the survival of the city, and a theme of this-worldly sacrifice.[21] These, respectively, individualising and totalising modalities of power define the parameters of modern political reason. Foucault's suggestion is that this political rationality finds its initial expression on Foucault's account in the emergence of two sets of doctrines: the *reason of state* and the *theory of police*. Consequently, before examining the relations between this political rationality, the humanist will to truth, and panoptic and confessional technologies, we will sketch these doctrines in order to flesh out the nascent form of this political rationality.

The emergence of the doctrine of 'reason of state' is situated by Foucault as a specific moment within a general problematics of government which arises in the sixteenth and seventeenth centuries; a problematics formed by the intersection of two processes, one of which relates to 'the establishment of the great territorial, administrative and colonial states', while the other 'with the Reformation and Counter-Reformation, raises the issue of how one must be spiritually ruled and led on this earth in order to achieve eternal salvation' (G p. 88). Broadly speaking, three types of political theory co-exist within this period. Firstly, there is Machiavelli's *The Prince* which is read as a treatise concerning the prince's ability to keep his principality. Secondly, there is the emergence of social contract theories which construct ideas of political obligation around an account of sovereignty. Thirdly, there is the doctrine of reason of state which establishes a distinct mode of political rationality in which the political government of things is located in relation to the economic government of the family and the moral government of the self. This third mode of political thinking specifies itself initially through an oppositional reading of Machiavelli's text. The character of this reading is to locate Machiavelli's text as situating the prince 'in a relation of singularity and externality, and thus of transcendence, to his principality' (G pp. 89–90). The relationship between the prince and his principality is synthetic rather than natural and, consequently, is perpetually subject to both external and internal threat. The fragility of this relation, it is argued, leads to the conclusion that the objective of exercising political power is to strengthen the principality as the prince's relation with his territory and subjects. To this 'Machiavellian' characterisation of politics as concerned with the prince's capacity to retain his principality, the theorists of *raison d'état* oppose the idea of an art of government. How is this difference demarcated? Firstly, the theorists of *raison d'état* note:

> that practices of government are, on the one hand, multifarious and concern many types of people: the head of a family, the superior of a convent, the teacher or tutor of a child or pupil; so that there are several forms of government of which the prince's relation to his state is only one particular mode; while, on the other hand, all these other types of government are internal to the state or society.
>
> (G p. 91)

The question of specifying the particular mode of governing applicable to the state as such is conceptualised as both distinct from, and related to, the question of government in general. Foucault notes, for example, La Mothe Le Vayer's typology in which morality as self-government, economics as government of the family and politics as government of the state are specified as having their own distinct rationalities while also linked within a framework of continuity.[22] Whereas the doctrine of the prince is structured around the problematic of justifying a radical distinction between political power and any other kind of power, the doctrine of *raison d'état* structures itself in terms of the task of founding the continuity of the art of government in both ascending and descending modes. Ascending continuity, Foucault argues, 'means that a person who wishes to govern the state well must first learn how to govern himself, his goods and his patrimony' (G p. 91), while descending continuity is based on the idea that 'when a state is well run, the head of the family will know how to look after his family, his goods and his patrimony, which means that individuals will, in turn, behave as they should' (G p. 92); this descending continuity is the site of emergence of the science of *police* (which we will address shortly). In both ascending and descending modes, the pivotal site for this continuity is the government of the family, that is, *economy*: 'This is . . . the essential issue in the establishment of the art of government: introduction of economy into political practice' (G p. 92). In this theoretical development, then, the government of the state 'will therefore mean to apply economy, to set up an economy at the level of the entire state, which means exercising towards its inhabitants, and the wealth and behaviour of each and all, a form of surveillance and control as attentive as that of the head of a family over his household and his goods' (G p. 92). The second moment of demarcation between the theorists of *raison d'état* and 'Machiavellian' politics, which is tied to this 'economic' moment, concerns the location of government as 'the right disposition of things' such that in contrast to the 'Machiavellian' situating of sovereignty as exercised on a territory and, thereby, its inhabitants, this notion of government attends to 'not territory but rather a sort of complex composed of men and things':

> The things with which in this sense government is to be concerned are in fact men, but men in their relations, their links, their imbrication with those other things which are wealth, resources, means of subsistence, the territory with its specific qualities, climate, irrigation, fertility, etc.; men in their relation to that other kind of things, customs, habits, ways of acting and thinking, etc.; lastly, men in their relation to that other kind of things, accidents and misfortunes such as famine, epidemics, death, etc.
>
> (G p. 93)

This element in the doctrines of *raison d'état* similarly demarcates it from theories of sovereignty, Foucault argues, in that whereas theories of sovereignty (e.g. Pufendorf) involve a commitment to the politics of the 'common good' conceived of as submission to sovereignty, the notion of government provided by the theorists of *raison d'état* 'is defined as a right manner of disposing things so as to lead not to the form of the common good, as the jurists' texts would have said, but to an end which is "convenient" for each of the things that are to be governed' (G p. 95). Government, in this sense, concerns the formulation of tactics for managing a plurality of particular aims (such as wealth production, provisions for the people and the increase in the population), rather than simply the imposition of laws onto men.[23]

Within the theory of the art of government which finds its initial elaboration in the doctrine of *raison d'état*, then, Foucault identifies the formation of a specific type of political rationality in which the totalising power of the state is linked to an individualising power. The formation of this type of political rationality, Foucault argues, is intimately connected from the beginning with the formation of the administrative apparatus that attends the emergence of the modern state; moreover, it is also connected on Foucault's account with the appearance of a set of analyses concerned with knowledge of the state (i.e. statistics). How is it though that this doctrine of *raison d'état* displaces or colonises the other types of political rationality which are present in this period, namely, 'Machiavellian' politics and social contract theory? To address this question of the development of the art of government we must examine Foucault's account of mercantilism and the Cameralists' science of police.

The argument Foucault develops is to suggest that the grounding of the art of government in the idea of *raison d'état*, that is, in the idea that 'the state is governed according to rational principles which are intrinsic to it' (G p. 97), actually acts to impede the development of the art of government. Foucault's point here is that while there are undoubtedly military, economic and political reasons for the blockage in the development of the art of government, there are also specific 'mental and institutional structures' which impede its development, most notably, the priority of 'the problem of the exercise of sovereignty, both as a theoretical question and as a principle of political organisation' (G p. 97). To illustrate this claim Foucault instances the development of mercantilism as the first attempt to institute an art of government in terms of both political practices and knowledge of the state, yet as an attempt which was impeded by its own forms of knowledge and practice. Foucault comments:

> The objective was sovereign's might, the instruments those of sovereignty: mercantilism sought to reinsert the possibilities opened by a consciously conceived art of government within a mental and institutional structure, that of sovereignty, which by its very nature stifled them.
>
> (G p. 98)

The matrix of sovereignty remains rigidly dominant as is illustrated by the attempts of contract theorists to derive an art of government from a theory of sovereignty and, while the theme of sovereignty constitutes the framework for political reflection, the art of government necessarily remains immobilised. At the same time, the theory of government has insufficient force to displace the matrix of sovereignty in so far as 'an economy of enrichment still based on a model of the family was unlikely to be able to respond adequately to the importance of territorial possessions and royal finance' (G p. 98). How does the 'governmentalisation' of the state develop given these blockages? Although the theory and practice of government remains trapped within the matrix of sovereignty through the seventeenth century, Foucault argues that a number of processes lead to the renewal of the theme of government in the eighteenth century in relation to 'the recentring of the theme of economy on a different

191

plane from that of the family' and the emergence of 'the problem of population'.

Foucault's claim is that the emergence of the problem of population (which attends the demographic expansion of the eighteenth century) creates the conceptual space within which the model of the family is displaced and the idea of economy resituated. Fundamental to this transformation is the role of statistics: [24]

> Whereas statistics had previously worked within the administrative frame and thus in terms of the functioning of sovereignty, it now gradually reveals that population has its own regularities, its own rate of deaths and diseases, its cycles of scarcity, etc.; statistics shows also that the domain of population involves a range of intrinsic aggregate effects, phenomena that are irreducible to those of the family, such as epidemics, endemic levels of mortality, ascending spirals of labour and wealth; lastly it shows that, through its shifts, customs, activities, etc., population has specific economic effects: statistics, by making it possible to quantify these specific phenomena of population, also shows that this specificity is irreducible to the dimension of the family.
>
> (G p. 99)

This emergence of population as a phenomenon possessing its own regularities irreducible to the model of the family leads to the resiting of the family as an element within population which functions as an instrument for its government rather than a model for government. While, on the one hand, the theme of population allows the remobilisation of the theme of government through a displacement of the model of the family, this remobilisation is complemented, on the other hand, by the location of population (rather than the power of the sovereign) as the ultimate end of government for which the family becomes a privileged instrument. In other words, the *telos* of government under the figure of population becomes those plural ends immanent to population (its welfare, its condition, its wealth, longevity, health, etc.), while the techniques of government are similarly conceived as immanent to the phenomenon of population itself. Within this matrix of governmentality, the population is constituted as both *subject* and *object* of government: 'the population is the subject of needs, of aspirations, but it is also the object in the hands of government, aware, *vis-à-vis* the government of what it wants, but ignorant of what is being done to it' (G p. 100). At the same time, this type of political rationality operates in terms of both individualising and totalising modalities of power constructed around the idea of 'interests': [25]

> Interest at the level of the consciousness of each individual who goes to make up the population, and interest considered as the interest

of the population regardless of what the particular interests and aspirations may be of the individuals who compose it, this is the new target and the fundamental instrument of the government of population: the birth of a new art, or at any rate a range of absolutely new tactics and techniques.

(G p. 100)

The formalisation of this notion of the government of population at the level of knowledge gives rise to the science of political economy or, more specifically, the emergence of a type of government which operates through interventions in the field of population and economy is intimately linked to the development of a *savoir* in which the relations between population and economy are subject to rational examination and calculation. The process Foucault is describing in this account, then, concerns the movement 'from a regime dominated by structures of sovereignty to one ruled by techniques of government' (G p. 101). Integral to this process is the development of the Cameralist science of police;[26] consequently, before concluding our discussion of Foucault's genealogy of biopolitics, it is necessary to examine the role this development played in the 'governmentalisation' of the state.

The science of police is connected by Foucault to both mercantilism and the development of statistics as a political arithmetic in the context of the development of the great administrative monarchies. Foucault's analysis operates by focusing this science of police as a utopia, as a practice and as a discipline by referring respectively to the work of Turquet, Delamare and von Justi. In 1611, Turquet presented his work *AristoDemocratic Monarchy* to the Dutch States General; in this work, Turquet proposes that four great officials concerned with the judiciary, the military, the exchequer and the police rank beside the king. The role of the police official in this system is to encourage virtuous habits amongst the subjects of the state through two boards which addressed people concerning, respectively, the positive dimensions of life (education, occupations, etc.) and the negative dimensions of life (poverty, unemployment, public health, etc.), and two boards which addressed things concerning, respectively, production (manufacturing, markets, trade, etc.) and the 'demesne' (the control of private property, the upkeep of the infrastructure, etc.). What is of interest to Foucault in this text which is 'contemporary with the great theoretical discussions on reason of state and the administrative organisation of monarchies' (PPC p. 78) are three themes: firstly, the police, while being formally an element of the state along with the judiciary, military and exchequer, actually directs itself to everything; secondly, the police takes man as its object, that is, not a judicial subject but a living, working subject; thirdly, the police intervene to ensure and highlight the vigour of the state, and to foster positive and productive relations between men. In other words, the police represent, in Turquet's utopia, the formation of secular pastoralism. At this stage, Foucault turns to Delamare's *Traité de la police*, an adminstrative manual published in 1705, to examine the practices outlined for the use of civil servants. Delamare's encyclopaedia of police is presented in eleven sections concerning religion, morals, health, supplies, roads and public buildings, public safety, the liberal arts, trade, factories, manservants and factory workers, and the poor. What logic of intervention operates here? Foucault notes three answers given by Delamare: (i) the role of the police is to see to men's happiness, (ii) to see to the regulation of men's social relations, (iii) to see to living, to life. The third of these answers, Foucault argues, subsumes the previous two such that the role of the police can be seen as leading men to the maximum degree of happiness to be enjoyed in this life:

> The police deal with religion, not, of course, from the point of view of dogmatic orthodoxy but from the point of view of the moral quality of life. In seeing to health and supplies, the police deal with the preservation of life. Concerning trade, factories, workers, the poor, and public order, the police deal with the conveniences of life. In seeing to the theater, literature, and entertainment, their object is life's pleasure. In short, life is the object of the police.
>
> (PTI p. 157; cf. PPC pp. 80–1)

The issue of police is connected in this context to three developments: firstly, a technicisation of the philosophical project of classifying needs which attempts to determine 'the correlation between the utility scale for individuals and the utility scale for the state' (PTI p. 157); secondly, the location of human happiness as an object of politics which is not simply an end but rather a condition and instrument for the survival and development of the state; thirdly, the identification of society and men as social beings (in contrast to a number of men simply living together) as the object of the police. Finally, then, Foucault turns to the science of police as an academic discipline by focusing on von Justi's *Elements of Police*. Although the object of the police in this text is still defined as men as living social beings, Foucault argues that von Justi's text marks a fourfold advance over that provided by Delamare. Firstly, von Justi locates more precisely the central paradox of police: 'to develop those elements constitutive of individuals' lives in such a way that their development also fosters that of the strength of the state' (PPC p. 82). Secondly, von Justi draws a distinction between *die Polizei* and *die Politik* whereby the latter refers to the negative task of fighting the external and internal enemies of the state, while the former has the positive task of fostering 'both citizens' lives *and* the state's strength' (PPC p. 82). Thirdly, von Justi explicitly introduces the theme of population understood as the end of government. Finally, von Justi provides not simply a list of prescription but also a conceptual grid through which the state can be observed: 'Von Justi combines "statistics" (the description of states) with the art of government. *Polizeiwissenschaft* is at once an art of government and a method of analysis of a population living on a territory' (PPC p. 83). The role of the police, in summary, is one of managing individuals and populations through a *savoir* which defines both the ends of the police and its instruments.

Having sketched out this modality of political rationality in which individualisation and totalisation are linked as the 'governmentalisation' of the state by attending to its formulation within the science of police (although this is only an initial form of this rationality[27]), we can return to our opening question and conclude this chapter by focusing on the relationship between this political rationality, panoptic and confessional technologies, and the humanist will to truth. An appropriate starting point to this discussion is to note that both panoptic and confessional technologies operate to link individualisation and totalisation at the level of knowledge through the construction of 'types' such as the *delinquent* and the *hysterical woman*, where the construction of these 'types' marks the intersection of tactics of individualisation (e.g. the case history) and tactics of totalisation (e.g. statistical norms). It may be noted further that the construction of 'types' through these technologies itself allows for an ever-increasing refinement of 'types' through a proliferation of 'sub-types' (e.g. Ferrus's typology of delinquents). This 'feedback' feature of panoptic and confessional technologies emerges when we note that, through the construction of 'types', both of these technologies also link individualisation and totalisation at the level of practice in so far as they function as 'laboratories of power' instituting regimes of discipline through which regulatory controls are articulated, while these regimes themselves re-articulate the domain of regulation. In other words, panoptic and confessional technologies provide more or less privileged instruments for the articulation of a 'policing' of individuals and populations.

However, in noting the commonality of these technologies with respect to the political rationality which Foucault terms 'biopolitics', we should not overlook the differences which mark panoptic and confessional technologies in terms of the relationship between the forms of disciplinary practice through which they function and the forms of knowledge which they generate (and which articulate their operation). In the case of panoptic technologies, the disciplinary focus is provided by the body as subject to causative processes such that dysfunctional elements within the constitution of an individual's *nature* may be re-aligned or overcome through regimes of training. In other words, this technology operates through the external environment of the individual (e.g. housing) and acts to produce a form of knowledge which locates the individual as a natural object. In the case of confessional technologies, the disciplinary focus is provided by the self as the site of meaning such that dysfunctional elements within the constitution of an individual's *identity* may be re-aligned or overcome through regimes of interpretation. In other words, this technology operates through the internal environment of the individual (e.g. dreams) and acts to produce a form of knowledge which locates the individual as a reflexive subject. What emerges in this brief sketch is the siting of the two poles of humanistic discourse, namely, the simultaneous identification of 'Man' as known object and knowing subject which Foucault analyses in *The Order of Things*.

In our examination of the ambivalence of this humanist will to truth which emerges in the form of three philosophical doubles, we noted that this ambivalence endows the humanist will to truth with a dynamic structure. Having located the grounds of this epistemological grammar by reference to confessional and panoptic technologies, we can note the way in which the dynamic form of this will to truth itself articulates the reproduction of biopolitics. This becomes clear if we note that both panoptic and confessional technologies operate through an identification of the truth of our being either in terms of our essential nature as determined objects or in terms of our authentic identity as free subjects; consequently, the 'failure' of these technologies to achieve the recon-ciliation of our empirical nature or identity with our essential nature or authentic identity does not denote that they should be abandoned; on the contrary, within the matrix of humanist discourse, it necessarily entails that they need to be refined at the level of knowledge and intensified at the level of practice. As Dreyfus and Rabinow acutely note:

> Bio-power spread under the banner of making people healthy and protecting them. When there was resistance, or failure to achieve its stated aims, this was construed as further proof of the need to reinforce and extend the power of experts. A technical matrix was established. By definition, there ought to be a way of solving any technical problem. Once this matrix was established, the spread of bio-power was assured, for there was nothing else to appeal to: any other standards could be shown to be abnormal or to present merely technical problems. We are promised normalization and happiness through science and law. When they fail, this only justifies the need for more of the same.
>
> (Dreyfus and Rabinow 1983: 196)

Biopolitics and humanism are, thus, the practical and theoretical articulations of the fate of modern culture as constituting modern sub-jectivity as a profoundly ambivalent phenomenon whereby resistance reproduces power relations.

10

THE POLITICS OF CRITIQUE
Foucault, maturity and modernity

I do not know whether we will ever reach mature adulthood. Many things in our experience convince us that the historical event of the Enlightenment did not make us mature adults, and we have not reached that stage yet.

(FR p. 49)

For Foucault, as for Nietzsche and Weber, our will to truth constitutes the central problem of modern culture; indeed, we might suggest that our *modernity* consists precisely in our becoming conscious of our will to truth as a problem. Yet the form of this dilemma in Foucault's genealogies is distinct from those forms presented by Nietzsche and Weber in so far as it is neither a question of the collapse of our structures of recognition as an engendering of nihilism nor a question of that reduction of our structures of recognition to material interests and instrumental rationality which signifies disenchantment; rather, Foucault's problem is that of the *hegemony* of humanism, that is, structures of recognition which embody the dynamic ambivalence of the humanist will to truth. Moreover, in so far as Foucault's account of modern culture is animated by a concern with the possibility of human autonomy, the critical potential of his genealogical project is predicated on its capacity to disclose and ground structures of recognition immanent to modern culture which articulate this possibility. To examine this positive moment within Foucault's project of historical ontology, we will begin by specifying further the form of the problem posed by the ambivalence of our will to truth before examining his attempt to confront this dilemma.

THE 'DOUBLE BIND' OF HUMANISM

To clarify Foucault's concern with the ambivalence of our will to truth, it is useful to examine his critique of humanism with respect to the question of ethics. After all, if Foucault's critique is to have force, it must provide more than the 'genetic' argument that modern humanist discourses emerge in the context of the development of normalising modalities of power by showing that these discourses, in some way, act to reproduce the technical matrix of biopolitics.[1] To initiate discussion of this topic, our focus will be the juridico-discursive conception of power and the repressive hypothesis which, Foucault argues, characterises humanist thought. We will move from this to a consideration of humanist ethics, before trying to illustrate how the immanent blindness of humanism to forms of power which 'produce' subjects entails the reproduction of biopolitics.

In examining humanist conceptions of power, Foucault focuses on three 'models', namely, the liberal account of power, the Marxist notion of power and the psychoanalytic concept of power.[2] Each of these accounts of power, Foucault argues, locates the exercise of power in terms of a negative relation to the subject – as oppression, as domination, as repression – which occludes the productivity of power, its capacity to constrain us through constituting our selves as particular kinds of subjects (e.g. delinquent, pervert). By analysing Foucault's critique of these humanist conceptions of power, we will be able to specify the notion of power which was sketched out in our methodological reflections on Foucault's project.

The liberal notion of power, developed within the juridical discourse of social contract theory, offers an understanding of power articulated through a discourse of natural rights:

> [In] the case of the classic, juridical theory, power is taken to be a right, which one is able to possess like a commodity, and which one can in consequence transfer or alienate, either wholly or partially, through a legal act or through some act that establishes a right, such as takes place through cession or contract. Power is that concrete power which every individual holds, and whose partial or total cession enables political power or sovereignty to be established.
>
> (P/K p. 88)

As Foucault points out, this understanding of power is predicated on 'the idea that the constitution of political power obeys the model of a legal transaction involving a contractual type of exchange' (P/K p. 88) where examples of total and partial cession may be provided by Hobbes and Locke respectively.[3] In thinking of power within this theoretical matrix, the crucial relationship is that between the sovereign body constituted through the act of cession and the contract which specifies the terms of the relationship between sovereign and subjects:

> A power so constituted risks becoming oppression whenever it over extends itself, whenever – that is – it goes beyond the terms of the contract. Thus we have contract-power, with oppression as its limit, or rather as the transgression of this limit.
>
> (P/K p. 91)

In this context, the concern of political theory is with specifying the legitimacy or illegitimacy of particular forms of the exercise of political power.[4] The illegitimate exercise of power is thus conceptualised negatively in terms of a breach of the contract made with, and by, rational subjects. Foucault's critical claim – which in itself is hardly original – is that the language of rights, of political emancipation, serves to conceal the presence of domination rather than to eliminate it:

> the theory of sovereignty, and the organisation of a legal code centred upon it, have allowed a system of right to be superimposed upon the mechanisms of discipline in such a way as to conceal its actual procedures, the element of domination inherent in its techniques, and to guarantee to everyone, by virtue of the sovereignty of the State, the exercise of his proper sovereign rights.
>
> (P/K p. 105)

Prima facie, this critique would appear to locate Foucault in that radical tradition of which Marx's essay *On the Jewish Question*[5] is an exemplary instance. It is, after all, a central tenet of Marxism that the rights granted to the subject as a juridical fiction veil the domination of the subject as a sensuous material being. However, the Marxist account of power in terms of a class domination produced by a specific mode of production similarly operates in terms of an understanding of power as establishing a negative relation to the subject in which the juridico-economic form of power is transformed and reproduced:

> Broadly speaking, in the first case [liberalism] we have a political power whose formal model is discoverable in the process of exchange, the economic circulation of commodities; in the second case [Marxism], the historical *raison d'être* of political power and the principle of its concrete forms and actual functioning, is located in the economy.
>
> (P/K p. 89)

What emerges in this conception of power is the idea of a domination which operates in terms of an alienation of man from his species-being (his essential human nature as a conscious, communal, creative being) articulated through the social relations which attend the organisation of the forces of production. This notion of power as repressing one's authentic identity finds a non-economic formulation in the psychoanalytic conception of power which emerges with Freud and Reich; thus one might note the critique of Marxism's economic understanding of power presented in Freud's *Civilisation and its Discontents*.[6] However, the commonality between these approaches, which finds its articulation in Marcuse's *Eros and Civilisation*, effaces the division between economic and sexual understandings of power in so far as both are predicated on an ethics of authenticity. To put this another way, we may say that Marxism

199

and psychoanalysis exhibit a common epistemological grammar, namely that of modern humanism as it is expressed in the analytic of finitude. The problematic structure of this conception of power is that it remains blind to those exercises of power which operate through forms of knowledge which are predicated on an identification of our essential nature or authentic identity and, consequently, facilitates the operation of these modalities of power. This is made manifest in Foucault's critique of the repressive hypothesis in which the identification of power as that which represses our authentic (sexual) identity produces a politics of resistance taking the form of an endless desire for liberation which calls for ever deeper and more refined confessional techniques, where it is precisely these techniques for constituting ourselves as authentic beings which enable the normalisation of our conduct, that is, the conducting of our conduct through 'scientific' norms. Foucault specifies this point with respect to humanist ethics:

> [M]ost of us no longer believe that ethics is founded in religion, nor do we want a legal system to intervene in our moral, personal, private life. Recent liberation movements suffer from the fact that they cannot find any principle on which to base the elaboration of a new ethics. They need an ethics, but they cannot find any other ethics than an ethics founded on so-called scientific knowledge of what the self is, what desire is, what the unconscious is, and so on.
>
> (FR p. 343)

It is in this context that we can grasp Foucault's notion of biopolitics as a technical matrix in which the epistemological grammar of humanism entails that resistance in operating through 'an ethics founded on so-called scientific knowledge' reproduces the technical matrix through which technologies of normalisation are articulated. We should be clear, moreover, before addressing Foucault's understanding of power, that the emergence of the liberal scheme of oppression and the Marxist and psychoanalytic schemes of repression are not presented by Foucault simply as masks which enable the operation of technologies of normalisation; rather, Foucault's approach must be grasped in terms of the specification of forms of social struggle. To clarify this issue, we may note that Foucault distinguishes three types of struggle: struggles against religious, ethnic and sexual discrimination, struggles against social and economic exploitation, and struggles against subjection (or subjectification). The point of this typology is twofold. Firstly, Foucault's suggestion is that the juridical conception of power emerges in the context of struggles against discrimination and the repressive conception of power develops in the context of struggles against exploitation, while his own conception of power addresses struggles of subjection.[7] Secondly, Foucault claims that, while struggles against forms of domination and exploitation have not disappeared, 'the struggle against forms of subjection – against the submission of subjectivity – is becoming more and more important' (SP p. 213). It is the conjunction of these two elements that locate the juridical and repressive accounts of power which characterises humanism as both providing resources through which the operation of domination and exploitation has been at least partially countered and inadvertently enabling the operation of forms of subjection.

At this juncture, let us return to Foucault's mode of analysing power which we have already addressed in our methodological reflections in terms of the idea of the 'conducting of conduct' and the 'agonism' of power and resistance. The significant point to note with respect to this notion of power in the present context is that Foucault addresses the way in which our conduct is conducted by reference to our constitution as particular kinds of subjects (e.g. delinquents, perverts). In other words, it is through the scientific siting of our empirical nature or subjective identities with respect to our essential nature or authentic identities that we are subjected to systems of constraint, that is, the conducting of our conduct, which operate to constitute us as 'normal' subjects.[8] We can sharpen this notion of power by noting that what is at stake, for Foucault, is our ability to transform ourselves, that is, to transgress the systems of constraint which conduct our conduct. The dilemma posed by humanism is that it ties our capacity to transform ourselves to the intensification of power relations in so far as self-transformation reproduces the politics of truth or, more specifically, the quest for authenticity which articulates the exercise of power relations.

To conclude this section, therefore, we may note that the problem posed by the hegemony of humanist structures of recognition, for Foucault, is not that of eliminating oppression or repression through either the specification of criteria of legitimacy or the elimination of constraints[9] but rather, that of examining how the growth of capabilities, which constitute our capacity to transform ourselves, can be disconnected from the intensification of power relations (FR p. 48). To articulate this disconnection Foucault must provide an anti-humanist ethics which displaces both the quest for authenticity and the politics of truth which attends it.

AN ANTI-HUMANIST ETHICS

To examine how Foucault seeks to articulate such a disconnection through the formulation of an anti-humanist ethics, we can begin by returning to his reflections on Kant and, more particularly, Baudelaire. In these reflections on the 'attitude of modernity', we will show that Foucault outlines an ethics which opposes the ethic of authenticity characteristic of humanism and, thereby, expresses the possibility of destabilising the technical matrix of biopolitics, that is, the 'double bind' of humanism.

In commenting on Kant's essay on enlightenment, Foucault identifies the outline of the 'attitude of modernity' in Kant's location of the present as difference in history; how though, if at all, does this relate to Kant's siting of ethics as 'an applied form of procedural rationality' (FR p. 372)? Foucault characterises Kant's ethics as follows:

> Kant says, 'I must recognise myself as a universal subject, that is, I must constitute myself in each of my actions as a universal subject by conforming to universal rules.' . . . Thus Kant introduces one more way in our tradition whereby the self is not merely given but is constituted in relationship to itself as subject.
>
> (FR p. 372)

The significant point for Foucault in Kant's formulation, its modernity, lies not in the emphasis on universality but in the notion of self-constitution. This aspect of Foucault's position has been pertinently characterised by Hacking:

> Among the radical novelties of Kant was the notion that we *construct* our ethical position. Kant said we do this by recourse to reason, but the innovation is not reason but construction. Kant taught that the only way the moral law can be moral is if we make it. Foucault's historicism combined with that notion of constructing morality leads one away from the letter and law of Kant, but curiously preserves Kant's spirit.
>
> (Hacking 1986: 239)

What it is in Kant's spirit which is preserved here is precisely that spirit of modernity embodied in this notion of construction which we have already shown as animating Nietzsche's and Weber's ethics. This point becomes clear when we turn to Foucault's focus on the elaboration of the *ethos* of modernity in Baudelaire:

> The deliberate attitude of modernity is tied to an indispensable asceticism. To be modern is not to accept oneself as one is in the flux of the passing moments; it is to take oneself as object of a complex and difficult elaboration: what Baudelaire, in the vocabulary of his day, calls *dandysme*. . . . This modernity does not 'liberate man in his own being'; it compels him to face the task of producing himself.
>
> (FR pp. 41–2)

In the context of Foucault's ethical concerns, the significance of Baudelaire's elaboration of *dandysme* is that it radicalises Kant's position by opposing an ethics of creativity to an ethics of authenticity. The connection between this ethics of creativity and Foucault's anti-humanism is drawn out in the following passage contra Sartre:

From the idea that the self is not given to us, I think there is only one practical consequence: we have to create ourselves as a work of art. In his analyses of Baudelaire, Flaubert, etc., it is interesting to see that Sartre refers work of creation to a certain relation to oneself – the author to himself – which has the form of authenticity or inauthenticity. I would like to say exactly the contrary: we should not have to refer the creative activity of somebody to the kind of relation he has to himself, but should relate the kind of relation one has to oneself to a creative activity.

(FR p. 351)[10]

What is presented in this passage is the immanent relationship between Foucault's anti-humanist mode of analysis and the idea of an ethics of creativity, a relationship which is isomorphic with Foucault's outlining of enlightenment contra humanism in terms of 'the principle of a critique and the permanent creation of ourselves in our autonomy' (FR p. 44). We should also note, at this stage, that Foucault's reflections on Kant and Baudelaire serve a secondary purpose in providing a sketch of the genealogy of Foucault's own theoretical apparatus. The importance of this point is to illustrate that the possibility of Foucault's genealogical project and of an ethics of creativity are reflexively located as immanent to modern culture as specific historical configurations of knowledge and ethics. How though does this notion of an ethics of creativity denote a rupture with the humanist 'double bind'?

Let us begin by recalling that the problem posed by humanism is that its elaboration of a politics of truth entails that ethics is predicated on a notion of authenticity which produces and reproduces forms of subjection. In other words, humanist ethics embodies a juridical/ repressive conception of power which locates the exercise of power in terms of the domination of one's essential nature or the repression of one's authentic identity. By contrast, Foucault's anti-humanist ethics embodies his notion of power as that which constrains our ability to transform ourselves, this being elaborated through its grounding not on a claim as to the truth of what we are but in the anti-humanist claim that there is no essential truth of what we are.[11] In other words, Foucault's rejection of the project of philosophical anthropology leads to the elaboration of an ethics which can articulate our struggles with forms of subjection by locating the identities elaborated by 'scientific experts' as aesthetic constructions. The significance of this ethics is that it displaces the form of self-relation predicated on authenticity and a discourse of truth through which the 'double bind' of modern subjectivity is articulated, that is, it disconnects the 'feedback' relationship between the growth of capabilities and the intensification of power relations by undermining the authority of 'truth' to determine our being. We expand on this by noting that, in so far as our self-relations are formulated in terms of a discourse of truth, this entails our recognition of the authority of the truth-teller to legislate norms for us; consequently, the politics of humanism is articulated around competing discourses of truth and, thus, of the legitimacy of the claims to authority made by different kinds of 'scientific expert', that is, their entitlement to legislate for us. What remains constant within this politico-epistemic grammar is a 'logic of legislation' whereby we are subjected to determinations of our identities which constrain our capacity to transform ourselves. It is in this context that Foucault's specification of an ethics predicated on a self-relation of creativity enacts a rupturing of this politico-epistemic grammar which displaces it with a politico-aesthetic grammar and thereby undermines both the figure of the expert as legislator and the logic of legislation which denotes the 'double bind' of humanism, that is, its simultaneous commitment to, and undermining of, the space of freedom.

To indicate the general character of Foucault's anti-humanist ethics and its implications with respect to the 'double bind' of humanism does not, however, complete the task of exploring the nature of Foucault's genealogical project as a mode of critique. On the contrary, our investigations to this stage have still only elaborated Foucault's position with regard to its concern to overcome the 'double bind' of humanism; what is still needed is a specification of this ethics and, more particularly, of the politics of this ethics.

ETHICS AS POLITICS

To fulfil this task, we need to focus on the topics of the form of asceticism which characterises this ethics and the *telos* which constitutes its parameters. Indirectly, we have already touched on each of these to the extent that we may define the asceticism of this ethics in terms of transgression and its *telos* as the self as work of art. What though do these definitions signify in the context of Foucault's reflections?

In locating the *practique de soi* of anti-humanist ethics in terms of the idea of transgression, Foucault is both specifying his Nietzschean commitment to autonomy as the extra-moral activity of self-overcoming and yet also transforming our understanding of the activity of self-overcoming. The latter point has been neatly expressed by Thiele: 'Foucault politicized what Nietzsche had internalised: the will to struggle' (Thiele 1990b: 923). What is being indicated here is Foucault's departure from the elements of a philosophical anthropology which remain in Nietzsche's work and are expressed in his presentation of modern subjectivity in terms of the struggle of psycho-physiological drives internal to the nihilistic individual as human type.[12] While Foucault follows Nietzsche in locating the will to struggle as integral to an ethics of creativity, he develops Nietzsche's critique of the metaphysics of mentalistic language by abandoning the residual naturalism of Nietzsche's position. In this context, we can broadly characterise Foucault's position in terms of a Nietzschean commitment to autonomy as struggle which is made manifest as if mediated through the critique of mentalist vocabularies articulated in the philosophy of language of the later Wittgenstein.[13] This position exhibits itself in Foucault's situating of the 'agonism' of power and freedom in relation to social practices and discourses or, more precisely, in the struggles through which social practices and discourses are produced, reproduced and transformed. The Nietzschean concern with self-overcoming as the struggle against the submission of subjectivity is thereby reproduced as a struggle against the forms of subjection embodied in humanist discourses and their attendant social practices. This entails that the activity of self-overcoming is constituted through transgressing social practices, that is, self-overcoming is thoroughly situated within relations of intersubjectivity. To draw out the implications of this formulation of the ascetic activity of an ethics of creativity, we need to turn to the *telos* of this ethics, namely, the constitution of self as a work of art.

By locating our activity of self-transformation within historically contingent relations of intersubjectivity, Foucault may be read as claiming that our becoming-in-the-world is always already a becoming-with-others.[14] Indeed, Foucault's concern with the hegemony of humanist structures of recognition may be located in part as a concern with humanism's desire to impose the law of the Same, that is, to institute a closure of our capacity for self-transformation through the elimination of alterity (i.e. its reduction to normality). In this context, our ontological 'thrown-ness' exhibits itself as a relation to the 'thrown-ness' of multiple others whose difference is a condition of possibility of our own self-transformation and whose multiplicity is constitutive of the field of possibilities disclosed to our aesthetic activity. The meaning of this ontological argument has been pertinently elaborated through a contrast with the emphasis on the monological character of aesthetic self-creation stressed by Nietzsche:

> While Nietzsche's monological artist escapes the normalizing gaze, in his particular manner of doing so he risks creating in *oblivion* to the multiplicity that must be confronted as the ontological basis of freedom. . . . In contrast, Foucault's understanding of artistic existence in which we seek to give ourselves form takes place at the limits of our being in *dialogue with* that which is different from us or that within us which finds no place within the reigning identities.
>
> (Coles 1991: 105)

We can draw out the significance of this understanding of artistic existence by noting that the intersubjective situatedness of our aesthetic labour on ourselves entails that just as our ascetic activity aims beyond itself towards a certain mode of being, that is, a certain form of subjectivity, so too it aims beyond itself in the sense of aiming towards relations of intersubjectivity which foster this mode of being.[15] Ethics is always already politics. To explore this idea further we can turn to Foucault's comments on Baudelaire and the aesthetics of modernity.

Opening this discussion we may note Foucault's citation of one of Baudelaire's precepts: ' "You have no right to despise the present" ' (FR p. 40). This designation of the attitude of modernity expresses neatly Foucault's own rejection of a nihilistic contempt for the present in favour of a more complex relation in which our present-ness figures as an achievement which is both heroic and ironic. The character of this ironic heroization, this tense conjunction of distance and passion, is expressed as follows:

> For the attitude of modernity, the high value of the present is indissociable from a desperate eagerness to imagine it, to imagine it otherwise than it is, and to transform it not by destroying it but by grasping it in what it is. Baudelairean modernity is an exercise in which extreme attention to what is real is confronted with the practice of a liberty that simultaneously respects this reality and violates it.
>
> (FR p. 41)

If we transpose these general remarks into our concern with an ethics of creativity, what emerges is a conception of our self-relation as practice of self-transformation which seeks to engage with the constitution of one's subjectivity as a reality whose heroic aspect ironically requires its transformation. We should not suppose though that the activity of self-transformation entails a frenzied or wanton transgression of limits. On the contrary, our respect for the reality of what we are, even as it impels us to transform ourselves, demands a reflective process which, put negatively, involves a determination of the 'main danger', that is, those systems of constraint which most threaten to foreclose the possibilities of transgressive activity, and, put positively, entails a determination of the specific practices of freedom through which we most radically constitute *and* express our autonomy. As Foucault has expressed this:

> My point is not that everything is bad, but that everything is dangerous, which is not exactly the same as bad. If everything is dangerous, then we always have something to do. So my position leads not to apathy but to a hyper- and pessimistic activism. I think that the ethico-political choice we have to make every day is to determine which is the main danger.
>
> (FR p. 343)

Foucault's use of the compound term 'ethico-political' in this passage refers us again to a recognition that our activity of self-transformation is situated within our relations with others. Consequently, in seeking to resist those social practices which would foreclose the possibility of struggle *per se*, we are engaged in maintaining the possibility of both our struggles and the struggles of others. This ethics-as-politics is, moreover, integrally linked to the expression of a concern with human dignity which respects alterity in that Foucault's conception of autonomy as the ongoing aesthetic labour we express through struggle entails that the ground of human dignity is our capacity to be otherwise than we are. As one commentator acutely notes: 'One's dignity is not that one *is* something, but that one may *become* many things' (Thiele 1990b: 919). Thus, in so far as our activity of struggle against constraints maintains the possibility of struggle, we are grounding both our own autonomy and our respect for the dignity of others (even though they may not share our specific struggles). We can make this discussion both more concrete and more precise by noting that, within this domain of ethico-political activity, it is the 'enhancement of struggle – not its mere production or exacerbation – [which] must form the criterion of political judgement' (Thiele 1990b: 922). We can pertinently recall at this juncture Foucault's comment that 'a system of constraint becomes truly intolerable when the individuals who are affected by it don't have the means of modifying it' (PPC p. 294). Thus, as I sit here writing while the spectre of Nazi ideology and genocide once more rises to haunt Europe, it is important to note that fascism in so far as it presents a politics of exclusion, a politics which defines itself by subjecting specific others to non-transformable constraints, constitutes a significant danger from the perspective of Foucault's political agonism, a danger which requires resistance if we are to maintain the possibility of human dignity.

The distinctive understanding of politics which emerges from this account can be set out as an opposition to the reduction of the political to the technical which attends humanism. The space of the political is presented as the space of struggle in which the question 'who are we?' remains perpetually open to negotiation and re-negotiation, rather than being located as the site of a transcendental determination of our being. Concomitantly, politics is the activity of struggle in which we produce and reproduce our freedom through its exercise.[16] Moreover, the specificity of our modernity *qua* politics is revealed in the ethos of 'ironic heroization' as our '*belonging to the questioning of that to which we belong*' (Coles 1991: 108). In other words, our political modernity lies in our belonging together as our belonging to the question 'who are we?' and our maturity lies in this belonging together as our belonging to the openness of this question.

To conclude our reflections on Foucault's anti-humanist ethics and the conception of politics as struggle which emerges from it, we can note that Foucault, contra humanist critics such as Habermas, does provide us with reasons for resisting exercises of power in that he locates autonomy as constituted through the activity of struggle in which one creates oneself. However, the question which emerges at this stage concerns how these reasons, given Foucault's anti-foundationalism, are to be grounded. To express this alternatively, our question concerns the politics of grounding Foucault's anti-humanist ethics. It is, after all, not enough simply to locate this ethics as an immanent possibility within modern culture; rather the question of how this possibility is to be actualised emerges. To address this topic, we will begin by focusing on Foucault's understanding of the activity of critique and the role of the intellectual, before moving to a consideration of genealogy as a form of intellectual and political practice.

INTELLECTUALS AND THE ACTIVITY OF CRITIQUE

In our reflections on Foucault's methodology, it was noted that, like Nietzsche and Weber, he commits himself to a stance of value-freedom as an engaged refusal to legislate for others. Foucault's critical activity is oriented to human autonomy yet his formal account of the idea of autonomy as the activity of self-transformation entails that the content of this activity is specific to the struggles of particular groups and individuals. Thus, while the struggle against humanist forms of power/knowledge relations denotes the formal architectonic interest of genealogy as critique, the determination of the 'main danger' which denotes the 'filling in' of this interest is contingent upon the dominant systems of constraint confronted by specific groups and individuals. For example, the constitution of women as 'hysterical', of blacks as 'criminal', of homosexuals as 'perverted' all operate through humanist forms of power/knowledge relations, yet the specificity of the social practices and discourses engaged in producing these 'identities' entails that while these struggles share a general formal interest in resisting the biopolitics of humanism, their substantive interests are distinct. It is against this context that Foucault's stance of value-freedom can be read as embodying a respect for alterity.

The implications of this stance for intellectual practice become apparent in Foucault's distinction between the figures of the 'universal' and 'specific' intellectual. Consider the following comments:

> In a general way, I think that intellectuals – if this category exists, which is not certain or perhaps even desirable – are abandoning their old prophetic function. And by that I don't mean only their claim to predict what will happen, but also the legislative function that they so long aspired for: 'See what must be done, see what is good, follow me. In the turmoil that engulfs you all, here is the pivotal point, here is where I am.' The Greek wise man, the Jewish prophet, the Roman

208

legislator are still models that haunt those who, today, practice the profession of speaking and writing.

(PPC p. 124)[17]

The 'universal' intellectual, on Foucault's account, is that figure who maintains a commitment to critique as a legislative activity in which the pivotal positing of universal norms (or universal procedures for generating norms) grounds politics in the 'truth' of our being (e.g. our 'real' interests).[18] The problematic form of this type of intellectual practice is a central concern of Foucault's critique of humanist politics in so far as humanism simultaneously asserts and undermines autonomy. *If*, however, this is the case, what alternative conceptions of the role of the intellectual and the activity of critique can Foucault present to us? Foucault's elaboration of the figure of the 'specific' intellectual provides the beginnings of an answer to this question:

> I dream of the intellectual who destroys evidence and generalities, the one who, in the inertias and constraints of the present time, locates and marks the weak points, the openings, the lines of force, who is incessantly on the move, doesn't know exactly where he is heading nor what he will think tomorrow for he is too attentive to the present.
>
> (PPC p. 124)

The historicity of thought, the impossibility of locating an Archimedean point outside of time, leads Foucault to locate intellectual activity as an ongoing attentiveness to the present in terms of what is singular and arbitrary in what we take to be universal and necessary. Following from this, the intellectual does not seek to offer grand theories but specific analyses, not global but local criticism. We should be clear on the latter point for it is necessary to acknowledge that Foucault's position does entail the impossibility of 'acceding to a point of view that could give us access to any complete and definitive knowledge of what may constitute our historical limits' and, consequently, 'we are always in the position of beginning again' (FR p. 47).[19] The upshot of this recognition of the partial character of criticism is not, however, to produce an ethos of fatal resignation but, in so far as it involves a recognition that everything is dangerous, 'a hyper- and pessimistic activism' (FR p. 343). In other words, it is the very historicity and partiality of criticism which bestows on the activity of critique its dignity and urgency. What of this activity then?

We can sketch the Foucault account of the activity of critique by coming to grips with the opposition he draws between 'ideal' critique and 'real' transformation. Foucault suggests that the activity of critique 'is not a matter of saying that things are not right as they are' but rather 'of pointing out on what kinds of assumptions, what kinds of familiar, unchallenged, uncontested modes of thought the practices we accept rest' (PPC p. 154).

209

This distinction is perhaps slightly disingenuous, yet Foucault's point is intelligible if we recognise his concern to disclose the epistemological grammar which informs our social practices as the starting point of critique. This emerges in his recognition that 'criticism (and radical criticism) is absolutely indispensable for any transformation':

> A transformation that remains within the same mode of thought, a transformation that is only a way of adjusting the same thought more closely to the reality of things can merely be a superficial transformation.
>
> (PPC p. 155)

The genealogical thrust of this critical activity is 'to show that things are not as self-evident as one believed, to see that what is accepted as self-evident is no longer accepted as such' for 'as soon as one can no longer think things as one formerly thought them, transformation becomes both very urgent, very difficult, and quite possible' (PPC p. 155). The urgency of transformation derives from the contestation of thought (and the social practices in which it is embedded) as the form of our autonomy, although this urgency is given its specific character for modern culture by the recognition that the humanist grammar of this thought ties us into the technical matrix of biopolitics.

The 'specificity' of intellectual practice and this account of the activity of critique come together in the refusal to legislate a universal determination of 'what is right' in favour of the perpetual problematisation of the present. It is not a question, for Foucault, of invoking a determination of *who* we are as a basis for critique but of locating *what* we are now as the basis for a reposing of the question 'who are we?' The role of the intellectual is thus not to speak on behalf of others (the dispossessed, the downtrodden) but to create the space within which their struggles become visible such that these others can speak for themselves.[20] The question remains, however, as to the capacity of Foucault's work to perform this critical activity through an entrenchment of the ethics of creativity as the structures of recognition through which we recognise our autonomy in the contestation of determinations of who we are.

GENEALOGY AS EXEMPLARY CRITIQUE

If Foucault cannot appeal to a legislative politics grounded in either philosophical foundations or world-historical figures, the central question must concern how the ethics of creativity he outlines is to be entrenched. We can approach this question through a consideration of Foucault's genealogical accounts as *exemplary*, by which I am referring to their *showing* of this ethics.[21] This topic has already been illustrated in our consideration of genealogy as embodying the ethos of 'ironic heroization' by which

210

Foucault characterises the 'attitude of modernity' exhibited in Baudelaire's conception of *dandysme*. Again, it has also been elucidated through Foucault's conception of humanist power/knowledge relations as constituting us as particular kinds of subjects whose identities are determined by a discourse of truth and of humanist ethics/knowledge relations as tying the growth of capacities to the intensification of power relations through an ethics of authenticity. Yet again, we have noted that genealogy as an intellectual enterprise involves an immanent relation to resistance as the condition of possibility of genealogy in so far as resistance is constitutive of the historical form of time. The issue to be addressed in this section, given all of these points, concerns the exemplarity of genealogy as a form of *practical* critique.

To this end, I will begin by considering a comment Foucault makes concerning the relationship of his genealogies to the public:

> R. Rorty points out that in these analyses I do not appeal to any 'we' – to any of the 'we's' whose consensus, whose values, whose traditions constitute the framework for a thought and define the conditions in which it can be validated. But the problem is, precisely, to decide if it is actually suitable to place oneself within a 'we' in order to assert the principles one recognises and the values one accepts; or if it is not, rather, necessary to make the future formation of a 'we' possible, by elaborating the question. Because it seems to me that the 'we' must not be previous to the question; it can only be the result – and the necessarily temporary result – of the question as it is posed in the new terms in which one formulates it.
>
> (FR p. 385)

In what sense does this passage disclose Foucault's position as embodying an exemplary rather than legislative stance? It should be noted firstly that the politics of genealogy as ethical practice revealed in this passage exemplifies that refusal to ground politics in an identification of the 'truth' of who we are (e.g. as communicative beings with an interest in emancipation) by which Foucault differentiates the ethics of creativity from an ethics of authenticity. Perhaps more significant, however, is the second feature, namely, the location of genealogical practice as constitutive of communities of judgement, whereby this constitutive character is grounded in the capacity of genealogy to articulate an understanding of the constitution of modern subjectivity which exemplifies the politics of struggle it advocates. On the latter point, we may note that *genealogy as intellectual struggle with the epistemological grammar of humanism is itself the isomorphic correlate of practical struggles with the technical grammar of biopolitics*. In other words, genealogy is always already an engagement in those struggles which it seeks to facilitate both at the level of its formal architectonic interest in human autonomy as this is articulated through

211

its deconstruction of the humanist will to truth and its problematisation of the form of the social practices/discourses constitutive of our subjectivity, and at the level of the substantive 'filling in' of this architectonic interest through its specific genealogical accounts as embodying interests in particular social practices/discourses which constrain certain groups and individuals (e.g. women as 'hysterical').

It is concomitant with the formal architectonic interest of genealogy as a form of intellectual practice and the specific substantive interests of genealogical studies that we can identify the formal community and substantive communities that this practice seeks to constitute. With respect to the formal interest, genealogy is oriented to the construction of a community constituted by an ongoing questioning of its own construction – that is, a 'we' whose belonging together is a belonging to the question 'who are we?' – in the sense that it is in such questioning that (the space of) our autonomy is constituted. To give this concrete clarity, we might note that a genealogy of the 'hysterical woman', for example, is oriented to the problematisation of this mode of subjectifying women and thus to constituting a space of reflection within which those subjected to this system of constraint are able to locate the response to the question 'who are we?' as contestable and, thus, to become otherwise than 'we are' through the contestation of 'who we are'. We should note, moreover, that precisely in so far as any genealogical account embodies both a universal formal interest in autonomy and a particular substantive interest in autonomy, it exemplifies that openness to alterity which marks Foucault's dialogical ethics in that particular struggles operate both to transform constraints and to maintain the general possibility of struggle.

We can perhaps summarise the exemplarity of genealogy as critique by noting that genealogy is immanently committed to the value of autonomy in so far as human autonomy denotes the condition of possibility of genealogy. To this we may add the point that any given genealogy is predicated on an ethical judgement as to the value of problematising specific forms of identity (e.g. 'hysterical women') in the interest of the autonomy of those subjected to this form of subjectivity. In this context, the capacity of genealogy as critique to ground or entrench Foucault's ethics of creativity is identical with the capacity of genealogy to constitute communities of judgement who recognise the value of autonomy or, more precisely, the capacity of genealogies to constitute both substantive and formal communities of judgement.

To conclude this chapter, let us recall that Foucault's position is not without its costs *qua* the humanist dreams of enlightenment in that it forgoes the temptation of a universal normative legislation in favour of an activity of critique in which we are always already beginning again and a politics for whom the question 'who are we?' is not subject to closure. Perhaps though these humanist dreams are all too nightmarish for us today and these 'costs' are themselves signals of the slow, all too slow, movement to maturity in which the historical spirit of enlightenment and the philosophical ethos of modernity find their home.

CONCLUSION

Thought thinks its own history (the past), but in order to free itself from what it thinks (the present) and be able finally to 'think otherwise' (the future).

(Deleuze 1988: 119)

It was suggested in the opening chapter of this text that Kant bequeaths us a double problematic in which the relationship between autonomy and time intersects with an ambivalence in the relationship between ethics and politics. The argument focused on the theme of maturity as the site of this double problematic, suggesting that Nietzsche, Weber and Foucault are all centrally concerned with constructing a form of historical thinking which reconstructs the relationship between autonomy and its conditions of realisation in modern culture in order to critically articulate the conditions of maturity. To begin to conclude, therefore, we may focus separately on these questions of the character of their historical thinking, the genealogies of modernity constructed, and the politics of maturity which emerge.

THOUGHT AND TIME

It was argued that the need to develop a form of critical thinking which recognises its own historicity, its own present-ness, emerged in the context of the historical antinomy which characterises Kant's philosophy. In other words, Nietzsche, Weber and Foucault confront the task of elaborating a mode of thinking which can articulate an understanding of its own historical conditions of possibility.

In Nietzsche, the principle of this thinking is provided by the idea of *will to power* and is elaborated through a focus on the *structures of recognition*, where these are the synthetic *a priori* judgements of a culture. Within this theoretical apparatus, Nietzsche accounts for the development of our history as the outcome of the interaction between the inner logic of worldviews and the conditions of 'willing', that is, the capacity of our synthetic *a priori* judgements to maintain our experience of ourselves as goal-directed agents. In Weber, this genealogical thinking is constructed around the *'switchman'* metaphor and is elaborated through an analysis of the *structures of recognition*, where these are located in terms of the world-images which articulate our ideal and material interests. Weber analyses social change in terms of the dynamic of charisma and routinisation, the differentiation between spheres of life, and the inner logic of worldviews. Again, however, the focus of this analysis is placed on the capacity of our worldviews to articulate our experience of ourselves as goal-directed agents. For Foucault, the principle of a historical ontology of ourselves is sited through the articulation of *knowledge, power and ethics* as constituting *structures of recognition*, where these are specified in terms of social practices and rationalities. Foucault accounts for historical change in terms of the relationship between patterns of possibility and actuality with regard to social practices and rationalities, wherein the contingent character of actuality emerges as the outcome of multiple sites of engagement of power and resistance, both power-knowledge relations and ethics-knowledge relations being located *qua* structures of recognition as 'intentional and non-subjective'.

Reflecting on these forms of historical thinking, of thinking historically, we can note that Foucault's thinking marks a departure from that of Nietzsche and of Weber in one central respect, namely, whereas as their focus on worldviews allows for the possibility of world-historical individuals who articulate a transformation of our worldviews, Foucault's emphasis on the intentional but non-subjective character of the totality of power-knowledge and ethics-knowledge relations entails that the transformation of our structures of recognition cannot be produced through a 'Subject' of history. We will return to the implications of this point in considering the critical character of these forms of thinking.

GENEALOGIES OF MODERNITY

In constructing their genealogies of modernity, Nietzsche, Weber and Foucault may be situated as performing a double task: on the one hand, they are specifying the emergence of the conditions of their own thinking, the present which their thought inhabits and which motivates its thinking of today as 'difference' in history, and, on the other hand, they are analysing and specifying the ambivalence of modern culture in terms of a will to truth which has become conscious of itself as a problem. In setting out their accounts, we have focused largely on the latter task.

Nietzsche's account of the ambivalence of modernity may be read in terms of his concern with the production of human types with the capacity for autonomy through Christian asceticism (this being understood in terms of the capacity for the reflexive constitution of 'inner distance'), yet where this same historical process undermines the cultural grounds of value requisite to the actualisation of this capacity in so far as our will to truth becomes nihilistic. A similar concern animates Weber for whom modernity is simultaneously characterised by the constitution of individuals with the capacity for autonomy and the collapse of cultural grounds for realising this capacity (disenchantment), while also being increasingly characterised by institutional structures which facilitate the reduction of ideal to material interests (rationalisation). For Foucault, the constitution of modern culture can be located in terms of the conjunction of biopolitical practices and humanist rationalities. The implication of this conjunction is that the growth of our capacities for autonomy remains tied to the intensification of power relations which increasingly constrain our ability to transform ourselves, that is, to create ourselves in our autonomy.

Again we may note a shift in emphasis occurring with Foucault in so far as his analysis locates the ambivalent character of modern culture in terms of the *hegemony* of humanist structures of recognition, rather than in terms of the collapse of our structures of recognition (Nietzsche) or the reduction of our structures of recognition from an articulation of ideal and material interests to simply material interests (Weber). We should also note in this context the deepening gaze of this trajectory of thought from cultural values (Nietzsche) to cultural values and institutions (Weber) to cultural rationalities and practices (Foucault). However, it is the implications of these diagnoses of the modern condition to which we must turn in order to focus on the theme of maturity.

MATURITY AND CRITIQUE

In considering the operation of genealogy as critical, the central question becomes that of how it articulates the relationship between the possibility of autonomy in modern culture and the realisation of this possibility, namely, the question of maturity. Two moments need to be specified in thinking through Nietzsche, Weber and Foucault with respect to this question: firstly, how do they conceive of maturity? and, secondly, how do their various modes of thinking operate as critique by articulating the realisation of maturity? We will examine each of these moments in turn.

We can begin by noting that Nietzsche, Weber and Foucault think of autonomy in terms of a relation of probity which governs the ongoing labour of self-construction in which one reflexively directs one's activity. Moreover, each recognises that the realisation of autonomy in modernity requires a specification of this relation of probity in modern culture. In the case of Nietzsche, this emerges with the doctrine of eternal recurrence as a delineation of the universal structure of probity in modern culture. By contrast, Weber seeks to specify the demands of probity in relation to the distinct life-spheres of modern culture, arguing that the form of

216

scientific probity and political probity, although sharing certain formal elements, must be understood as distinct. Finally, Foucault locates probity in terms of the dialogic activity of constructing oneself as a work of art through the transgression of constraints.

At this juncture, the second moment – the moment of the relation of ethics and politics – arises: how are these understandings of maturity to be facilitated? The pertinency of this question derives its urgency from anti-foundational stances adopted by these three thinkers which entail that they cannot ground their thinking as critique through a transcendental 'ought', that is, by reference to the Kantian recourse to a God's eye view. It is, moreover, within the space of this question that the tensions of Kant's essay on enlightenment emerge in the form of a politics which problematises its own ethical status. In this context, we focused on the tensions within the trajectory of thought addressed by showing how Nietzsche's politics takes two distinct forms: on the one hand, an appeal to the figure of the legislator, that is, the world-historical *Übermensch* who attempts to constitute a 'sovereign culture' on the basis of a generalised economy of violence, and, on the other hand, an attempt to constitute a community of judgement through a local economy of exemplarity grounded in the figure of the quiet *Übermensch*. It was argued that the notion of the world-historical *Übermensch* transforms and reproduces the Kantian problematic of a politics which undermines its own ethical ends, while the notion of the quiet *Übermensch* entails an abandonment of the project of global critique. These two forms of politics – legislation and exemplarity – were then shown to be interwoven in Weber's portrayal of the mutuality of the charismatic politician and the scientific genius in which legislation is grounded in exemplarity. Yet, as we noted, Weber's distinction between science and politics entails that his thought even as it takes on one role must refuse the other, while already within this portrayal the tensions between a utopian gesture and its denial struggle with each other. Finally, we examined how Foucault avoids the Kantian problematic by embracing a form of political thinking which exemplifies its ethical commitments, that is, Foucault's genealogies are political engagements which retain their ethical responsibilities to otherness by refusing the gesture of legislation and limiting themselves to an economy of exemplarity which attempts to constitute a generalised formal community of judgement and localised substantive community of judgement. At the same time, Foucault's rejection of the idea of the world-historical individual displaces this economy of exemplarity from the individual genius to a mode of thinking, a philosophical *ethos*, in which we are always already beginning again.

This argument ends on this note with the idea of the 'genius of thought', the struggle of thought with itself as it tries to 'think otherwise' in its preserving of the openness of the ethical question 'what is it to be

217

human?' and of the political question 'who are we?', an openness which marks the space of freedom and its exercise.

GLOSSARY

This glossary is intended to provide guidelines for grasping the central concepts used in this study; these guidelines are not attempts to offer definitive definitions of terms. It will be noted that I do not offer entries on the concepts *maturity, modernity* and *critique*; this is simply because these concepts are the sites of contest within which this study engages the thought of Nietzsche, Weber and Foucault, that is, the elucidation of the specific senses they each give to these terms is a central task of this text.

Anti-humanism This approach displaces the idea of the constituent subject as the foundation of reason, history and truth. It entails the rejection of the project of philosophical anthropology as the attempt to provide a determinate answer to the question 'What is Man?' in the idea of a transcendentally free and creative subject. Anti-humanism locates the subject as a contingent historical product and claims that the answer to the question 'What is Man?' is always already futural, that is, can never be finally given (cf. *ethics of creativity*).

Archaeology The attempt to uncover the *'positive unconscious'* of knowledge, that is, the rules which govern what statements fall within the domain of being up for grabs as true or false. Archaeology is the method by which Foucault attempts to specify the 'historical *a priori*' on the basis of which certain forms of knowledge (and not others) become possible (cf. *episteme*).

Bad conscience The consciousness of guilt which, on Nietzsche's account, articulates the opposition of consciousness and the instincts, that is, 'the existence on earth of an animal soul turned against itself, taking sides against itself' (GM II 16 p. 85). It motivates the denigration of the body which appears in the opposition of reason and affectivity that characterises our *will to truth*. This achieves its highest form in the Christian opposition of spirit and flesh which assigns individuals' suffering to the weakness of their spirit in the face of the desires of the flesh.

Biopolitics The form of modern political reason in which the ancient right

219

to take life or let live is displaced by a power to foster life or disallow it to the point of death. This political rationality develops about two poles – a disciplining of the human body and a regulation of the population – and is interwoven with the development of the human sciences. Biopolitics proceeds by transforming political questions into technical-scientific questions through mechanisms such as the *panopticon* and the *confessional*.

Charisma   This idea refers to the extraordinary personal quality or 'gift of grace' by which an individual constitutes a community which both accepts the ideas and recognises the (legitimate) authority of this individual. On Weber's account, the concept of charisma is central to an account of how new beliefs revolutionise social life (cf. *routinisation*). This concept is also the root of the idea of *calling* in Weber (cf. *vocation*).

Confessional technologies   Ensembles of practices which tie individuals to the *true self* or *authentic identity* which they can discover, with the help of experts (e.g. psychologists, psychiatrists and psychoanalysts), through the self-examination of consciousness and the practice of confession. The *telos* of these technologies is the production of normal individuals as moral truth-telling citizens. These technologies are interwoven with the constitution of the modern individual as knowing subject and the emergence of the interpretive human sciences. Confessional technologies, like panoptic technologies, operate through the construction of 'types' (e.g. the hysterical woman) which link individualisation (the case history) and totalisation (the statistical analysis) in the policing of individuals and populations (cf. *biopolitics*, *subjectification* and *ethics of authenticity*).

Disenchantment   Like Nietzsche's idea of *nihilism*, this concept refers to the loss of grounds upon which to regard human life and activity as valuable or meaningful. More specifically, the idea of disenchantment signals Weber's account of the withdrawal of the highest values from the public sphere and, concomitantly, the reduction of the social world to categories of calculation.

Dispositif   Variously translated as 'apparatus' and 'grid of intelligibility', this conceptual tool denotes the isolation of specific (types of) relations of power and knowledge (e.g. *biopolitics*) such that the construction of this grid of intelligibility allows Foucault to uncover the structure of the practices organised as an apparatus for constituting subjects and objects. The *dispositif* differs from the *episteme* in that it includes non-discursive as well as discursive practices.

Episteme   This concept denotes the *archaeological* attempt to specify the 'historical *a priori*' on the basis of which certain forms of knowledge (and not others) become possible. Foucault presents the *episteme* as *both* the totality of relations which exist between the sciences at the level of discursive regularities *and* the rules of formation which govern what statements become possible as either true or false. This ambivalence leads Foucault to abandon the idea of the *episteme* and to develop the idea of *dispositif* as part of his more general move from *archaeology* to *genealogy*.

Eternal recurrence This complex doctrine is described by Nietzsche as the highest formula of affirmation and takes the form of an affective thought-experiment whereby the individual is subjected to the idea that he or she will live the same life over and over again as a test of strength. It may be read as (i) the attempt to constitute a *pathos of distance* which grounds human value in the idea of the self as a work of art, (ii) a formalisation of Kant's categorical imperative which abandons the presupposition of the universalisability of contents and (iii) the ethics of the *Übermensch*.

Ethics of adaptability The ethics of the fully adjusted inhabitants of a bureaucratic age (i.e. the last man) in which human beings have lost the sense of wonder which led them to reflect on the character of human existence and do not strive to transcend the immediate horizon of material needs. Both Nietzsche and Weber associate this ethics with ideas such as *utilitarianism*.

Ethics of authenticity A form of self-relation which is predicated on a metaphysical/scientific determination of what it is to be human and concerns itself with reflexively realising this essence. This is an ethics constructed in terms of the truth of our being which locates autonomy in terms of the realisation of this truth.

Ethics of creativity A form of self-relation which is predicated on the aesthetic idea that the self is not given but constituted and concerns itself with reflexively constructing the self as a work of art. This is an ethics constructed in terms of the art of becoming which locates autonomy in terms of the activity of becoming otherwise than one is.

Genealogy A historical reconstruction of how we have become what we are which acts as an immanent critique of what we are and which is directed towards the practical achievement of human autonomy.

Humanism The grounding of reason, history and truth in the figure of the transcendentally free and creative subject. Humanism, at least in its modern form, exhibits itself as the project of philosophical anthropology which attempts to offer a determinate answer to the question of what it is to be human (cf. *ethics of authenticity*).

Ideal-type A conceptual tool constructed through the one-sided accentuation of certain (culturally significant) elements of reality to form a unified analytical construct (e.g. the Protestant ethic) which is not a description of reality but a means of expression to such a description.

221

Life-sphere Weber uses this complex concept to refer to analytically distinct modes of human activity which each involve their own criteria concerning meaningful social action, that is, their own immanent norms and obligations. He identifies six such modes: economics, politics, religious, intellectual (scientific), aesthetic and erotic; and argues that modernity is characterised by the increasing separation of these spheres from one another.

Nihilism The condition whereby the highest values devalue themselves. Nihilism is a product of our *will to truth* turning on, firstly, the Christian moralism which produced it and, secondly, itself. Nihilism names both an epochal condition – the death of God – and a psychological condition – the lack of grounds on which to regard human activity as valuable or meaningful. It also names a possibility: the possibility of the *Übermensch*.

Objectification The process by which an entity is constituted as an object of power/knowledge relations. This concept refers both to the practices through which man is rendered an object of knowledge and the knowledges through which man is practically objectified (cf. *panoptic technologies*).

Panoptic technologies Ensembles of practices which operate by tying individuals to their *true being* or *essential nature* as this is determined by expert observers (e.g. behaviourists) through processes of classification and experimentation. The *telos* of these technologies is the production of normal individuals as productive and docile bodies. These technologies are interwoven with the constitution of the modern individual as an object of knowledge and the emergence of the structural human sciences. Panoptic technologies, like confessional technologies, operate through the construction of 'types' (e.g. the delinquent) which link individualisation (the case history) and totalisation (the statistical analysis) in the policing of individuals and populations (cf. *biopolitics*, *objectification* and *ethics of authenticity*).

Pathos of distance That sense of power (i.e. affective experience of oneself as a goal-directed agent) predicated on *social* distance (the pre-reflective noble), *metaphysical* distance (the reflective slave/Christian) and *artistic* distance (the *Übermensch*) which grounds the meaning and value of one's existence and is constitutive of 'inner distance' as 'that longing for an ever-increasing widening of distance within the soul itself' (BGE 257 p. 173).

Personality This formal concept refers to a constant relation to particular ultimate values and meanings of life which govern purposes and are constitutive of goal-directed agency. Weber argues that personality in modernity necessarily takes the form of *vocational* work. In other words, man must ground the dignity of his life through work within a given *life-sphere*.

Politics of truth   This idea opposes the humanist desire to ground a politics in a truth which will set us free with the suspicion that it is the grounding of politics in truth which is the proper political question. Here the humanist opposition of truth and power is displaced by Foucault's Nietzschean understanding of truth and power (and ethics) as co-productive (cf. *power/knowledge*).

Power/knowledge   This does *not* refer to the dialectical identity of power and knowledge but, rather, to the idea that forms of rationality open up fields of possible practices, while modes of practice open up fields of possible rationalities. The precise relationship between any given relations of knowledge and of power cannot be deduced but, rather, must be analysed by attending to the discursive and non-discursive practices which constitute specific power/knowledge relations.

Rational discipline   Practices whose *telos* is the transformation of self into an obedient instrument of authority, that is, the process whereby training transforms the execution of an order from the domain of conscious action to that of automatic behaviour. This concept, which anticipates Foucault's concept of discipline, is central to Weber's analysis of bureaucratisation as an aspect of the *rationalisation* of modern cultural life.

Rationalisation   This complex ideal-typical concept refers both to the process of the adoption of certain types of rational conduct by individuals and, concomitantly, to the spread of formal (instrumental) rationality in modern culture (cf. *rational discipline*). Rationalisation is *not* a homogeneous developmental process but a complex, and sometimes contradictory, set of relations and practices.

Ressentiment   This concept denotes the rejection and negation of the relationship between self and world which motivates the spirit of revenge embodied in the slave revolts in morals and exhibits itself in the construction of the transcendent metaphysical world and the idea of the soul, where these constructs enable the slaves' experience of themselves as *free* (goal-directed) agents.

Routinisation   The systematisation of a set of beliefs by a priestly stratum and/or the accommodation of this set of beliefs to a particular stratum of believers. This concept is used by Weber to account for the ways in which the revolutionary impact of a set of beliefs is gradually accommodated and entrenched within everyday life (cf. *charisma*).

Structures of recognition   The *a priori* judgements of a culture which articulate our recognition of ourselves and others. Formally, these entrenched judgements are necessary for the possibility of identity formation, while their substantive character governs the type of (structure of) identity formed. Thus, for example, Nietzsche's concept of nihilism refers to the process of destruction of our structures of recognition and the paralysis of agency which this destruction engenders.

Subjectification The process by which an entity is constituted as a subject of power/knowledge relations. This concept refers both to being a subject *of* knowledges and to being subjected *by* practices (cf. *confessional technologies*).

Übermensch Nietzsche's conception of the mature individual as one who affirms his relationship to the world (i.e. embraces the idea of *eternal recurrence*) in giving style to his character (i.e. making his life a work of art). Nietzsche seems to deploy two contrasting 'models' of the *Übermensch*: on the one hand, the idea of the *world-historical Übermensch* as lawgiver is represented by the figure of Napoleon and, on the other hand, the idea of the *quiet Übermensch* as monological artist is represented by Goethe.

Vocation (Beruf) This concept is deployed by Weber as a secularisation of Luther's concept of a religious calling and refers to one's inner calling to the norms and obligations of a given *life-sphere* (e.g. science, politics and art). A calling is characterised by the combination of passionate devotion and inner distance with respect to one's work. It is closely connected with Weber's ideas of *charisma* and *personality*.

Will to Power This concept is deployed by Nietzsche both to *explain* cultural change in terms of the capacity of our entrenched cultural judgements (cf. *structures of recognition*) to facilitate our experience of ourselves as goal-directed agents and to *evaluate* those judgements in terms of their capacity to enable the formation of autonomous agents. Nietzsche distinguishes between other-worldly and this-worldly types of cultural judgement. Thus the doctrine of eternal recurrence may be read as Nietzsche's formulation of a this-worldly cultural judgement which facilitates the formation of autonomous agents *contra* the doctrine of Christianity which Nietzsche reads as an other-worldly set of judgements which can enable the formation of goal-directed agents but which exhibit debilitating effects with respect to the production of autonomous agents.

NOTES

1 KANT AND THE QUESTION OF MATURITY

1 For alternative readings of this text, see Onara O'Neil (1986) and John Christian Laursen (1986). Foucault's reading of Kant's essay will be addressed in Chapter 8.
2 Kant seems close here to Nietzsche's criticism of the ascetic priest (cf. GM III).
3 See O'Neil (1986) and Laursen (1986) for interesting comments on the theme of publicity.
4 Kant's optimism with respect to the future consonance of public and private uses of reason takes on a peculiarly naive look when compared with Weber's discussions of bureaucracy; cf. Chapters 6 and 7.
5 On this issue, see the excellent discussion in Patrick Riley's (1982) chapter on Kant.
6 Kant locates the antinomy of causality as providing his impetus towards philosophy in a letter to Garve cited in M.A. Gillespie (1984: 30; also cf. 183 fn. 14).
7 See Gillespie (1984: 33).
8 See, for example, Kant's essay 'On the Proverb: That may be True in Theory, But is of No Practical Use' in Kant (1983: 61–92).
9 See Y. Yovel (1980: 102) for a discussion of this issue.
10 This recalls Rousseau in the final chapter of *The Social Contract* in which Rousseau's specification of the tenets of the civic religion provides self-interested reasons for *not* acting in a self-interested manner (Rousseau 1968).
11 Yovel (1980: 21–3).
12 Yovel (1980: 21–2).
13 On this point, see Owen (1993) for a consideration of freedom and necessity in Kant, Nietzsche and Weber.
14 One of the many objections which might be made to the reading of Kant offered here is its failure to address the implications of the Third Critique *qua* Kant's politics. The argument for the significance of the Third Critique has been made forcefully in Steven M. Delue (1985) which interestingly seems to push towards a Nietzschean concern with the uniqueness and incomparability of persons. However, for a reading which problematises both Delue and myself, see the extremely sophisticated reading of the Third Critique in Caygill (1989) and also Caygill (1988) for a discussion of the problem of judgement which emerges in this context.

2 THE TRANSFORMATION OF CRITIQUE: NIETZSCHE AND GENEALOGY

1 This topic is addressed by Deleuze (1988: 89–94) in terms of Nietzsche's fulfilment of the task of critique through a rupture with Kant's critical philosophy. Although this is a reading I have much sympathy with, Deleuze may be overstating the case with respect to this rupture; on this, see Michael Bowles (1992). An interesting overview of the relationship of Kant and Nietzsche is given in Keith Ansell-Pearson (1987).

2 Compare Nietzsche's comments here with Hegel's introduction to *Phenomenology of Spirit* (1977).

3 For an interesting discussion of this issue, see Tracy Strong (1988: ch. 2).

4 See Strong (1988: chs 2, 3).

5 See Strong (1988: ch. 3) and also the discussion of this topic in Alan Schrift (1990: chs 5, 7).

6 On this point, see Schrift (1990: ch. 5) and Alan Megill (1984: 94–9).

7 On the various uses of the idea of reification, see the discussion in Gillian Rose (1978: 28–51).

8 Nietzsche's concern here yet again is with the eliding of the problem of history in Kant's thought; it would not be overstating the case to say that this concern with history becomes one of the dominant themes of post-Kantian philosophy together with the unconscious and language. This can be located through Foucault's reading of the modern *episteme* in *The Order of Things*, especially the chapter 'Man and his Doubles'.

9 We can distinguish two levels of perspectivism in Nietzsche only the latter of which is immediately relevant to our concerns; these may be termed 'ontological perspectivism' and 'value perspectivism'. On the former, see GS 374 p. 336. The whole question of perspectivism is difficult but this has thrown up a number of interesting discussions of the topic. See, for example, Strong (1988: ch. 10) for a careful reading of perspectivism contra epistemology, Schrift (1990: ch. 6) for the location of perspectivism with respect to Nietzsche's account of language and the idea of genealogy, and Maudmarie Clark (1990: ch. 5) for an excellent analytical discussion of the implications of perspectivism *qua* truth.

10 In other words, Nietzsche does not recognise the Kantian distinction between constitutive and regulative uses of reason.

11 An interesting overview of the question of the will *qua* Nietzsche is given in Keith Ansell-Pearson (1991a).

12 For a brilliant and much fuller discussion of will to power which has greatly influenced my own reading, see Mark Warren (1988a: ch. 4).

13 See BGE 36 pp. 48–9 and also Warren (1988a: 126–9).

14 Nietzsche's emphasis on the two modes of constructing a 'centre of gravity' may be compared with Weber's distinction between this-worldly and other-worldly forms of rationality; cf. Chapter 5.

15 Although specific to modernity, Nietzsche's ideal of autonomy is related to the pre-reflective autonomy of the ancients, hence his concern with doing a genealogy and not simply a history.

3 THE GENEALOGY OF MODERNITY: NIETZSCHE, ASCETICISM AND NIHILISM

1 Nietzsche's notion of 'breeding' (*Zucht, Züchtung*) should not be taken as

implying a programme of, for example, eugenics, but rather in the sense in which given modes of culture act to cultivate certain forms of subjectivity and not others, although the German, like the English, has both connotations. For an argument which suggests that Nietzsche does include a strong biological element in his thinking, see Detwiler (1990: 107–14).

2 Perhaps one might qualify this by noting that there is no sharp distinction between instinct and consciousness for animals, whereas it is precisely this relation which Nietzsche takes up with respect to man as a historical animal.

3 Keith Ansell-Pearson notes that Nietzsche does not use the notion of *Recht* in this passage and suggests that 'it is important to bear in mind that when Nietzsche speaks of this "right" to make promises . . . he means a "right" in the sense of a privilege bestowed on the individual by society and by his peers' (Ansell-Pearson 1991b: 255 fn. 93).

4 In this sense, reification denotes the process whereby the taken-for-granted or common-sense stock of ideas constitutes the horizon of a community, that is, constitutes a community *qua* community.

5 There is an insightful discussion of this topic in Deleuze (1983: ch. 4).

6 Ansell-Pearson (1991b: 134–49) provides an illuminating reading of the topic of *bad conscience*.

7 Warren (1988a: 20–30) provides an interesting reading of this issue which runs across that offered here.

8 It might be suggested that *bad conscience* is prior to *ressentiment* as suggested by GM II 16; however, this seems to miss the question of enclosure not just within the walls of society but also of peace which I emphasise. Deleuze (1983: ch. 4) provides support for this strategy of reading Nietzsche.

9 Interestingly Nietzsche's argument here seems to anticipate that elaborated by MacIntyre with respect to debates around the topic of incommensurability (MacIntyre 1977).

10 For a fuller discussion of this topic which has been crucial to my own reading, see Strong (1988: chs 6, 7).

11 See Strong (1988: 161–82).

12 It has been argued, for example, that Nietzsche views the Western concept of truth as articulated through the Socratic identification of truth and goodness (Ansell-Pearson 1986: 501).

13 We should emphasise the fact that Nietzsche's primary objection is to St Paul (AC 42 pp. 154–5), whereas his attitude to Christ is more ambivalent if finally negative (Strong 1988: 123–30).

14 See Z, Of Self-Overcoming.

15 This raises a difficulty for Nietzsche in so far as his concern with the establishment of a culture characterised by squandering the super-abundance and overflow of creative energy also requires that this culture be capable, unlike the Renaissance, of reproducing its energy even as it squanders it.

16 One might develop Nietzsche's criticism of Marx from this perspective. Love (1986) offers an interesting reading of this topic.

4 THE POLITICS OF THE *ÜBERMENSCH*: NIETZSCHE, MATURITY AND MODERNITY

1 My use of the notion of *structures of recognition* is in part a response to the standard and rather uninteresting Hegelian critiques of Nietzsche and in part a setting up of an issue which will be of considerable significance for my

readings of Weber and Foucault. I should acknowledge here that this notion emerged under the influence of Warren (1988a) and owes much to his discussion of will to power as offering a post-metaphysical account of agency.

2 See Strong (1989: 162) for pertinent comments on this theme.

3 As with my earlier use of the notion of entrenchment, I think Nietzsche is anticipating certain Wittgensteinian themes here, a viewpoint shared by Strong (1988) and Heller (1988) amongst others.

4 Nietzsche's point here operates against Hegel's reading of modernity; this is predicated, I suggest, on the fundamentally different relations of autonomy and time in their accounts. For Hegelian critiques of Nietzsche on this issue, see Walker (1991) and Houlgate (1986).

5 This point is crucial to understanding Nietzsche's commonality with Weber and Foucault in that it is not simply the lack of appropriate structures of recognition but the progressive undermining of the possibility constituting them which gives urgency to modern thought for these thinkers.

6 My reading here owes much to Nehamas (1985: 170–99) even if my argument may develop slightly differently. For an interesting critique of Nehamas on this topic, see Shapiro (1989: 86–9).

7 On the relation of this tragic understanding of responsibility to the Greeks, see Strong (1988: 166–7).

8 This also displaces an understanding of reason as opposed to affectivity, a theme explored in Blondel (1991) and Owen (1993).

9 My argument here runs against that elaborated by Keith Ansell-Pearson who suggests that Nietzsche's politics are geared towards the constitution of a culture characterised by a high degree of social stratification as the condition for a noble culture (Ansell-Pearson 1991b: 200–4); although there is much textual evidence for this view, I suggest that it does not cohere with the transformation of humanity wrought under the aegis of Christian asceticism.

10 Again I owe a debt to Nehamas (1985), although my argument shifts from his concerns. It is interesting to note relative to contemporary thought that the critique of the author develops simultaneously with an increasing interest in Nietzsche (cf. for example FR pp. 101–20).

11 This point is crucial in so far as it reiterates the historical specificity of Nietzsche's writing and of the form of philosophy in which he engages.

12 As this hopefully makes clear, the operation of the thought of eternal recurrence demands the capacity for self-reflection bred under the aegis of Christian asceticism.

13 Today we are perhaps all too aware of how such transformative reinventions of the past may be utilised to justify expressions of *ressentiment*; the rise of neo-Nazi movements in Europe and its connection to revisionist histories of the Holocaust signals the pertinence of Nietzsche's thinking.

14 This has been addressed in detail in Ansell-Pearson (1991b: 176–85); cf. also Stamburgh (1972) for a detailed exploration of eternal recurrence with respect to the theme of time.

15 Cf. Ansell-Pearson (1991b: 176–85); also Small (1990a).

16 For discussions of this topic, see Schutte (1984: 63–75), Schacht (1983: 253–66), Heidegger (1984), Magnus (1978), Small (1990b), amongst others.

17 Weber, it seems to me, makes this error (PE: p. 232 fn. 66) by following Simmel's reading of Nietzsche (Simmel 1986).

18 Ansell-Pearson (1992) comments interestingly on this issue and also raises the topic of the relation of eternal recurrence to women. Although I do not take up the latter issue, it has been central to much recent writing (cf. Ansell-Pearson 1993). Oliver (1984, 1988) provides a series of excellent

interventions around Nietzsche and women. See also Owen (1993) for some thoughts on this topic with respect to the politics of genealogy.

19 In so far as this experience constitutes a ground of value which reproduces itself, Nietzsche avoids the problem posed by the Renaissance of a squandering which exhausts itself.

20 Cf. EH GM p. 313 where Nietzsche explicitly cites Zarathustra as the teacher of a counter-ideal to Christian asceticism. Also Magnus (1973) and Nehamas (1980).

21 On this issue, see the interesting piece by Nancy (1990) brought to my attention by Bernstein's essay (1991).

22 See my discussion of Weber's concept of 'personality' in Chapter 7 with respect to this topic, and also Owen (1994).

23 It should be noted here that Nietzsche is not operating with the *Gemeinschaft/Gesellschaft* distinction popularised by Tönnies.

24 Again compare with the discussion of Weber in Chapters 5 and 7.

25 See Keith Ansell-Pearson (1991a, c) on this point.

26 See Keith Ansell-Pearson (1991b: 152–99).

27 On this point, Strong (1989) is informative with respect to Emerson's influence on Nietzsche.

28 Conway (1989) offers a superb reading of this issue although I think Nietzsche's texts are more ambivalent than he perhaps allows. His reading of *Thus Spake Zarathustra* is elaborated in Conway (1988, 1990).

29 This comment might be read as providing a certain legitimation to the idea that Nietzsche aestheticises politics.

30 Certain similarities between Nietzsche and Machiavelli are indicated in Ansell-Pearson (1991b: 192; cf. also 240 fn. 71); cf. also Strauss (1975). I should point out that I read Machiavelli as a profoundly ironic writer at least with respect to *The Prince* (Machiavelli 1961).

31 This is, in part, similar to the reading of Nietzsche's politics offered by Keith Ansell-Pearson (1991b: 202–6) although he reads the notion of a sovereign culture differently from myself.

32 Tracy Strong has noted that, in his last letters and notebooks prior to his descent into madness, Nietzsche declared himself ready to rule the world (Strong 1988: 153). One could alternatively read these comments as ironic; this is the strategy taken up persuasively by Dan Conway (1989) as part of his wider strategy of reading Nietzsche as an ironic thinker (1988, 1990).

33 This point is made by Dan Conway (1989) and also informs Robert Pippin's reading of *Thus Spoke Zarathustra* (1989).

34 Cf. Keith Ansell-Pearson (1991b: 194–9).

35 Cited as the epigram to Strong (1989).

36 Cited in Strong (1988: 153).

5 GENEALOGY AS CULTURAL SCIENCE: WEBER, METHODOLOGY AND CRITIQUE

1 See, for example, Fleischmann (1964), Turner (1982), Eden (1983), Schroeder (1987), Hennis (1988: 146–62), Warren (1988b, 1992), Scaff (1989: 127–33), Strong (1992), Owen (1991a, 1994).

2 Cf. Owen (1991a) for an outline of this argument.

3 Burger (1976) and Oakes (1988) offer the most detailed elaboration of this claim.

4 Rickert (1962) does not explicitly mention Nietzsche as the source of this

argument, yet he is clearly referring to a perspectival theory of knowledge of the sort that Nietzsche elaborates.

5   For Weber, methodological activity is justified only in so far as shifts in the cultural problems of the age demand shifts in the conceptual apparatus deployed to examine them. In this context of shifting problems, method-ological activity is a requirement of intellectual probity. Cf. MSS p. 113.

6   Weber's point here may be interestingly compared with Kuhn's insistence that a paradigm switch involves a change in the ways one goes about doing science and what counts as science (Kuhn 1970).

7   Weber's reference here is to Eduard Meyer's *Zur Theorie und Methodik der Geschichte* as a contribution to the methodological debate within the cultural sciences in Germany. See Tenbruck (1987) for a discussion of Weber and Meyer.

8   This topic is the central concern of Lassman and Velody (1989: 159–204) which brilliantly explores the tensions generated within Weber's reflections by this commitment to reflexivity.

9   Cf. Löwith (1982) and Lassman and Velody (1989) on this issue. It may be noted that it is profoundly ironic that science at the very moment it is set adrift from its various cultural anchorages becomes, paradoxically, the reference point and source of legitimation for other secular philosophical anthro-pologies. I am grateful to Charles Turner for bringing this to my attention. The politics of this paradox is, of course, a central concern for Foucault; cf. Chapters 9 and 10.

10   In a superb essay, Sheldon Wolin (1984) explores Weber's methodological writing as a form of political education with respect to the vocations. This reading has been of considerable importance for the interpretation of the vocation essays offered in Chapter 7.

11   Cf. Lassman and Velody (1989: 173–9) on this topic.

12   We should note here that the retreat of the highest values is simultaneously the retreat of the political understood as the space of the struggle of values, whereby 'politics' is located as simply a technical exercise.

13   Cf. also PE p. 29.

14   This 'leap of faith' required of the scientist can be interestingly contrasted with Kant's 'matters of faith' in so far as both Kant and Weber are concerned with the conditions of meaningful action.

15   For orthodox readings, cf. the collection edited by Rogers (1969) and Käsler (1988: 180–4) amongst others. With respect to the relevance of the ideal-type to contemporary social theory, cf. Hekman (1983: 18–60).

16   This, it will be recalled, is also the requirement which attaches to Nietzsche's principle of will to power; cf. Chapter 2.

17   Compare with the comments Nietzsche's makes on grammar and world-images (BGE 20).

18   For a Kantian interpretation of the switchman metaphor, see Schroeder (1992: 7–27). Despite my disagreements with this reading, it has influenced my own approach to this topic.

19   Actually, as Nietzsche recognised, the former of these is presupposed in the idea of charisma in so far as this concept represents the genius of the founder of the religion; cf. GS 353 pp. 296–7.

20   Weber's approach here parallels Nietzsche's concern with the synthetic *a priori* judgements of a culture. One may read Weber's position here as a refinement of the Nietzschean hypothesis of will to power.

21   For two alternative readings of personality, cf. Portis (1978) and Schroeder (1991).

22   Cf. Wolin (1984) and Lassman and Velody (1989) for similar arguments.

6 THE GENEALOGY OF MODERNITY: WEBER, ASCETICISM AND DISENCHANTMENT

1 On the question of thematic unity, cf. Tenbruck (1980), Hennis (1988: 21–61) and Schroeder (1992: 1–32). My position might be located as between those elaborated by Hennis and Schroeder.

2 This is explored in Owen (1991a) and a similar interest is expressed in Scaff (1989).

3 For readings of the East, cf. Schroeder (1992: 33–71); this topic is also addressed in B. Turner (1974) and more critically in B. Turner (1981).

4 Schroeder (1992: 72–84) distinguishes between the period of the covenant, the period of the kingdom and the post-exilic period, while Schluchter (1981: 200) notes that five periods may be distinguished: the period of the covenant, the period of the kingdom, the period of exile, and the post-exilic period which can be spilt into the periods before and after the destruction of the Second Temple. For my purposes, the post-exilic period can be taken as a single unity, and thus I operate with four periods.

5 Cf. AC 25 pp. 135–6 and also my comments on Nietzsche's reading of Judaism in Chapter 3.

6 Weber's analysis here recalls Nietzsche's focus on internal and external threats (cf. Chapter 3). We may also note in passing certain similarities with Nietzsche's analysis of panhellenism (Caygill 1993).

7 Compare with Nietzsche (GM I) on nobles and slaves.

8 This affinity between Nietzsche's and Weber's analyses, albeit that Weber's account is much more specific and detailed, may be read as lending support to my suggestion that Weber's switchman metaphor can be seen as a refinement of the Nietzschean hypothesis of will to power.

9 I am not directly concerned with the accuracy of Weber's analysis but with how this informs his reading of modernity. For criticisms of Weber, cf. Zeitlin (1984).

10 In moving straight from ancient Judaism to Protestantism, I am taking it as read that Catholicism represented a regression with respect to rationalism; cf. Schroeder (1992: 84–96).

11 See, for example, Marshall (1982) and Poggi (1983).

12 We may note in passing that this Weberian distinction applies neatly to the two forms of politics we noted as operating in Nietzsche's texts.

13 'Strictly speaking, the charismatic force of the Protestant worldview is derived from two sources: one is the idea of the radical transcendence of God, originating from Israelite prophets, and the other the combination of the ideas of the calling and of predestination found in Luther and Calvin' (Schroeder 1992: 111 fn. 12).

14 Compare with Nietzsche (GM III 18) on priests and work as sublimation.

15 Cf. my reading of Nietzsche's interpretation of Protestantism in Chapter 3.

16 Cf. Paden (1988) for an interesting reading of this aspect of Puritanism.

17 Compare with the reading of Nietzsche in Chapter 3 and cf. also Owen (1991a).

18 SV pp. 140–1.

19 Compare with Nietzsche's perspective on Christianity as the synthesis of philosophical and theological dialectics (cf. Chapter 3).

20 Cf. Merton (1973) on the issue of puritanism and science.

21 Cf. Schluchter (1979: 32–59) for interesting comments on this theme, particularly p. 43 fn. 113 for a consideration of the category of secularisation.

22 It is interesting to note that this concern with values and structures was

considered the proper domain of the sociology of science (until the emergence of post-empiricist philosophies of science) and Weber's essay on science as a vocation was read as an early contribution to this field; cf. Lassman and Velody (1989: 163–7).

23 In contrast with the current state of universities, this conception takes on an almost utopian glow.

24 We might note in passing that for Catholics the separation of the value spheres is meaningless at the level of worldviews.

25 Cf. Troeltsch (1931, 1989) with respect to Protestantism, natural law and science.

26 Cf. Landshut (1989) on this topic.

27 Compare with the reading of Nietzsche in Chapter 3.

28 Cf. Alexander (1987) for some interesting comments on this theme.

29 Wright Mills (1959: 171).

7 THE POLITICS OF 'PERSONALITY': WEBER, MATURITY AND MODERNITY

1 We should note that Weber's notion of 'personality' is not simply reducible to a concern with resisting the processes of rationalisation and disenchantment but belongs within the broader tradition of German intellectual culture. Albrow (1990: 42–77) explores the theme with respect to Weber's relations to Kant, Nietzsche and Goethe; however, his location of Weber as presenting a Kantian ethic fails to recognise the commonality of Nietzsche's and Weber's concern with intellectual integrity and the purely formal character of the idea of 'personality' in Weber. Hinton Thomas (1983) offers a useful contextual guide on this question by illuminating the influence of Nietzsche in German culture during the period of Weber's life with respect to the close connection of the themes of *Individualität* and *Persönlichkeit*. This question is also explored in Scaff (1989) in the context of Weber's relation to Simmel and the Weber Circle, while C. Turner (1992: 47–59) explores the tensions around this notion in respect of politics.

2 Cf. the section on Nietzsche's reading of the Reformation in Chapter 3.

3 This topic is explored through a contrast with Sartre in Alexander (1987).

4 The similarities between this fear of the entrenchment of an ethic of adaptation and Nietzsche's fear of the rise of the 'last man' are striking. In both cases, this concern is directed at the twin perils of a materialist culture linked to a utilitarian form of thinking.

5 In the light of Weber's analysis, Kant's injunction to members of civic posts to instrumentalise themselves with respect to the performance of their civic roles takes on an excessively naive look.

6 Foucault's concern with biopolitics may be read as sharing this concern. For a discussion of Weber and Foucault with respect to rationalisation, cf. O'Neil (1986).

7 In other words, as in Nietzsche and Foucault, the concern with autonomy is immanently related to the project of genealogy.

8 Although on this question of aestheticism, see the story cited in Hennis (1988: 165) in which Weber adopts a musical analogy to express his position.

9 Cf. GS 290 p. 232.

10 Owen (1993) explores this in greater detail.

11 Cf. Z, Of the Vision and the Riddle, p. 178.

12 Cf. Simmel (1986); support for this is given in Hennis (1988: 146–62).

13 This distinction between Nietzsche and Weber should be read lightly in so far as both problematise the distinction between life and work; cf. Owen (1991a: 86–7).

14 It should be noted that the criteria of probity in the spheres of science and politics are distinct in terms of the substantive commitments that they require, not in the formal elements they exemplify. The tragic character of Weber's personality is often read in terms of this conflict as Wittenberg (1989) notes.

15 In suggesting that Weber's switchman metaphor articulates a refinement of the Nietzschean hypothesis of will to power, we might argue that the character of this refinement lies in the capacity of Weber's analyses to exhibit the relation of cultural and institutional features of modernity in a way which Nietzsche's examinations of nihilism may not convincingly achieve.

16 It should be noted that my argument stands or falls with this claim.

17 The question of exemplarity which is exhibited here with respect to the grounding of legislation in charismatic authority constitutes a central problematic for modern thought from, at least, the time of Rousseau's depiction of the role of the legislator in *The Social Contract* (Rousseau 1968) and relates this issue firmly to the question of genius raised by Kant (1987: §47–50).

18 It may be that my agreement with Brubaker on this issue underestimates the richness of the concept of *Zweckrationalität*. On this issue, and in general for a brilliant reading of the question of politics in Weber's work, see Charles Turner (1992: 146–70).

19 Eden (1982, 1983) offers a fascinating reading of Weber with respect to this issue around the theme of leadership and the possibility of a liberal politics without liberal ideology; cf. also Warren (1988b).

20 Cf. SV p. 151 where Weber distinguishes between the scientist with a calling and the technician.

21 This theme is central to Foucault's critique of the human sciences in terms of their immanent connection with biopolitics; cf. Chapter 9.

22 In other words, I am suggesting that Machiavelli's *The Prince* (1961) can be read as an essay on what it is to have a vocation for ruling, albeit one which does not express the same religious musicality as Weber's essays on science and politics.

23 Reading the two vocation essays as fundamentally complementary was a commonplace with respect to Weber's contemporaries (Wittenberg 1989), a strategy which is also taken up in ways which exhibit certain parallels with my own reading by Schluchter (1979: 65–113). For an opposed reading of these essays, see Schroeder (1992: 112–37).

24 On the tragic character of Weber's exclusion, cf. Wittenberg (1989).

8 GENEALOGY AS HISTORICAL ONTOLOGY: FOUCAULT, METHODOLOGY AND CRITIQUE

1 Cf. also PPC p. 95.

2 Foucault's reading of Kant is taken up with respect to the self-reflective character of Foucault's own work in Coles (1991), Dreyfus and Rabinow (1986) and Gordon (1986).

3 This aspect is highlighted by Deleuze in his reflection on Foucault's thinking (1988: 119–23).

4 Foucault's sense of his relation to the Frankfurt School is sketched in an interview with Gérard Raulet (PPC pp. 17–46).

5 Despite their Kantian form, this remains true of Habermas's discourse ethics and it is this which (amongst other issues) creates problems for his account; cf. Benhabib (1986: 330–1).

6 On Foucault, Kant and self-construction, cf. Hacking (1986).

7 For criticisms offered of Foucault from this perspective apart from Habermas's own (1986; 1987: 238–93), cf. Dews (1987: 144–219; 1989) and McCarthy (1990). Ironically, both Dews and McCarthy are more sensitive to Foucault's position and offer more sophisticated critiques than Habermas's rather heavy-handed hammering.

8 The centrality of the figure of Baudelaire to this question is established by Benjamin's classic study (1983). Foucault's comments may be interestingly compared with Habermas's (1987: 1–11).

9 This has led some critics to charge Foucault with aesthetic decisionism (Wolin 1986); however, for a more judicious approach which also indicates the differences between Nietzsche and Foucault, see Coles (1991), especially p. 105.

10 A good discussion of this ethos of critique is given in Dreyfus and Rabinow (1986).

11 Humanism as it is embodied in the project of philosophical anthropology may be read as an attempt to provide an answer to Kant's question 'What is Man?', that is, to foreclose the question of what it is to be human. For Foucault the question of what it is to be human is always futural. I am grateful to Joanna Hodge for pointing this out to me through her work on Heidegger; cf. Hodge (1994).

12 The theme of a liminal thinking is one which increasingly inhabits the philosophical domain; cf. Wood (1991) and Cornell (1992).

13 Foucault's concept of *episteme* can be interestingly compared with Kuhn's notion of a *paradigm* (disciplinary matrix), yet Foucault's concerns are operating at a quite distinct philosophical level to Kuhn's in so far as Foucault attempts to draw out the constitutive conditions of utterances across disciplines, that is, to map a regime of truth. This topic has been considered by Major-Poetzl (1982).

14 For an interesting account of Foucault's notion of epistemological breaks which highlights his relations to Bachelard and Cauguilheim, see Gutting (1989: especially ch. 1).

15 This seems to be the error of Merquior (1985: 56–75) amongst others.

16 I borrow this useful phrase from Ian Hacking. See his discussion of the idea of styles of reasoning in this context (1982).

17 For an alternative reading, cf. Gutting (1989: ch. 6).

18 Habermas is referring here to remarks of Paul Veyne on Foucault (Habermas 1987: 414 fn. 22).

19 The question of Foucault's fidelity to Nietzsche has been critically addressed by Pizer (1990) and Ansell-Pearson (1991d).

20 Cf. OT pp. 330–4 for a fuller discussion of the metaphysics of origins in modern thought.

21 Foucault reflects further on this anti-essentialist theme in his essay on Deleuze's *Différence et Repetition* and *Logique du sens* (LMC pp. 165–96).

22 Cf. Clark (1990) on Nietzsche's account of truth.

23 We should note that genealogy has a formal architectonic interest in autonomy, yet this interest is 'filled in' in different ways by the direction of given genealogical accounts.

24 Cf. MSS p. 112.

25 I am grateful to Arpad Szakoiczai for pointing out to me how Foucault's late reflections combine archaeology and genealogy.

26 There are numerous essays on Foucault's notion of power; a few interesting

ones include Philp (1983), Taylor (1984, 1985, 1989), Connolly (1985), Thiele (1986), Hoy (1988), Fraser (1989: chs 2, 3, 4) and Patton (1989).

27 Patton (1989) is excellent on the question of power as relating to capacities.

28 Thus, contra Dews (1987: 144–99), I suggest that Foucault does not dissolve the relation between reason, consciousness and freedom but problematises certain ways of thinking this relation. This is elaborated in the following section of this chapter.

29 More precisely, we might say that it is a question of the relationship of rationalities and social practices.

30 Dews (1987: 171–99) seems to make this suggestion along with Fraser (1989), Habermas (1987) and Taylor (1984), but see Foucault's comment on this reading of his work cited in Keenan's excellent paper (1987: 12).

31 This is the heart of the argument, my reading of Foucault's methodology stands or falls with this claim.

32 Cf. Thiele (1986: 256).

33 For an example of the sense of Foucault's claim about the intelligible and non-subjective character of power relations, see P/K pp. 202–3.

34 This is not to say that an individual or group may not constitute a dominant vector but rather that they may not constitute a determining vector.

35 Contra Nietzsche and Weber, Foucault appears to be prepared to let the becoming of history become. For the problems raised by Nietzsche's unwillingness to accept this position, cf. Ansell-Pearson (1991b: 222).

36 Cf. UP p. 37.

37 Cf. GS 290 and for Foucault's comments on this question FR p. 351.

38 Foucault may be gesturing towards this when he notes the double meaning of the term 'subject' (SP p. 212).

39 In other words, I am suggesting that Foucault's methodology like Weber's is to be read as a refinement of the Nietzschean hypothesis of will to power.

40 This emphasis on an ethical showing (exemplarity) as opposed to an ethical saying (legislation) is a central concern of this text. It is perhaps the failure of Hegelian critics of Foucault to register the order of exemplarity which leaves them confused by the relation between the richness of his empirical studies and the apparent lack of normative grounds.

41 Habermas (1987), Fraser (1989), Taylor (1984), Dews (1987) and others all focus their criticisms around this claim, although Dews (1989) also focuses on the theme of subjectivity.

42 This has been noted somewhat damningly by Jay (1986).

43 Habermas completely fails to recognise this Nietzschean stance, perhaps because of his blindness to the idea of an ethics of exemplarity. In this context, it is worth noting the discussion on the role of intellectuals between Foucault and Deleuze (LMC pp. 205–17) with respect to their formulation of the opposition of the universal and specific intellectual. This contrast is interestingly explored in Rajchman (1985: ch. 3).

44 Although requiring investigation, I suspect that the topic of time is liable to problematise any attempt to reconcile Foucault and Habermas.

9 THE GENEALOGY OF MODERNITY: FOUCAULT, HUMANISM AND BIOPOLITICS

1 We should note here that genealogy has a formal architectonic theoretical interest in accounting for our constitution as subjects of knowledge and a formal architectonic practical interest in our constitution as autonomous

subjects. Roughly, I am concerned with the first of these in this chapter, and the second in the following chapter.

2 In other words, the project of philosophical anthropology may be read as an attempt to close the ethical openness of the question 'what is it to be human?'

3 Genealogy as scepticism, where scepticism should perhaps be understood ethically in a Levinasian sense; cf. Critchley (1992: 156–69).

4 For two more extended discussions of *The Order of Things* around the modern episteme, cf. Dreyfus and Rabinow (1983: 26–43) and Gutting (1989: 181–217).

5 One might suggest Lange's materialism as representative of this category which in itself raises interesting questions about Nietzsche's position. For comments on Nietzsche's relation to Lange, cf. Stack (1991: 30–58).

6 The history of twentieth century Marxism may be read in terms of the tensions between positivism (e.g. Second International) and eschatology (e.g. the Frankfurt School).

7 We can read, for example, Freud and the psychoanalytic tradition in the light of this comment.

8 I am not entirely convinced that Foucault avoids this third double given his comments on history in 'Is It Useless to Revolt?'

9 For further reflections on Foucault's question, cf. Perrot (1980).

10 Needless to say confessions are still coerced; it is simply that the element of coercion is secret in so far as its visibility disqualifies the confession as truth.

11 Locke's *Two Treatises on Government* (II.1 §8) provides a classic exemplar of this form of reasoning (Locke 1960: 312–13).

12 Locke notably thinks of punishment in terms of deterrence (II.1 §8; cf. Locke 1960: 313).

13 Again Locke (II.1 §8) is a clear exemplar of this style of reasoning.

14 The figure of the delinquent emerges as the re-unification of these two lines of objectification. On the difficulty of everyday conduct as a site of signs and role of this difficulty, cf. Foucault's essay on the concept of the dangerous individual (PPC pp. 125–51) which represents one of the clearest expositions of his critique of humanist discourses (Owen 1991b).

15 In 'Technologies of the Self' Foucault explores this question around the topic of asceticism with respect to Cassian.

16 This analytical/cellular and natural/organic body marks the site of humanism, cf. OT ch. 8.

17 This is interestingly explored by Macherey (1992) in terms of Foucault's articulation of a natural history of norms.

18 Cf. TS pp. 46–9.

19 This shift from a familial model of government to a location of the family as a simultaneous site and instrument of government is sketched around the idea of population as the end of government (G pp. 99–101).

20 Cf. HS pp. 146–7.

21 Cf. PPC pp. 60–7.

22 Cf. G p. 91.

23 Gordon (1991: 8–14) offers a clear exposition of Foucault on this topic.

24 Cf. Hacking (1991: 181–96) for observations on giving an account of the emergence of statistics.

25 An illuminating essay on the question of interests is provided by Burchill (1991: 119–50) which also explores parallels between Foucault and Pocock.

26 Cf. Gordon (1987: 293–316) on the topic of Cameralism and also for comments on the relationship of Foucault's thinking on this theme and Weber's approach to it.

27 See, for example, the collection edited by Burchill *et al.* (1991).

10 THE POLITICS OF CRITIQUE: FOUCAULT, MATURITY AND MODERNITY

1 Dreyfus and Rabinow (1983: 188–97) provide a cogent reading of this topic although lacking the input of Foucault's late work, Hooke (1987) deals with this theme implicitly within a discussion of the question of resistance, while Donnelly (1992) offers a critical perspective on Foucault's deployment of the idea of biopower.

2 Cf. Foucault's 'Two Lectures on Power' (P/K pp. 78–108).

3 Hobbes offers an account of the total cession of rights as the ground of that absolutism requisite to the preservation of order (peace and security), while Locke's account of natural rights implies only a cession of the right to execute the law of nature to the sovereign body. Sabine (1937: 392–401, 442–57), for example, provides an explication of these positions.

4 It is, of course, this question which Rousseau's elaboration of 'popular sovereignty' through the 'general will' is meant to resolve (Rousseau 1968).

5 Cf. Marx (1975: 211–41).

6 Cf. Freud (1975: 49–51).

7 This threefold exposition of power might be compared with the position elaborated by Lukes, except that Foucault is engaged in making a historical claim and also rejects the idea of 'real interests' which underpins (and undermines) Lukes's account. See Hoy (1986: 123–47) for an interesting discussion of this topic.

8 A clear exposition of this theme is given in Foucault's essay on the concept of the dangerous individual (PPC pp. 125–51).

9 Cf. PPC p. 294.

10 Immediately following this passage, Foucault notes that his view is much closer to Nietzsche's in GS 290 than Sartre's.

11 In other words, Foucault preserves the possibility of an ethical thinking – a responsibility to otherness – by refusing to foreclose on the question of what it is to be human.

12 For a reading of Nietzsche along these lines, cf. Thiele (1990a).

13 Foucault, as I read him, may be taken as developing Wittgenstein's insights into the operation of language games by showing how they are rooted in the historical emergence, development and transformation of power relations. In this context, it is interesting to note that the contested character of concepts signals their location within conflicting forms of self- and other-relations.

14 Cf. Coles (1991) for a sensitive exposition of this issue.

15 Parallel arguments are suggested by Thiele (1990b) and Coles (1991).

16 Cf. FR p. 245; this point is highlighted in Thiele (1990b).

17 This topic has been explored in detail by Bauman (1987).

18 For a defence of Habermas on this issue, cf. White (1988: 69–89, 144–53); interestingly White's position has developed into an attempt to reconcile modern and postmodern positions around the tension between a responsibility to act and a responsibility to otherness, or (in my terms) a legislative or exemplary politics (White 1992).

19 It is this recognition which leads thinkers like White (1992) to question the political value of Foucault in so far as they read him as engaged in a mode of thinking which entails a perpetual withholding from action. I suggest that, on the contrary, Foucault's work is about constituting communities of action.

20 Foucault's engagement in groups like the GIP served precisely this purpose, for example.

21 This emphasis on *showing* has recently been emphasised with respect to

deconstruction (Critchley 1992), while Whitford (1991) appears to make a similar case for Irigaray.

BIBLIOGRAPHY

NIETZSCHE

Beyond Good and Evil, tr. R.J. Hollingdale, Harmondsworth: Penguin, 1973.
The Birth of Tragedy/The Case of Wagner, tr. W. Kaufmann, New York: Random House, 1967.
Daybreak, tr. R.J. Hollingdale, Cambridge: Cambridge University Press, 1982.
The Gay Science, tr. W. Kaufmann, New York: Random House, 1974.
On the Genealogy of Morals/Ecce Homo, tr. W. Kaufmann and R.J. Hollingdale, New York: Random House, 1969.
Human, All Too Human, tr. R.J. Hollingdale, Cambridge: Cambridge University Press, 1986.
Philosophy and Truth, tr. D. Breazeale, Brighton: Harvester, 1979.
Twilight of the Idols/The Anti-Christ, tr. R.J. Hollingdale, Harmondsworth: Penguin, 1968.
Thus Spoke Zarathustra, tr. R.J. Hollingdale, Harmondsworth: Penguin, 1961.
The Will to Power, tr. W. Kaufmann and R.J. Hollingdale, New York: Random House, 1968.
Untimely Meditations, tr. R.J. Hollingdale, Cambridge: Cambridge University Press, 1983.

WEBER

Ancient Judaism, tr. H.H. Gerth and D. Martindale, Glencoe, Ill.: Free Press, 1952.
Economy and Society (2 vols), ed. G. Roth and C. Wittich, New York: Bedminster, 1968.
From Max Weber: Essays in Sociology, tr. H.H. Gerth and C. Wright Mills, London: Routledge & Kegan Paul, 1948.
Gesemmelte Aufsätz zur Wissenschaftslehre [Collected Essays on Methodology], Tübingen: J.C.B. Mohr, 1973.
The Methodology of the Social Sciences, tr. E.A. Shils and H.A. Finch, Glencoe, Ill.: Free Press, 1949.
'The Nation State and Economic Policy [Freiburg Address]', *Economy and Society* 9 (4): 428–49, 1980.
'Politics as a Vocation', in *From Max Weber*, pp. 77–128.
The Protestant Ethic and the Spirit of Capitalism, tr. T. Parsons, London: Allen & Unwin, 1930.
'Science as a Vocation', in *From Max Weber*, pp. 129–56.
'The Social Psychology of World Religions', in *From Max Weber*, pp. 267–301.
The Sociology of Religion, tr. E. Fischoff, London: Methuen, 1965.

Roscher and Knies: the Logical Problems of Historical Economics, tr. G. Oakes, New York: Free Press, 1975.

FOUCAULT

The Archaeology of Knowledge, tr. A.M. Sheridan-Smith, London: Tavistock, 1972.

Discipline and Punish, tr. A.M. Sheridan-Smith, Harmondsworth: Penguin, 1977.
The Foucault Reader, ed. P. Rabinow, Harmondsworth: Penguin, 1984.
'Governmentality', in *The Foucault Effect*, ed. G. Burchell, C. Gordon and P. Miller, London: Harvester Wheatsheaf, 1991, pp. 87–104.
The History of Sexuality, vol. 1, tr. R. Hurley, Harmondsworth: Penguin, 1978.
Language, Counter-Memory, Practice, tr. D.F. Bouchard and S. Simon, Ithaca, N.Y.: Cornell University Press, 1977.
The Order of Things, London: Tavistock, 1970.
Power/Knowledge: Selected Interviews and Other Writings 1972–77, ed. C. Gordon, London: Harvester Wheatsheaf, 1980.
Politics, Philosophy, Culture: Interviews and Other Writings 1977–84, ed. L.D. Kritzman, London: Routledge, 1988.
'The Political Technology of Individuals', in *Technologies of the Self*, ed. L.H. Martin, H. Gutman and P.H. Hutton, London: Tavistock, 1988, pp. 145–62.
'Questions of Method', in *The Foucault Effect*, ed. G. Burchell, C. Gordon and P. Miller, London: Harvester Wheatsheaf, 1991, pp. 73–86.
'The Subject and Power', in H. Dreyfus and P. Rabinow, *Michel Foucault: Beyond Structuralism and Hermeneutics* (1st edition), Brighton: Harvester, 1982.
'Technologies of the Self', in *Technologies of the Self*, ed. L.H. Martin, H. Gutman and P.H. Hutton, London: Tavistock, 1988, pp. 16–49.
The Use of Pleasure, tr. R. Hurley, New York: Pantheon, 1985.
'Is it Useless to Revolt?', *Philosophy and Social Criticism*, 8: 5–9, 1981.

GENERAL

Albrow, M. (1990) *Max Weber's Construction of Social Theory*, London: Macmillan.
Alexander, J. (1987) 'The Dialectic of Individuation and Domination: Max Weber's Rationalization Theory and Beyond', in S. Lash and S. Whimster (eds) *Max Weber, Rationality and Modernity*, London: Allen & Unwin.
Ansell-Pearson, K. (1986) 'The Exoteric Philosophy of Friedrich Nietzsche', *Political Theory* 14 (3): 310–40.
Ansell-Pearson, K. (1987) 'Nietzsche's Overcoming of Kant and Metaphysics: From Tragedy to Nihilism', *Nietzsche-Studien* 16: 310–40.
Ansell-Pearson, K. (1991a) 'Nietzsche and the Problem of the Will in Modernity', in K. Ansell-Pearson (ed.) *Nietzsche and Modern German Thought*, London: Routledge, pp. 165–92.
Ansell-Pearson, K. (1991b) *Nietzsche Contra Rousseau*, Cambridge: Cambridge University Press.
Ansell-Pearson, K. (1991c) 'Nietzsche on Autonomy and Morality: the Challenge to Political Theory', *Political Studies* 32 (2): 270–87.
Ansell-Pearson, K. (1991d) 'The Significance of Michel Foucault's Reading of Nietzsche', *Nietzsche-Studien* 20: 267–83.
Ansell-Pearson, K. (1992) 'Who is the *Übermensch*? Time, Truth, and Woman in Nietzsche', *Journal of the History of Ideas* 53 (2): 309–31.

Ansell-Pearson, K. (1993) 'Nietzsche, Woman, and Political Theory', in P. Patton (ed.) *Nietzsche, Feminism and Political Theory*, London: Routledge, pp. 27–48.

Aron, R. (1970) 'The Logic of the Social Sciences', in D. Wrong (ed.) *Max Weber*, Englewood Cliffs, N.J.: Prentice Hall, pp. 77–89.

Bauman, Z. (1987) *Legislators and Interpreters*, London: Polity.

Beetham, D. (1974) *Max Weber and the Theory of Modern Politics*, London: George Allen & Unwin.

Benhabib, S. (1986) *Critique, Norm, Utopia: A Study of the Foundations of Critical Theory*, New York: Columbia University Press.

Benjamin, W. (1983) *Charles Baudelaire*, London: Verso.

Bergmann, F. (1988) 'Nietzsche's Critique of Morality', in R.C. Solomon and K.M. Higgins (eds) *Reading Nietzsche*, Oxford: Oxford University Press, pp. 29–45.

Bernstein, J. (1991) 'Autonomy and Solitude', in K. Ansell-Pearson (ed.) *Nietzsche and Modern German Thought*, London: Routledge, pp. 192–215.

Blondel, E. (1991) *Nietzsche: The Body and Culture*, tr. S. Hand, London: Athlone Press.

Bowles, M. (1992) *An Enquiry Concerning the Extent of Nietzsche's Repetition of Kant's Critical Philosophy*, Ph.D. Thesis, University of Essex.

Brubaker, R. (1984) *The Limits of Rationality: An Essay on the Social and Moral Thought of Max Weber*, London: Allen & Unwin.

Bruun, H.H. (1972) *Science, Values and Politics in Max Weber's Methodology*, Copenhagen: Munksgaard.

Burchill, G. (1991) 'Peculiar Interests: Civil Society and Governing "The System of Natural Liberty" ', in G. Burchill, C. Gordon and P. Miller (eds) *The Foucault Effect: Studies in Governmentality*, London: Harvester Wheatsheaf, pp. 119–50.

Burchill, G., Gordon, C. and Miller, P. (eds) (1991) *The Foucault Effect: Studies in Governmentality*, London: Harvester Wheatsheaf.

Burger, T. (1976) *Max Weber's Theory of Concept Formation*, Durham, N.C.: Duke University Press.

Caygill, H. (1988) 'Post-Modernism and Judgement', *Economy and Society* 17 (1): 1–20.

Caygill, H. (1989) *The Art of Judgement*, Oxford: Basil Blackwell.

Caygill, H. (1993) 'Philosophy and Cultural Reform in the Early Nietzsche', in K. Ansell-Pearson and H. Caygill (eds) *The Fate of the New Nietzsche*, London: Avebury Press, pp. 109–22.

Clark, M. (1990) *Nietzsche on Philosophy and Truth*, Cambridge: Cambridge University Press.

Coles, R. (1991) 'Foucault's Dialogical Artistic Ethos', *Theory, Culture and Society* 8: 99–120.

Connelly, W.E. (1985) 'Taylor, Foucault and Otherness', *Political Theory* 13: 365–76.

Conway, D. (1988) 'Solving the Problem of Socrates: Nietzsche's *Zarathustra* as Political Irony', *Political Theory* 16 (2): 257–80.

Conway, D. (1989) 'Overcoming the *Übermensch*: Nietzsche's Revaluation of Values', *Journal for the British Society for Phenomenology* 20 (3): 211–24.

Conway, D. (1990) 'Nietzsche contra Nietzsche: The Deconstruction of Zarathustra', in C. Koelb (ed.) *Nietzsche as Postmodernist*, Albany, N.Y.: State University of New York Press.

Cornell, D. (1992) *The Philosophy of the Limit*, London: Routledge.

Critchley, S. (1992) *The Ethics of Deconstruction*, Oxford: Basil Blackwell.

Deleuze, G. (1983) *Nietzsche and Philosophy*, tr. H. Tomlinson, London: Athlone.

Deleuze, G. (1988) *Foucault*, Minneapolis, Minn.: Minneapolis University Press.

DeLue, S.M. (1985) 'Kant's Politics as an Expression of the Need for his Aesthetics', *Political Theory* 13 (3): 409–29.

241

Detwiler, B. (1990) *Nietzsche and the Politics of Aristocratic Radicalism*, Chicago, Ill.: University of Chicago Press.

Dews, P. (1987) *Logics of Disintegration: Post-Structuralist Thought and the Claims of Critical Theory*, London: Verso.

Dews, P. (1989) 'The Return of the Subject in Late Foucault', *Radical Philosophy* 51: 37–41.

Donnelly, M. (1992) 'On Foucault's Uses of the Notion of "Biopower" ', in T.S. Armstrong (tr.) *Michel Foucault Philosopher*, London: Harvester Wheatsheaf, pp. 199–204.

Dreyfus, H. and Rabinow, P. (1983) *Michel Foucault: Beyond Structuralism and Hermeneutics*, Chicago, Ill.: University of Chicago Press.

Dreyfus, H. and Rabinow, P. (1986) 'What is Maturity? Habermas and Foucault on "What is Enlightenment?" ', in D.C. Hoy (ed.) *Foucault: A Critical Reader*, Oxford: Basil Blackwell, pp. 109–22.

Eden, R. (1982) 'Doing Without Liberalism: Weber's Regime Politics', *Political Theory* 10 (3): 379–407.

Eden, R. (1983) *Political Leadership and Nihilism*, Tampa, Fla.: University Presses of Florida.

Fleischmann, E. (1964) 'De Nietzsche à Weber', *Archives Européennes de Sociologie* 5: 190–238.

Fraser, N. (1989) *Unruly Practices: Power, Discourse and Gender in Contemporary Social Theory*, London: Polity.

Freud, S. (1975) *Civilisation and its Discontents*, London: The Hogarth Press.

Gillespie, M.A. (1984) *Hegel, Heidegger, and the Ground of History*, Chicago, Ill.: University of Chicago Press.

Gordon, C. (1986) 'Question, Ethos, Event: Foucault on Kant and Enlightenment', *Economy and Society* 15: 63–83.

Gordon, C. (1987) 'The Soul of the Citizen: Max Weber and Michel Foucault on Rationality and Government', in S. Lash and S. Whimster (eds) *Max Weber, Rationality and Modernity*, London: Allen & Unwin.

Gordon, C. (1991) 'Governmental Rationality: an Introduction', in G. Burchill, C. Gordon and P. Miller (eds) *The Foucault Effect: Studies in Govermentality*, London: Harvester Wheatsheaf, pp. 1–52.

Gutting, G. (1989) *Michel Foucault's Archaeology of Scientific Reason*, Cambridge: Cambridge University Press.

Habermas, J. (1986) 'Taking Aim at the Heart of the Present', in D.C. Hoy (ed.) *Foucault: A Critical Reader*, Oxford: Basil Blackwell, pp. 103–9.

Habermas, J. (1987) *The Philosophical Discourse of Modernity*, Cambridge: Polity.

Hacking, I. (1982) 'Language, Truth and Reason', in M. Hollis and S. Lukes (eds) *Rationality and Relativism*, Oxford: Basil Blackwell, pp. 48–66.

Hacking, I. (1986) 'Self-Improvement', in D.C. Hoy (ed.) *Foucault: A Critical Reader*, Oxford: Basil Blackwell, pp. 235–40.

Hacking, I. (1991) 'How Should We Do the History of Statistics?', in G. Burchill, C. Gordon and P. Miller (eds) *The Foucault Effect: Studies in Governmentality*, London: Harvester Wheatsheaf, pp. 181–96.

Hegel, G.W.F. (1977) *Phenomenology of Spirit*, tr. A.V. Miller, Oxford: Oxford University Press.

Heidegger, M. (1979) *Nietzsche. Volume One: The Will to Power as Art*, tr. D.F. Krell, London: Routledge.

Heidegger, M. (1982) *Nietzsche. Volume Four: Nihilism*, tr. F.A. Capuzzi, San Francisco, Calif.: Harper & Row.

Heidegger, M. (1985) *Nietzsche. Volume Two: The Eternal Recurrence of the Same*, tr. D.F. Krell, New York: Harper & Row.

Heidegger, M. (1987) *Nietzsche. Volume Three: The Will to Power as Knowledge and as Metaphysics*, tr. J. Stambaugh, F.A. Capuzzi and D.F. Krell, San Francisco, Calif.: Harper & Row.

Hekman, S. (1983) *Weber, the Ideal Type and Contemporary Social Theory*, Notre Dame, Ind.: Notre Dame University Press.

Heller, E. (1988) *The Importance of Nietzsche*, Chicago, Ill.: Chicago University Press.

Hennis, W. (1988) *Max Weber: Essays in Reconstruction*, London: Allen & Unwin.

Hinton, T. (1983) *Nietzsche in German Politics and Society 1890–1918*, Manchester: Manchester University Press.

Hodge, J. (1994) *Heidegger and Ethics*, London: Routledge.

Hooke, A.E. (1987) 'The Order of Others: is Foucault's Anti-humanist Against Human Action?', *Political Theory* 15: 38–60.

Houlgate, S. (1986) *Hegel, Nietzsche, and the Criticism of Metaphysics*, Cambridge: Cambridge University Press.

Hoy, D.C. (1986) 'Power, Repression, Progress: Foucault, Lukes and the Frankfurt School', in his *Foucault: A Critical Reader*, Oxford: Basil Blackwell, pp. 123–48.

Hoy, D.C. (1988) 'Foucault: Modern or Postmodern?', in J. Arac (ed.) *After Foucault*, New Brunswick, N.J.: Rutgers University Press, pp. 12–41.

Iggers, G. (1968) *The German Conception of History*, Middletown, Conn.: Wesleyan University Press.

Jay, M. (1986) 'In the Empire of the Gaze: Foucault and the Denigration of Vision in Twentieth-century French Thought', in D.C. Hoy (ed.) *Foucault: A Critical Reader*, Oxford: Basil Blackwell, pp. 175–204.

Kant, I. (1963) *Critique of Pure Reason*, tr. N. Kemp Smith, New York: St Martin's Press.

Kant, I. (1981) *Grounding for the Metaphysics of Morals*, tr. J.W. Ellington, Indianapolis, Ind.: Hackett.

Kant, I. (1983) *Perpetual Peace and Other Essays*, tr. T. Humphrey, Indianapolis, Ind.: Hackett.

Kant, I. (1987) *Critique of Judgement*, tr. W.S. Pluhar, Indianapolis, Ind.: Hackett.

Käsler, D. (1988) *Max Weber: an Introduction to his Life and Work*, Cambridge: Polity.

Keenan, T. (1987) 'The "Paradox" of Knowledge and Power: Reading Foucault on a Bias', *Political Theory* 15 (1): 5–37.

Kuhn, T. (1970) *The Structure of Scientific Revolutions*, Chicago, Ill.: University of Chicago Press.

Landshut, S. (1989) 'Max Weber's Significance for Intellectual History', in P. Lassman and I. Velody (eds) *Max Weber's 'Science as a Vocation'*, London: Unwin Hyman, pp. 87–111.

Lassman, P. and Velody, I. (1989) 'Max Weber on Science, Disenchantment and the Search for Meaning', in their *Max Weber's 'Science as a Vocation'*, London: Unwin Hyman, pp. 159–204.

Laursen, J.C. (1986) 'The Subversive Kant: The Vocabulary of "Public" and "Publicity" ', *Political Theory* 14 (4): 584–603.

Locke, J. (1960) *Two Treatises on Government*, Cambridge: Cambridge University Press.

Love, N.S. (1986) *Marx, Nietzsche, and Modernity*, New York: Columbia University Press.

Löwith, K. (1982) *Max Weber and Karl Marx*, tr. H. Fantel, London: Allen & Unwin.

Löwith, K. (1989) 'Max Weber's Position on Science', in I. Velody and P. Lassman (eds) *Max Weber's 'Science as a Vocation'*, London: Unwin Hyman, pp. 138–56.

Macherey, P. (1992) 'Towards a Natural History of Norms', in T.S. Armstrong (tr.) *Michel Foucault Philosopher*, London: Harvester Wheatsheaf, pp. 176–92.

Machiavelli, N. (1961) *The Prince*, tr. G. Bull, Harmondsworth: Penguin.

MacIntyre, A. (1977) 'Dramatic Narratives, Epistemological Crises, and the Philosophy of Science', *The Monist* 60: 453–72.

MacIntyre, A. (1984) *After Virtue*, London: Duckworth.

Magnus, B. (1973) 'Nietzsche's Eternalistic Counter-Myth', *Review of Metaphysics* 26: 604–16.

Magnus, B. (1978) *Nietzsche's Existential Imperative*, Bloomington, Ind.: Indiana University Press.

Major-Poetzl, P. (1982) *Michel Foucault's Archaeology of Western Culture*, Chapel Hill, N.C.: University of North Carolina Press.

Marcuse, H. (1962) *Eros and Civilisation*, New York: Random House.

Marshall, G. (1982) *In Search of the Spirit of Capitalism: An Essay on Max Weber's Protestant Ethic Thesis*, London: Hutchinson.

Marx, K. (1975) *Early Writings*, Harmondsworth: Penguin.

McCarthy, T. (1990) 'The Critique of Impure Reason: Foucault and the Frankfurt School', *Political Theory* 18 (3): 437–69.

Megill, A. (1984) *Prophets of Extremity*, Berkeley, Calif.: University of California Press.

Merquior, J.G. (1985) *Foucault*, London: Fontana.

Merton, R. (1973) 'The Puritan Spur to Science', in his *Sociology of Science*, Chicago, Ill.: University of Chicago Press.

Minson, J. (1985) *Genealogies of Morals*, London: Croom Helm.

Nancy, J.-L. (1990) ' "Our Probity!" On Truth in the Moral Sense in Nietzsche', in L. Rickels (ed.) *Looking After Nietzsche*, Albany, N.Y.: State University of New York Press, pp. 67–88.

Nehamas, A. (1980) 'The Eternal Recurrence', *Philosophical Review* 99: 331–56.

Nehamas, A. (1985) *Nietzsche: Life as Literature*, Cambridge, Mass.: Harvard University Press.

Oakes, G. (1988) *Weber and Rickert: Concept Formation in the Social Sciences*, Cambridge, Mass.: MIT Press.

Oliver, K. (1984) 'Woman as Truth in Nietzsche's Writing', *Social Theory and Practice* 10: 185–99.

Oliver, K. (1988) 'Nietzsche's Woman: The Poststructuralist Attempt to Do Away with Women', *Radical Philosophy* 48: 25–9.

O'Neil, O. (1986) 'The Public Use of Reason', *Political Theory* 14 (4): 523–51.

O'Neill, J. (1986) 'The Disciplinary Society: from Weber to Foucault', *British Journal of Sociology* 37 (1): 42–60.

Owen, D. (1991a) 'Autonomy and "Inner Distance": a Trace of Nietzsche in Weber', *History of the Human Sciences* 4 (1).

Owen, D. (1991b) 'Foucault, Psychiatry and the Spectre of Dangerousness', *Journal of Forensic Psychiatry* 2 (3): 238–41.

Owen, D. (1993) 'Nietzsche's Squandered Seductions: "Woman", the Body and the Politics of Genealogy', in K. Ansell-Pearson and H. Caygill (eds) *The Fate of the New Nietzsche*, London: Avebury Press.

Owen, D. (1994) 'The Ruling Virtue: *Redlichkeit* in Nietzsche and Weber', *Journal of Nietzsche Studies*, forthcoming.

Paden, W.E. (1988) 'Theaters of Humility and Suspicion: Desert Saints and New England Puritans', in L.H. Martin, H. Gutman and P.H. Hutton (eds) *Technologies of the Self*, London: Tavistock, pp. 64–79.

Patton, P. (1989) 'Taylor and Foucault on Power and Freedom', *Political Studies* 37: 260–76.

Perrot, M. (ed.) (1980) *L'Impossible Prison: recherches sur la système pénitentaire au XIX siecle*, Paris: Seuil.

Philp, M. (1983) 'Foucault on Power: a Problem in Radical Translation?', *Political Theory* 11: 29–52.

Pippin, R. (1989) 'Irony and Affirmation in Nietzsche's *Thus Spake Zarathustra*', in M.A. Gillespie and T.B. Strong (eds) *Nietzsche's New Seas*, Chicago, Ill.: Chicago University Press.

Pizer, J. (1990) 'The Use and Abuse of "Ursprung": On Foucault's Reading of Nietzsche', *Nietzsche-Studien* 19: 462–78.

Poggi, G. (1983) *Calvinism and the Capitalist Spirit: Max Weber's Protestant Ethic*, London: Macmillan.

Portis, E.B. (1978) 'Max Weber's Theory of Personality', *Sociological Inquiry* 48: 113–20.

Rajchman, J. (1985) *Michel Foucault: the Freedom of Philosophy*, New York: Columbia University Press.

Rickert, H. (1962) *Science and History: a Critique of Positivist Epistemology*, tr. G. Reisman, New York: Van Nostrand.

Rickert, H. (1986) *The Limits of Concept Formation in Natural Science*, tr. G. Oakes, Cambridge: Cambridge University Press.

Rickert, H. (1989) 'Max Weber's View of Science', in P. Lassman and I. Velody (eds) *Max Weber's 'Science as a Vocation'*, London: Unwin Hyman, pp. 76–86.

Riley, P. (1982) *Will and Political Legitimacy*, Cambridge, Mass.: Harvard University Press.

Ringer, F. (1969) *The Decline of the German Mandarins*, Cambridge, Mass.: Harvard University Press.

Rogers, R.E. (ed.) (1969) *Max Weber's Ideal Type Theory*, New York: Philosophical Library.

Rose, G. (1978) *The Melancholy Science: An Introduction to the Thought of Theodor W. Adorno*, London: Macmillan.

Rousseau, J.-J. (1968) *The Social Contract*, tr. M. Cranston, Harmondsworth: Penguin.

Sabine, G. (1937) *A History of Political Thought*, London: George G. Harrup.

Scaff, L. (1989) *Fleeing the Iron Cage*, Berkeley, Calif.: University of California Press.

Schacht, R. (1983) *Nietzsche*, London: Routledge.

Schluchter, W. (1979) 'The Paradox of Rationalisation', in G. Roth and W. Schluchter (eds) *Max Weber's Vision of History*, Berkeley, Calif.: University of California Press.

Schluchter, W. (1981) *The Rise of Western Rationalism: Max Weber's Developmental History*, Berkeley, Calif.: University of California Press.

Schrift, A. (1990) *Nietzsche and the Question of Interpretation*, London: Routledge.

Schroeder, R. (1987) 'Nietzsche and Weber: Two Prophets of the Modern Age', in S. Lash and S. Whimster (eds) *Max Weber, Rationality and Modernity*, London: Allen & Unwin,

Schroeder, R. (1991) ' "Personality" and "Inner Distance": the Conception of the Individual in Max Weber's Sociology', *History of the Human Sciences* 4 (1): 61–78.

Schroeder, R. (1992) *Max Weber and the Sociology of Culture*, London: Sage.

Schutte, O. (1984) *Beyond Nihilism: Nietzsche Without Masks*, Chicago, Ill.: University of Chicago Press.

Seidman, S. (1983) 'Modernity, Meaning and Cultural Pessimism in Max Weber', *Sociological Analysis* 44 (4): 267–78.

Shapiro, G. (1989) *Nietzschean Narratives*, Bloomington, Ind.: Indiana University Press.

Simmel, G. (1986) *Schopenhauer and Nietzsche*, tr. H. Loiskandl *et al.*, Amherst, Mass.: University of Massachusetts Press.

Small, R. (1990a) 'Absolute Becoming and Absolute Necessity', *International Studies in Philosophy* 21: 125–34.

Small, R. (1990b) 'Nietzsche, Dühring, and Time', *Journal of the History of Philosophy* 28 (2): 229–50.

Stack, G. (1991) 'Kant, Lange and Nietzsche: Critique of Knowledge', in K. Ansell-Pearson (ed.) *Nietzsche and Modern German Thought*, London: Routledge, pp. 30–58.

Stamburgh, J. (1972) *Nietzsche's Thought of Eternal Return*, Baltimore, Md.: Johns Hopkins University Press.

Strauss, L. (1975) *Political Philosophy. Six Essays*, ed. H. Gilden, Indianapolis, Ind.: Bobbs-Merrill.

Strong, T.B. (1988) *Friedrich Nietzsche and the Politics of Transfiguration* (2nd edition), Berkeley, Calif.: University of California Press.

Strong, T.B. (1989) 'Nietzsche's Political Aesthetics', in M.A. Gillespie and T.B. Strong (eds) *Nietzsche's New Seas*, Chicago, Ill.: University of Chicago Press, pp. 153–74.

Strong, T.B. (1992) 'What Have We to Do with Morals? Nietzsche and Weber on History and Ethics', *History of the Human Sciences* 5 (3): 9–18.

Taylor, C. (1984) 'Foucault on Freedom and Truth', *Political Theory* 12: 152–83.

Taylor, C. (1985) 'Connolly, Foucault, and Truth', *Political Theory* 13: 377–85.

Taylor, C. (1989) 'Taylor and Foucault on Power and Freedom: a Reply [to Patton]', *Political Studies* 37: 277–81.

Tenbruck, F. (1980) 'The Problem of Thematic Unity in the Works of Max Weber', *British Journal of Sociology* 31 (3): 316–51.

Tenbruck, F. (1987) 'Weber and Meyer', in W.J. Mommsen and J. Osterhammel (eds) *Max Weber and his Contemporaries*, London: Allen & Unwin.

Thiele, L.P. (1986) 'Foucault's Triple Murder and the Modern Development of Power', *Canadian Journal of Political Science* 19: 243–60.

Thiele, L.P. (1990a) *Friedrich Nietzsche and the Politics of the Soul*, Princeton, N.J.: Princeton University Press.

Thiele, L.P. (1990b) 'The Agony of Politics: the Nietzschean Roots of Foucault's Thought', *American Political Science Review* 84: 907–25.

Troeltsch, E. (1931) *The Social Teaching of the Christian Churches* (2 vols), London: Allen & Unwin.

Troeltsch, E. (1989) 'The Revolution in Science', in P. Lassman and I. Velody (eds) *Max Weber's 'Science as a Vocation'*, London: Unwin Hyman, pp. 58–69.

Turner, B.S. (1974) *Weber and Islam: a Critical Study*, London: Routledge & Kegan Paul.

Turner, B.S. (1981) *For Weber: Essays on the Sociology of Fate*, London: Routledge & Kegan Paul.

Turner, B.S. (1982) 'Nietzsche, Weber and the Devaluation of Politics: the Problem of State Legitimacy', *Sociological Review* 30: 367–91.

Turner, C. (1992) *Politics and Modernity in the Work of Max Weber*, London: Routledge.

Walker, J. (1991) 'Nietzsche, Christianity, and the Legitimacy of Tradition', in K. Ansell-Pearson (ed.) *Nietzsche and Modern German Thought*, London: Routledge, pp. 10–29.

Warren, M. (1988a) *Nietzsche and Political Thought*, Cambridge, Mass.: MIT Press.

Warren, M. (1988b) 'Max Weber's Liberalism for a Nietzschean World', *American Political Science Review* 82 (1): 31–50.

Warren, M. (1992) 'Max Weber's Nietzschean Conception of Power', *History of the Human Sciences* 5 (3): 19–37.

White, S.K. (1988) *The Recent Work of Jurgen Habermas*, Cambridge: Cambridge University Press.

White, S.K. (1992) *Political Theory and Postmodernism*, Cambridge: Cambridge University Press.

Whitford, M. (1991) *Luce Irigaray: Philosophy in the Feminine*, London: Routledge.

Wittenberg, E. (1989) 'The Crisis of Science in Germany in 1919', in P. Lassman and I. Velody (eds) *Max Weber's 'Science as a Vocation'*, London: Unwin Hyman, pp. 112–21.

Wittgenstein, L. (1958) *Philosophical Investigations*, tr. G.E.M. Anscombe, Oxford: Basil Blackwell.

Wolin, R. (1986) 'Foucault's Aesthetic Decisionism', *Telos* 67: 71–86.

Wolin, S. (1984) 'Max Weber: Legitimation, Method and the Politics of Theory', in W. Connolly (ed.) *Legitimation and the State*, Oxford: Basil Blackwell, pp. 63–87.

Wood, D. (1991) *Philosophy at The Limit*, Oxford: Basil Blackwell.

Wright Mills, C. (1959) *The Sociological Imagination*, Oxford: Oxford University Press.

Yeats, W.B. (1974) *Selected Poetry*, London: Pan.

Yovel, Y. (1980) *Kant and the Philosophy of History*, Princeton, N.J.: Princeton University Press.

Zeitlin, I. (1984) *Ancient Judaism*, Cambridge: Polity.

NAME INDEX

SUBJECT INDEX

191–2, 195; punitive 171, 182,
187–8; sexual 182, 184, 187–8
Reformation 55–7, 61, 188
relativism 85–6, 126
religion 101–3, 108, 115
Renaissance 55–7, 63, 79
ressentiment 5, 38, 40, 42–3, 45–6, 48,
50–3, 56, 62, 65, 68, 70–1, 103
routinisation 5, 96, 106, 215

science 5, 54–9, 84–5, 87–90, 93–4,
98–100, 112–17, 121, 123–4,
127–31, 133–9, 144, 181, 185–6,
193, 195, 217
self-overcoming 3, 28, 55, 74, 127,
158, 204–5
sex 182–7
sexuality 6, 164, 182, 184, 187, 200
slave 29, 31, 41–3, 47, 51–3, 68, 107
sovereign 164, 167, 198; culture
78–9, 217; individual 31, 37, 68
sovereignty 37, 39–40, 54, 189–92,
198–9
structures of recognition 64–5, 67,
76, 95, 124, 148, 151, 156–7,
159–61, 187, 197, 201, 205, 210,
214–16
subjectivity 6, 27–8, 72, 148–50, 152,
156–7, 159–60, 169, 187, 196,
203–6, 211–12

teleological 12, 14, 98, 128, 157
telos 3, 28, 37, 39, 62, 65, 120–1, 126,
157–8, 180, 183, 187, 192, 204–5
tragic 66, 83, 90, 136–9
transgression 143, 204–6, 217
truthfulness 57–9

Übermensch 5, 6, 63, 70, 74, 78, 79–82,
137, 157, 217
universality 13, 72, 74, 76, 101,
104–7, 172, 177, 202
utopian 5, 82–3, 119

value-freedom 85–6, 90, 94, 160, 208
values 4, 45, 62, 68, 71, 74–5, 84–6,
90, 115, 126, 130, 135–6, 158,
160; grounds of 5, 69, 121, 123,
216; ultimate 93, 111, 130–3, 135,
137–8
vocation 87, 89, 98, 116, 128, 136
vocational ethic 6, 128

will to power 4–6, 27–8, 30–3, 37,
68–70, 84, 95–6, 99, 214
will to truth 3, 5–6, 54, 58–9, 63, 73,
94, 101, 105, 115, 118, 147–8,
163, 166, 168–9, 188, 195–7, 212,
215
worldviews 5, 96–7, 106, 108–10,
115, 118, 120–1, 126, 128, 214